Wild colonial boys

Manchester University Press

Other books by Thomas Paul Burgess

A Crisis of Conscience: Moral Ambivalence and Education in Northern Ireland (Aldershot: Avebury/Ashgate, 1993).
Community Relations, Community Identity and Social Policy in Northern Ireland (Lewiston, NY: Edwin Mellen Press, 2002).
Highways, Crossroads and Cul de Sacs: Journeys into Irish Youth and Community Work, ed. with Peter Hermann (Bremen: Europäische Hochschulverlag, 2010).
The Contested Identities of Ulster Protestants, ed. with Gareth Mulvenna (London: Palgrave Macmillan, 2015).
The Contested Identities of Ulster Catholics, ed. (London: Palgrave MacMillan, 2018).

Novels

White Church, Black Mountain (Troubador Books, 2015; Bloodhound Books, 2021).
Through Hollow Lands (Urbane Books, 2018; Bloodhound Books, 2021).

'This overdue account of a Northern Irish punk story flies by as quickly as a Ramones classic. Sprinkling his tale with rock star anecdotes, Burgess is not above settling a few old scores, though this is balanced with plenty of finger-pointing at his own band and indeed himself.'

Eoin Brannigan, Editor-in-Chief,
Belfast Telegraph

'Paul Burgess writes, as Ruefrex played, an absolute storm: from the head and the heart, with attitude and with truth. If you weren't there, this is the book you need. If you *were* there, this is still the book you need.'

Glenn Patterson, author of
Two Summers

'Unabashed, unapologetic and outspoken. Thomas Paul Burgess provides a refreshingly honest account of his experiences as a punk musician from the "wrong" side of the divide in Northern Ireland. Well-worn historical narratives are upturned in an engaging, beautifully written chronicle of identity, class and the politics of anti-sectarianism.'

Russ Bestley, co-author of
The Art of Punk

'Not quite how I remember SLF, but still a very good read. Shows the determination one part of a band can have to make better the whole! If you are interested in the struggle to succeed, this is the book for you, no matter your type of music.'

Henry Cluney, Stiff Little Fingers

'An honest, articulate and no-bullshit account of a young songwriter/drummer and his band struggling to "keep it together" in the throes of impending success in the (still perilous) UK music scene. Paul enjoys the authority earned by having truly "been there".'

Mick Glossop, music producer

'*Wild colonial boys* is a beautifully written account of the band Ruefrex and their bid for success in Britain at a time of changing political perceptions. Offering a fresh window on the history of Northern Ireland punk, it takes a few swipes at icons along the way. A compelling read.'

Elvera Butler, founder of Reekus Records

'This is a storm of a book. A rollicking account of the punk revolution in popular music, intersecting with the story of the maligning of the Protestant working class as innately fascistic and unimaginative. Outrage through music was a creative response to the sectarian corralling of young people and sectarian branding. Paul Burgess was at the heart of it.'

Malachi O'Doherty, author of *How to Fix Northern Ireland*

Wild colonial boys

A Belfast punk story

Thomas Paul Burgess

Manchester University Press

Copyright © Thomas Paul Burgess 2024

The right of Thomas Paul Burgess to be identified as the author of this work has been asserted in accordance with the Copyright, Designs and Patents Act 1988.

Published by Manchester University Press
Oxford Road, Manchester, M13 9PL
www.manchesteruniversitypress.co.uk

British Library Cataloguing-in-Publication Data
A catalogue record for this book is available from the British Library

ISBN 978 1 5261 7337 9 paperback

First published 2024

The publisher has no responsibility for the persistence or accuracy of URLs for any external or third-party internet websites referred to in this book, and does not guarantee that any content on such websites is, or will remain, accurate or appropriate.

Typeset by Newgen

*A generation built from red-bricked streets,
all proud, and hard, and honourable men.
One same purpose, that of right and wrong,
family and jobs their main concern.
Another side the newsmen seldom tell,
days of heaven, nights of hell.*
                              'Days of Heaven', Ruefrex

*To keep us down in days gone by
you played the Orange card,
and European fields of war, like sheep,
we'd rush to guard.*

*Six county men have looked to you,
in past and present strife,
six county men again have found,
you're betting with their life.*

*And you're playing cards with dead men,
but you're losing every hand,
You cheat my people, past and present,
we've lived and died upon this land.*
               'Playing Cards with Dead Men', Ruefrex

*In memory of my late parents, Ruby and Tommy.
And for Mary.*

Contents

Preface	xi
Sleeve notes	xvi

Side 1: Origins: Belfast and Dublin (1974–84) 1

1. TC 3
2. 'Pastures not greener but meaner' 12
3. Anderson, Kelly and Greene 24
4. The Pride of Ardoyne 33
5. Bad vibrations 42
6. The boy looked at Clarkey 52
7. Lousy body 58
8. If you go down to the Harp today … 61
9. GOT-8 66
10. *Cross the Line* 72
11. 'Wasted Life' 79
12. The fly and the dandelion 85
13. The indignity of labour 92
14. A sense of Ireland 98
15. The Black Catholics 103
16. Of giants and sandcastles 111

Side 2: Second coming: London and Manchester (1985–87) 121
17 'The Wild Colonial Boy' 123
18 'Change of Attention' 130
19 Our Tune 138
20 Home thoughts from abroad 148
21 Hot to trot 152
22 If it ain't stiff, it ain't worth a fuck 161
23 The fourth estate 168
24 It's too late to stop now 180
25 Sarm East is east, Sarm West is west 191
26 Brixton nights 198
27 On *The Tube* with Sonnie Rae 205
28 Shane MacGowan's smile 211
29 Jumping the shark 217
30 Green and pleasant land 231
31 The return of the native 239

Coda: Legacy issues and the perils of misremembering 248
Appendix 1: Song lyrics referenced in text 254
Appendix 2: Ruefrex discography 271
List of illustrations 275
Dedications, acknowledgements and thanks 276
Index 277

Preface

I've always thought that it must take a gargantuan level of self-importance to assume that other people might want to read a memoir about your art, much less your life. That might be a consequence of my grounded upbringing or simply because I am from Belfast. Belfast people have an adroit way of deflating pomposity and one that takes no prisoners. You may, for example, be told that someone is 'up his own hole'. But my favourite put-down comes from my adopted hometown of Cork: 'If he were made of chocolate, he'd eat himself!' The task of writing a memoir, then, clearly gives pause for thought.

Furthermore, the academic in me felt distinctly uneasy at such a clearly subjective undertaking, so much so that what I have attempted to produce here is a kind of fusion of the factual with the anecdotal, a style that marries the autobiographical with aspects of the anthropological or musicological in exploring liminality.[1]

So it was with some trepidation that I decided to undertake this *obligation* (for that is what this task had become to me). My band Ruefrex, despite experiencing something like the fabled 'fifteen minutes of fame', is not as widely known or recognised as other Northern Irish punk contemporaries from that period – Stiff Little Fingers, The Undertones, Rudi, The Outcasts. Instead, we inherited that most bittersweet of epitaphs: 'The best band never to have made it.' And while there might be some consolation in that – and genuine delight in the support of those hard-core fans who have remained unswervingly faithful to this day – ultimately 'close, but no cigar' doesn't really cut it now, does it?

While our musical journey *did* enable us to rub shoulders with enough A-listers from the music business to provide some tasty vignettes for this book, those reminiscences are in no way my primary motivation for writing it. Rather, the driving force behind this memoir comes from a dilemma I have been unable to reconcile for most of my adult life; that is, the intrinsic tensions that have existed for young men from my community during the conflict (and beyond), young men who were in touch with their Ulster Loyalist heritage but uncomfortable with the triumphalist, confrontational, sometimes sectarian aspects of it.

You could find no band more fervently committed to the precepts of the Pistols or The Clash, more fully loyal to the edicts of Johnny Rotten and his credo 'I wanna be anarchy … get pissed, destroy!' than Ruefrex. Yet the realpolitik of the situation we lived in meant that it was hard to fuck over 'the Queen and her fascist regime' when only the forces of the Crown stood between you and Irish republican murder gangs on the rampage.

The conflicted allegiances of staying true to the cultural mores of my working-class Loyalist upbringing while challenging the conservative, reactionary behaviours inherent within that tradition have in some ways come to define me.

So, underpinning the story that follows is a sustaining hurt, an enduring sense of injustice, perhaps, that is more

Preface

than simply sour grapes. It is a conviction that Ruefrex's place in the pantheon of punk greats was hindered by a negative stereotyping that still bedevils my community to this day. We were stymied by the belief, held by liberal cultural gatekeepers, that great art in general, and edgy, subversive popular culture in particular, is the unimpeachable birth-right of the dispossessed, the revolutionary and the freedom fighter, and woe betide anyone from the liberal intelligentsia who might dare to suggest otherwise.

That was certainly the reality underpinning the British music scene of the early 1980s in which Ruefrex found themselves.

The 'greening' of alternative music in London at that time saw The Pogues, That Petrol Emotion, U2 and Dexys Midnight Runners all trade off their Irish credentials. Others like Elvis Costello, Oasis, The Smiths and John Lydon were eager to identify with their Catholic Irish roots.

This often manifested in a simplistic analysis of the Troubles and knee-jerk support for the 'armed struggle'. It also too often led to the catch-all comparison of my community to white Afrikaners, portrayed as little more than Planters, Imperialist usurpers or right-wing knuckle-draggers. While I was in London, I was constantly fielding exhortations of 'Troops Out!' from every quarter. My response to hecklers was a simple and unambiguous one: if British troops leave Northern Ireland, will you and your family go and live there? Will you endure the vortex of violence their removal will create, as you clearly expect me, my band and my family to?

In short, the London scene was at best suspicious, at worst antagonistic, towards four lads from the Shankill Road who, in press interviews, not only refused to apologise for their cultural legacy or identity but also wrote songs about it and were beginning to command favourable coverage in the national media.

Then, as now, my broad identification with Northern Irish politics was grounded in class terms, and, by extension, anti-sectarian terms. We believed that our community was as entitled to a legitimate expression/identification of its cultural identity as that of Republicans/nationalists. While aspects of this culture may seem unpalatable – even at odds sometimes with class consciousness – nevertheless, it was, and remains, rich, valid and worthy. And Ruefrex took pride in, and encouragement from, the many positives it offered.

Consequently, what follows here is to some degree a catharsis, an attempt to revisit the grass-root circumstances that acted as a catalyst for the music and fashioned an angry defiance that would carry us to the recording studios and the bright lights of London and beyond.

It is also a recollection of a shared rite of passage and a loss of innocence, an account of how the untrammelled dreams of adolescence were at first remarkably realised, then quickly sullied, of how unshakeable camaraderie and an unbreakable sense of shared purpose were lost in artistic compromise, personality clashes and that hoary old euphemism, 'musical differences'.

As an analogy, if this story were a football match, a Sky commentator would describe it as the proverbial 'game of two halves'. In the first half, the plucky 'giant killers' emerge from nowhere, punch above their weight and take the lead. In the second, they lose their midfield enforcer, score a few own goals and succumb to a lack of character and experience at the highest level.

While conducting research for this book, I revisited many of the reviews and interviews published during the band's sojourn in the public eye. But it was an excerpt

Preface

from a chapter by Professor Colin Coulter of Maynooth University – perhaps uniquely placed to comment with authority on Ruefrex – that offers the most insightful observation:

> Looking back, it becomes ever clearer that the band really were an anomaly in the recent history of the popular culture of this island – four working-class lads from unionist backgrounds, with fine tunes and radical politics, who had no time for the conventions that punk was meant to dissolve but would instead reproduce in a heartbeat. It is little wonder, then, that Ruefrex have been all but airbrushed out of the official narratives of Irish popular music history.[2]

TPB

NOTES

1. I tried to do something similar (but with a greater academic emphasis) in *The Contested Identities of Ulster Catholics* (London: Palgrave MacMillan, 2018). There, I invited broadly biographical chapters from some contributors but placed them in the ethnographical contextual framework of an investigation into cultural identity.
2. Colin Coulter, 'Ruefrex, 2014', in *In Concert: Favourite Gigs of Ireland's Music Community. Supporting Syrian Refugees.* Compiled by Niall McGuirk and Michael Murphy (Dublin: Hope Collective Publications, 2016), p. 147.

Sleeve notes

The Great Hall, Christchurch College, Oxford University, 1987

Professor Martin Goodman was aptly named. He was small with a broad, open face and a gap-toothed smile. Despite a look of almost boyish naïveté, something about his demeanour immediately suggested a life dedicated to poring over the Scriptures and the Torah. He might have been born with his kippah already fused onto the crown of his head.

The Dean of Hebrew and Jewish Studies at Oxford University had been assigned the task of mentoring a junior member from one of the smaller postgraduate colleges, where he was a fellow.

I had assumed that such a task would be onerous to an academic of his standing. If so, he did a good job disguising it. So when he casually suggested that I join him for dinner, I had expected the venue to be my own minor college of St Cross. 'No', he mildly admonished me, patient with my lack of knowledge of Oxford etiquette. St Cross was to be wholesomely commended for its hearty lunches; dinner, however, would be elsewhere. Would I be willing to join him in the Great Hall at his own college of Christchurch?[1]

Sleeve notes

Christchurch College! *The* Christchurch College, which boasted alumni that included thirteen British prime ministers, seventeen archbishops? The Christchurch of King Edward VII, King William II, the writers Lewis Carroll and W. H. Auden, the philosopher John Locke?

'Oh, it'll be high table. It's a terrible old fuss, I know, but you'll need to wear the batman gear. You *do* have a gown, don't you?'

'Of course, of course', I lied, pushing down my rising panic at what was unfolding.

'Seven thirty for eight, the Great Hall, Christchurch. Just tell the porter on the gate you're to be shown to the Senior Common Room'.

'Seven thirty it is. I'll look forward to it', I said, trying hard to appear unflappable.

'Bring a good appetite!' he threw back over his shoulder, along with his scarf.

I laughed (too loudly), wondered where I might borrow a gown from and waved with fragile bonhomie. And perhaps for the first time in my life, I realised the profundity of the old adage 'Be careful what you wish for ...'.

Only a few weeks earlier, and for the second time in less than a year, I had packed everything I owned into a small, faded lemon-coloured Vauxhall Chevette: an old Toshiba music centre and speakers, a small portable TV, a few boxes of records and cassette tapes, bags, and a suitcase stuffed with clothes, shoes and several framed photographs. The car radio was broken, so I had taken to driving with my Sony Walkman headphones clamped to my ears, effectively blocking out any exterior sounds. Not the safest way to make the Belfast–Stranraer–Oxford journey.

I had come up to Oxford University via the most circuitous and unlikely of routes and circumstances.

Wild colonial boys

A failed 11 Plus student from a troubled Belfast comprehensive, I was threatened with expulsion for running with 'the wrong crowd' and recall my schooldays as a catalogue of clashes with authority punctuated with occasional threats from paramilitary bullies. There *was* solace of a sort to be found in the herculean efforts of a talented and committed generation of young English and History teachers who earned their spurs in this toughest of learning environments. They were always open to imaginative ways to engage distracted and unsettled adolescents, and often planned lessons around the music and lyrics of David Bowie, The Velvet Underground, Pink Floyd or Bob Dylan, or enlivening the epoch-defining French Revolution and its aftermath with tales of artists, thinkers and patriots.

However, despite their best efforts and some stirrings of my embryonic intellect, the school system made it abundantly clear that higher education was not for the likes of me. Excluded from the grammar stream unless I was willing to endure the excruciating humiliation of being 'held back' for an extra year's study in order to do A levels, I was abandoned to the dead zone of the dreaded CSE class,[2] where learning a language was replaced by Technical Drawing and History and Economics were replaced by Woodwork and Metalwork. It seemed I was destined for an ill-suited apprenticeship in a city where traditional industries were in terminal decline.

But socially, I was accepted, on sufferance, by the older wisecracking 'A' level crowd. If my secondary education had imbued me with any legacy that might be considered constructive, it was my driven, single-minded determination to prove every last one of those fuckers wrong!

Like most young men from the Loyalist working-class heartland of the Shankill Road at that time, my peers might

Sleeve notes

be said to fall broadly into three categories: those who craved some degree of financial independence and who were willing to work in virtually any setting to achieve it (office or shop floor salaries; sales of everything from insurance to shoes); those who, with financial support from their parents and the public purse, were prepared to play the long game for greater (professional) reward on graduation from a university; and those who fell for the dubious attractions of the paramilitaries. It should be noted that these groups were by no means mutually exclusive.

I opted for the dosh. Bidding my younger classmates a less than fond 'fuck you', I left forever (or so I thought) the academic establishment that had needlessly prolonged my rite of passage to self-esteem, adulthood and acceptance. A permanent, pensionable clerk's job in Short Brothers & Harland was a job for life and I was deemed lucky to get it.

The aircraft and missile manufacturer was the sister company of Belfast's most iconic employer, Harland & Wolff. In the history of working-class culture in Belfast, thousands of young Protestant men had taken this route before me, and in a period when the order books for both firms looked increasingly thin, I was expected to keep the head down and be eternally grateful for entry to the so-called labour aristocracy.[3]

It was far from an ideal fit for me and in no time I was considering my options.

Higher education was a path that many of my peers were beginning to take. It was an opportunity that we largely embraced as our right back then and one that, with hindsight, fuelled educational and social mobility for the working classes in a manner only dreamed of today. It was a way out, a way to thwart predestination.

But this transitional flux was not taking place in a vacuum. It was 1977. Running parallel with my dreary travails – and underpinning my all-consuming need to break away from convention, challenge authority and kick over the traces – was the generation-defining, liberating and full-on participatory detonation of punk rock. In 1977, Messrs Strummer, Rotten and Vanian were opening different doors that we would rush to go through.

Rebellion was in some small way already stirring in me, from the publishing and clandestine photocopying of punk fanzines to rehearsed phone calls feigning illness to my unimpressed boss at Short's Sub-Contracts Department, hands blistered from gigging the night before and nursing a massive hangover.

Everything changed. Changed utterly. And so a gobbing, pogoing, two-fingered beauty was born.

And I had my band. And my band were the best. And we were going to ram it down their fucking throats and show them all!

* * *

Meanwhile, some years later, back at the Senior Common Room at Christchurch College, the vibe resembled something straight out of Harry Potter: balding men in tweeds and gowns, hair sprouting from ears and noses, puffing on pipes and sipping port, their heads suddenly turning to scrutinise the newcomer.

To my horror, Martin Goodman was nowhere to be seen.

Mercifully he arrived soon afterwards and brusque introductions were made. A professor of biomedical engineering here, a Senior Fellow in Greek rhetoric and oratory there. To say that my imposter syndrome was in overdrive is an understatement. But this sparkling bauble of establishment assimilation dangled right there in front of me and I was, for the moment anyhow, completely entranced by it.

Sleeve notes

Eventually, a dowdy college lickspittle shuffled in, carrying what looked like Black Rod's staff from the House of Commons and announced that dinner was served. I duly lined up, two abreast with Martin Goodman, and we filed in procession up a narrow stone staircase, emerging onto an elevated platform set for banquet.

It reminded me immediately of going out onstage with the band, and in many respects it was exactly that, a performance. Below in the semi-darkness, the progeny of England's elite sat illuminated by candles at long bench-like tables. The cream of the establishment, rich and thick. The walls were hung with watercolours of past masters and notable old boys. A rumble filled the hall as chairs were pushed back and the undergraduates rose in time-honoured tradition to greet our entrance. They stood like that until we were seated.

I struggled to keep an idiot grin off my face: 'How'd ya like me now suckas!' My euphoria was short-lived when I realised I would be expected to exchange witty dinner repartee with those around me. Once grace had been droned out (in Latin), everyone took their seats.

I was seated with Goodman on one side and a medieval French poetry expert on the other; a quantum physicist from Berkshire sat across from me. This was going to be a long and probably mortifying night!

Thinking quickly, I opted for an amalgam of street smarts and some superficially topical cherry-picking. This suggested knowledge in a variety of conversational topics that I did not necessarily possess. Monsieur d'Oisy was a definite no-no for conversation, and as for the Albert Einstein lookalike sitting across the table ... No, the social lubricant would have to be provided by my host, Martin Goodman. But Old Testament ruminations on the Torah seemed just as daunting. I needed to steer things onto surer ground. The

Song of Solomon and King David playing that secret chord on the harp for the Lord. Thank you, Sunday school catechism! Thank you, Leonard Cohen!

Did they agree there was a direct correlation between this and the preponderance of Jewish artists working in a variety of twentieth century media: Woody Allen, Benny Goodman, Norman Mailer, Saul Bellow, Phillip Roth, Bob Dylan? Did the chosen people possess some special God-given dispensation?

They took the bait. I had them!

As a child, my mother had taught me that people like the sound of their own voices, and in situations like this, it seemed obvious that I should encourage them. And did they ever! They talked and they talked – about the muse, about the human condition and its place in the arts, about the soul, about social protest and the creative act. You couldn't shut them up!

Off the hook, I sat back and let it all wash over me ... until I felt it was time.

'Did I mention that I was in a band?'

NOTES

1. Later to be featured as Hogwarts in the Harry Potter movies.
2. CSEs were introduced to provide qualifications to a broader range of schoolchildren. They were distinct from the GCEs (O levels), aimed at more academically able pupils, mostly those at grammar and independent schools (rather than secondary moderns).
3. In the nineteenth and early twentieth centuries, the phrase 'labour aristocracy' was used to define better-off members of the working class (as used, for example, by Jack London in *The People of the Abyss* (1903)).

Side 1

Origins: Belfast and Dublin (1974–84)

1
TC

In the beginning ... there was TC.

> Close friends get to call him TC,
> Providing it's with dignity!
> Top Cat!
> The indisputable leader of the gang.

At fifteen years of age, Tom Coulter – 'TC' – was, by some distance, the best street fighter in Loyalist North Belfast. From a hard-working family, and promising, if not delivering on, a strong performance at GCE O and A level, he differed somewhat from his more bovine rivals thanks to the wit, humour and panache he brought to bear on his dispensation of casual violence. Remarkably, even those who fell afoul of his attentions seemed to agree.

As all titular gun slingers know, there is always someone keen to prove that they are faster than you. As his second in prearranged duels with aspirational pretenders, I would discuss with him the relative merits of Doc Martens and Oxford boots (the latter having steel tips on the heels), pilot jackets and Wrangler jackets (the former having a fur collar which an adversary could grab hold of), and braces or studded belts (no competition, really).

Wild colonial boys

An agreed, if unwritten, code of conduct was observed by these street-corner gladiators – times, places, number of seconds allowed to attend; weapons were prohibited; and fights concluded when one or other protagonist admitted defeat. This might sound like something from *West Side Story*, a rumble between Jets and Sharks, but the contests were usually feral and bloody.

TC was the leader of the 'Debs', short for Debonairs. We prided ourselves on the fact that, distinct from the other street gangs, we delivered our blows with a singular flourish and brought a better class of mayhem to the fight. Drawing on *Clockwork Orange*'s Droog paraphernalia (as Ziggy Stardust and The Spiders had done) and James Moffat's *Skinhead* and *Suedehead* novels, our white parallel skinners sat meticulously atop our DM boots, and we sported a folded white handkerchief in the breast pockets of our immaculate three-quarter-length Crombies.[1] We regarded the prevalent Tartan gangs of the period with disdain, for the lemming-like way that they seemed to attract mass affiliation and for their dubious sartorial choices.

TC was my best mate, even though he was a year older and a few classes academically higher than me at Belfast Boys Model School in the north of the city. He was charismatic and manipulative in equal measure and found me a pliant and willing lieutenant. The initial appearance of what seemed to me his affluent home life (centred as it was around a detached house in a leafier part of Ballysillan) belied the herculean efforts of his working-class parents, unskilled manual labourers. Like many who wanted something better for their kids, they practised frugality in the extreme and pushed themselves to the limit to afford this property. TC boasted family links with the working-class

Shankill Road. In 1974–75, this was something of a badge of honour and one that I proudly wore myself.

My own early experience was also marked by humble beginnings. In 1971, just a few years earlier, I had been living in a two-up two-down in Jersey Street, Shankill Road. No hot water or central heating; a tin bath in front of the fire for ablutions; an outside toilet; a small bedroom shared with my older brother, David. Perhaps not surprisingly, this went some way to informing my subsequent views on matters of class equality and social justice and shaping the left-of-centre politics that would permeate my career and creative endeavours thereafter.

Older than me by six years, David always seemed preoccupied with his own circle. He was a much-feted footballer at that time and captain of the first eleven, a successful scholar and Deputy Head Boy to boot. I was invariably dismissed as Davy Burgess's wee brother.

My mother's family, the Sharpes, had been on the Shankill for generations. Born into relative poverty, Ruby had to drop out of Glenwood School to care for her six brothers and sisters when her mother, Letitia, died prematurely in childbirth and her father suffered a debilitating stroke. That she wasn't able to finish school remained a great source of regret to her in later years.

My father, Tommy, was an only child from the Lisburn Road in South Belfast. He set his cap at Ruby from the moment he first saw her. And despite being scrutinised closely by her brothers and rebuffed on a number of occasions, he finally got the girl.

My mother often told me that my father was never out of work a day in his life, but it was usually unskilled manual labour with few prospects. She exceeded his income by working as a supervisor in the Ladybird Clothing Factory in Agnes Street, off the Shankill Road. This ensured that my brother and I wore only the best of children's outfits, sometimes matching!

As was often the case in working-class families at that time, ours was covertly matriarchal. My father would hand in his pay packet at the end of the week and Ruby would give him something back for a bet and a few pints. She managed the household in every respect.

Throughout the Troubles, they brought us up to believe in that old adage 'There's good and bad on both sides' and to exercise a healthy scepticism regarding rabble-rousers and false prophets. They often lamented the loss of close friendships with Catholics due to the conflict, friends who could no longer cross the city to visit and vice versa. I have a poignant memory of my 'aunt' Lily Higgins from the Lower Ormeau Road, pleading tearfully with my mother to ensure that I did not wear my school uniform (with its identifying badge) if we visited them, both for our own safety and for theirs. It was undoubtedly my parents' stewardship and these experiences which shaped the anti-sectarian beliefs that I hold to this day.

At that time, the Shankill was increasingly suffering from the violence of street riots, bombs and a brutal redevelopment scheme that ripped the heart out of the community. So my mother sought to secure a better future for us by applying to the recently established Northern Ireland Housing Executive to be rehoused elsewhere. The Executive was charged with the equitable distribution of public housing, which had become a highly contentious issue due to the questionable sectarian allocation practices of unionist-controlled councils. Her decision to move us to a newly developed estate, Rathfern, on the northern outskirts of the city was driven by good intentions but it ultimately had deleterious consequences.

Still only thirteen, I was at first overwhelmed by the palace in which we now resided. We had a telephone, for God's sake! I promptly set about running up an enormous bill on the Dial-a-Disc service by repeated plays of 'Rockin' Robin' by The Jackson 5. It was the scorching summer of '72 and the excitement of running my first indoor, plumbed (cold) bath was palpable.

The nearby Carnmoney Hills – a rural idyll as far as I was concerned – provided a cherished green-scape for a boy, his dog and his Chopper bike, that was until, one day, I stumbled upon local men in army fatigues on manoeuvres who gestured angrily at me not to give away their position.

Soon, Loyalist murals began to appear on the newly pebbledashed gable walls of the estate, while older men, professing to be ex-British Army, recruited for the UDA in draughty, smelly municipal halls. They showed us local kids how to 'disarm an assailant', laughing as they slammed us down hard on mottled gym mats. Even then I noted that some of these men exhibited a rather unhealthy interest in the physical prowess of adolescent boys. The talk inevitably turned to firearms, and stories swirled and tentative assurances were given regarding 'taking the next step' as youngsters were targeted and drawn into the vortex of mounting violence.[2]

Further afield, chaos reigned. In 1972, there were over 12,000 shooting and bombing attacks in Northern Ireland. By 1974, the UDA were on the march and playing a central role in the Ulster Workers' Council strike. This led to the collapse of the power-sharing administration at Stormont headed by Ulster Unionist Brian Faulkner and including members of the nationalist SDLP and cross-community

Alliance Party. The strike paralysed Northern Ireland, cutting off electricity supplies and forcing Ulster Unionist members to resign from the executive. For young men, the domestic uncertainties around electricity and gas supplies turbocharged an already volatile civic and political environment that seemed to be sliding into outright anarchy.

So some of us felt excited, even flattered, when we were approached by the older boys and supplied with khaki uniforms and lead-filled, black Sellotaped iron pipes. The intention was that, for propaganda purposes, us young kids would be bussed to a site where we would swell the uniformed ranks of the protest march to Stormont. But when my mother became aware of this, I was dispatched forthwith to return these items to the older boys. She was a much more daunting prospect than the 'corporal' of the company to whom I reported – a greasy loser with an acne problem known as 'Harry half-a-head'. (The reasons for this moniker were not immediately obvious due to his penchant for tweed caps, worn in perpetuity.) My mother insisted that I informed him I would not be returning. In truth, I had decided as much for myself anyway.

Despite escaping the clutches of predatory paramilitaries, the daily commute to and from Belfast – to school for me and to the Ladybird factory for my mother – was increasingly problematic. For the inward leg, we depended on the good graces of a young, upwardly mobile couple she knew who had a brand-new bronze-coloured Ford Capri. It had an electric retractable aerial and was, without question, the coolest thing I had ever seen. However, getting home again was another matter entirely.

Smithfield Bus Station was located in a predominantly Catholic, republican and nationalist area of the city. It wasn't a place conducive to the well-being of schoolboys sporting the Red Hand of Ulster and Crown on their school blazer badges. Similarly, allegiance to Linfield and Glasgow Rangers football clubs – scrawled in black marker across school canvas haversacks – did little to commend us to the pupils of St Malachy's or St Patrick's College, Bearnageeha. We often found ourselves running the gauntlet between verbal abuse and physical assault on our daily journeys home.

It was around this period that I started to spend time with the older boys at school. One of them gave me my first lesson in class politics. If I was set upon by the Catholic boys, I was to look for those wearing a James Connolly badge in their lapel. This identified the wearer's sympathies with the Official IRA rather than the Provisionals. The logic ran that they were more likely to espouse socialist values and reject sectarianism for its own sake. In short, they might let you off with a warning, not a kicking.

The seniors of the Boy's Model School were a mine of both useful and useless information. They quoted Monty Python sketches verbatim and were wary of the 'Super-Prod' knuckle-draggers who gathered in sullen packs, comparing tattoos. But crucially, they shunned the tepid aural diet that had, up to that point, provided the soundtrack to my world. Not for them the pathetic mewling of The Osmonds, Bay City Rollers or David Cassidy, or the slow dance, disco foreplay of The Stylistics, The Chi-Lites or The Drifters.

Instead, music amongst the cool kids was a defining badge of honour, an indication of whether or not you could be trusted. Something to enthuse about, to escape into, to belong to. A club where all you needed to know about someone was whether they liked David Bowie, Lou Reed, Alice Cooper. Sure, there was Mud, Slade, The Glitter Band, T. Rex, and Sweet to stomp around the church hall disco to while giving out Carlsberg Special Brew-fuelled attitude

Wild colonial boys

and scowls. But there was also Roxy Music, Mott the Hoople, Cockney Rebel, Sparks. Later it was Black Sabbath, Hawkwind and King Crimson, even Peter Gabriel's Genesis.

Elite Lower Sixth cliques ran from lovers of cock rock exponents Led Zeppelin and Deep Purple to prog rock nerds who worshipped Emerson, Lake & Palmer and Yes. If so inclined, you could produce an interesting Venn diagram that took in the lot of them.

The liberation enjoyed through these new allegiances and alternative vistas was not matched at home, however, and soon we were on the move again, this time to Ballysillan, North Belfast.

Despite having to endure a bleak maisonette in the Sunningdale estate that had bars on the windows and damp and mould in the bedrooms, I was now at least amongst my boys, my comrades, the only troop to whom I would wish to belong.

I first spotted Tom Coulter in the school playground. Rumour had it that he headed up an elaborate protection racket in which, for a 10p outlay, you could mention his name and be showered with a never-ending supply of crisps, Mars Bars and Coca-Cola from the juniors who staffed the tuck shop. With one hand he was surreptitiously cramming crisps into his gob from a bag of Tayto Cheese & Onion concealed in his blazer pocket. With his other, he cradled copies of *Live at Max's Kansas City* by The Velvet Underground, *For Your Pleasure* by Roxy Music and *Billion Dollar Babies* by Alice Cooper. After some cursory checks of my bona fides, he had no compunction in letting me borrow all three.

Nothing, as they say, would ever be the same again.

NOTES

1 The street gang origins of Ruefrex remained a source of criticism from other Belfast bands, who referred to our followers and the band by the derogatory local term 'Spidermen'. A Crombie is a classic man's overcoat.
2 We later wrote and recorded a song entitled 'Playing Adult Games' which reflected this period. It featured on the *Political Wings* EP (see Appendix 1 for lyrics).

2
'Pastures not greener but meaner'

By 1974–75, North Belfast was well on its way to securing a moniker it shared with Cambodia's tragedy and which it would remain known by throughout the worst years of the conflict and beyond – 'the killing fields'.[1] The name chillingly reflected the patchwork quilt of unionist and nationalist areas bordering, and sometimes intersecting, each other in the north of the city, thus providing the opportunity for sectarian murder gangs to roam and randomly abduct, torture and kill innocents at will.

Bounded by hills, mountains and fields that often served as the dumping grounds for such atrocities, parts of North Belfast might appear to the untrained eye as much sought-after residential areas. The buildings are old, solid, semi-detached, red-brick, feel-goods; a nice garden front and back. They were originally built for the church-going bourgeoisie who filed dutifully home from their senior management tasks in the linen mills, tobacco factories and shipyards. But the leafy thoroughfares of Donegall Park Avenue and the tidy privets of Cavehill hid darker truths.

Eventually, the unionist merchant class watched their civic legacy go up in flames. But their love of property and capital meant that an economic scorched earth policy was

'Pastures not greener but meaner'

out of the question. And so they sold up, first to the skilled labourers they had so long affected a smug superiority over, and finally – unthinkably – to the emerging middle classes of professional, educated 'Fenians'. Resignedly, they abandoned these places of science, reason and commerce for a comfortable home in East or South Belfast and even further afield, to Bournemouth, Eastbourne or Torquay – the 'mainland'.

Elsewhere in Belfast, dark housing estates, lit by piss-orange streetlamps, ominously fringed those affluent verdant avenues, rendering night-time travel ill-advised. Loyalist Glenbryn bordered the republican Ardoyne, which stretched to the better-off Cliftonville Road. Catholic Ligoniel edged Protestant Ballysillan, which met with the prosperous North Circular Road.

The whole territory was a bewildering maze of football and Gaelic supporters' clubs, bookies, bowling greens, garden centres and bridge fraternities. Whether things were good or bad, the streets pretty much emptied after dark. In later years, that led to the death squads phoning up taxi cabs or pizza delivery companies located across the sectarian divide to lure drivers to a certain death: one minute walking unwittingly up a garden path, pepperoni deep-pan in one hand, garlic bread in the other, then *Crack! Crack! Crack!*

The madness of 1975 even invaded the apparent neutrality of the worlds of live music, show business and entertainment when the Ulster Volunteer Force (UVF) carried out a gun and bomb attack on the members of the Miami Showband.

The Stormont power-sharing executive had floundered; tentative Provisional IRA ceasefires and truces were short-lived; Direct Rule was reinstated to fill the dangerous vacuum. PIRA (Provisional Irish Republican Army)

Wild colonial boys

bombings increased at home and in London, and by late 1975, a poll published in the *Daily Telegraph* showed that 64 per cent of people in Britain wanted the British Army to be withdrawn from Northern Ireland. A more destabilised environment in which to grow up is hard to imagine.

For teenagers in North Belfast there was safety in numbers. The key was to ensure that the collective you belonged to was most assuredly non-paramilitary in nature. I've never been a great one for joining existing groups; I prefer to initiate them. This tendency most certainly helped me in avoiding membership of paramilitary organisations – this and an ever-vigilant mother, who scoured gangs of rioting youths, intervened and marched me, mortified, back home.

By this time, our gang, the Debs, had grown in number and our penchant for petty crime had progressed somewhat, from light shoplifting (clip-on earrings; Lady Esquire shoe polish to sniff while drinking Scotsmac, Clan Dew or Carlsberg Extra) to a fledgling protection racket.

'Heckle' was a popular junior member of the gang and hampered by a pronounced stutter, but he was happy to serve his apprenticeship through menial tasks and errands. This was just as well, as the initiation rites for the Debs were uncompromising and the hazing brutal.[2] It was bullying pure and simple and something of which I'm certainly not proud. But I had been at the sharp end of similar treatment when I was his age and was frankly relieved to be inside the tent this time round.

Part of Heckle's internship required him to make available his family home as a refuge for those of us absenting ourselves from the arduous school day. Both his parents were at work during the day, and tea, biscuits and Bowie's *Aladdin Sane* passed the day quite nicely for those of us availing of his hospitality. However, mischief was seldom

'Pastures not greener but meaner'

far away. When he was out of the room, TC's penchant for the dramatic saw him take a large pair of garden shears to the family's weekly wash that was drying on the clotheshorse. It left poor Heckle having to explain to his folks the butchered blouses and shortened trouser legs, and what exactly he was doing home during school hours in the first place.

At other times, Heckle's homework would be graded by TC and myself and comments appended in red ink accordingly: 'This book reeks of wine boy!' or 'Your critique of Orwell's *Animal Farm* seems to imply a sexual predilection for livestock!'

Heckle's older brother, 'Weeble', named after the popular children's toy of the time ('Weebles wobble but they don't fall down'), which he physically resembled, was not deemed suitable Debs material, so he did not enjoy the requisite protections afforded to gang members. Unfortunately for him, this rendered his newspaper round fair game. TC determined that Weeble should hand over the week's takings to us, rather than return them to the newsagent. He was simply to tell his boss that a gang of strangers had set upon and robbed him. At first Weeble complied, but after a while the credibility of his excuses began to wear thin. He made the cardinal error of asking us to 'rough him up a little ... not too much', just for authenticity's sake, and we, of course, were only too happy to oblige.

The core of the gang now consisted of TC (undisputed leader of the pack), me (disparagingly labelled 'Jap', an unwelcome sobriquet until the massive success of Bruce Lee and the oriental look), 'Stinkleroot' McKeown (so named because of his propensity for toxic farts), Jim 'Musky' Mawhinney (sometimes 'Muskrat' on account of his prominent front teeth), and Stephen Mills ('Lambsy' from the then popular cartoon series *It's the Wolf*).

Wild colonial boys

On the fringes of this collective was a truly intimidating figure: 'Croucher', aka 'Steamer'. A Praetorian Guard of sorts for TC, he unwisely confided in our leader about a regrettable drunken episode whereby he employed a stringless acoustic guitar to relieve himself when caught short. Taunting Croucher about this, however, was a risky business as only TC could confidently control his considerable menace.

On the whole, our activities were unpleasant and hostile for any unfortunate we alighted upon, but by the standards of the times, our actions could be considered nothing more than juvenile. Looking back now, I can see how we had unconsciously created our own kind of respite from the daily abhorrence of the adult world, an antidote to the horrors at large, a hermetically sealed bubble that we fiercely guarded from interlopers and celebrated through underage drinking and turf wars with peers who perhaps had the same idea. Bizarrely, this teenage gang warfare, while red in boot and fist, was somehow more acceptable, innocent even, when compared with the daily body count announced on the news.

Territory grabs inevitably took place at youth clubs and discos. Youth clubs tended to be church-run, ping-pong orientated and fuelled by orange cordial, so they were deemed lame. Discos were another matter entirely. They ticked all the boxes. Dress code was co-ordinated and rigorously observed, and copious amounts of cheap, retch-inducing alcohol was obtained through some older sibling or a stranger's good graces at the off-licence. Although the playlist for the evening was not entirely under our control, we could be assured our heroes would feature at some point. After all, we had to have our favourite soundtrack playing in the background when taking the field.

'Pastures not greener but meaner'

Outside, after the adrenaline rush of combat, there was the squiring of the local girls, involving 'lumbering' (heavy petting, perhaps resulting in a trophy love bite), and 'tits on the outside' (considered first base), graduating, if you were lucky, to 'tits on the inside'. Anything more was considered fantastical fabrication or almost unthinkable good fortune.

Finally, there was 'lashings of the old ultraviolence', as Alex from *Clockwork Orange* put it. Since we didn't venture across sectarian boundaries, for obvious reasons, this meant that disco-brawls kicked off against other Protestant gangs, playing away from home. It was a dicey enough business – if you were on another gang's patch and you got separated from your mates, you could expect a serious going over ... but that just added to the away-day buzz.

Sunningdale Disco, ostensibly run by the UDA, was our patch. But like Afghanistan or the Russian steppes, it could be taken by others, although not decisively held for any amount of time. If another gang were going to make an incursion, they let it be known well in advance, thus making an 'event' of the evening and offering all involved something to look forward to.[3]

We had known for some time that the Highfield Bootboys, fronted by their talismanic slayer of mere mortals, 'Sledger', were coming out to play. They were an established outfit that may have had its origins in the fabled Tartan gangs of the time.[4] Preparations had been in train for some time. On the night itself, the Debs met beforehand in Ballysillan Playing Fields and ran an eye over each other's apparel: bleached Wrangler jackets, skinners, parallels, DMs, and so on.

Talk turned inevitably to music. We recalled another night, a year or so earlier when, having met in similar circumstances, we had been uniformly excited by what had seemed a stellar *Top of the Pops* that evening: 'Sorrow' by Bowie; 'My Friend Stan' by Slade; 'Ballroom Blitz' by Sweet; 'A Hard Rain's A-Gonna Fall' by Bryan Ferry; 'Angel Fingers' by Wizzard; 'All the Way from Memphis' by Mott the Hoople; 'Angie' by the Stones; 'Rock On', an interesting song by some new cockney geezer (David Essex); and 'The Show Must Go On', a mind-melter from a little bloke dressed as a clown (Leo Sayer). We laughed at the memory. Our taste at thirteen years of age seemed infantile compared with the awakening adolescent sophistication of the fourteen- and fifteen-year-olds we were now.

I had my own fond memories of that night a year before. But I kept them to myself, for they involved feelings of fraternal love and respect that I had not yet learned to understand or articulate. Jim Mawhinney – 'Musky' – lived in Joanmount Park. We had become firm friends initially as classmates, then later as Debs, and for a period Musky and I were inseparable. He was what the comedian Ken Dodd might have looked like as a boy – pale skin, freckles, protruding, broken front teeth, and a mop of unruly red hair piled on top of a high forehead.

Something of a cartoon caricature, he was universally liked and unfailingly funny. In a world where credibility was determined by how game you were, he was – like me – deemed able to handle himself if necessary but otherwise not spoiling for a fight. When we squared up for the occasional sectarian street riot, the nationalist kids from the Bone and Ardoyne would call his name across the peace line or from outside their disco in Cliftondene, ribbing him mercilessly for wearing a pair of pink skinners[5] that he'd meant to dye red.

When I first joined the group and was tentatively negotiating the Debs' pack order, a fraught and delicate undertaking given TC's tendency to remove your privileges

'Pastures not greener but meaner'

unannounced should you appear too cocky, Musky was already popular and established. I had come out that evening, a callow thirteen-year-old, proudly sporting my brand new oxblood Doc Martens. Surely this would cut some ice with those who might still be mistrustful of me. As I drew close to the group I noticed him break away and approach me. Then, inexplicably, he dropped to his knees on the wet paving stones in front of me, reached out towards my boots and started unlacing them. I was somewhere between perplexed and mortified. Was it a joke at my expense? Were the others laughing? No, they had turned away and continued to chat. Before I could say anything, he explained: 'You've them laced up criss-crossed ... like in the shop. They have to go across. See ... in a straight line.' He pointed to his own. He worked away, the knees of his white skinners darkened by the dirty rain, until both boots were re-laced in a sartorially acceptable manner. It was hard to process, but something important had just happened. The hardman pretence had fallen away. There was a bonding of sorts, an acceptance. I belonged. It was the beginning of what we'd now call a bromance.

Back at the playing fields, talk turned to the forthcoming battle with Sledger and the Bootboys. Some of the others visibly tensed and the horseplay grew more robust. An underage stiffener was needed, while the high stone steps leading to the changing rooms were chosen as a look-out point, offering a clear vista in all directions and, therefore, early warning of any RUC patrols.

Howard Giffin was not a Debs member, but he was aligned with our cause and a valuable asset. From the lower Oldpark, he had a reputation for 'blade-work' and had ingeniously sewn a variety of straight-edged razors into the lapels and hem of his Crombie. A nice enough guy but clearly not to be fucked with. When he arrived, he announced that our alcohol needs for the evening had been taken care of, thanks to his home-brew kit, and produced a glass cider flagon filled with a foaming, dark green liquid.

Lambsy, always having something to prove, offered to down the first swig. Hooking his finger into the handle and resting the flagon on the crook of his elbow, he tilted his head back in the manner of an Appalachian hillbilly and took a mouthful.

'Not half bad,' he said, once he'd recovered.

'It'll get the job done!' Giffin said, proffering the pitcher to the rest of us.

'Give us it here!' we shouted in turn, and it was passed around almost ritualistically, with everyone happy to quaff it down.

'I feel it working already!' Musky declared.

The sound of girly giggling rose up from the cinder track below. The local girls were on their way to Sunningdale Disco. Good lassies all, and well able for the likes of us. They were a tight group, and attended the Girls' Model School, the female counterpart to our own. We recognised them from shared am-dram productions and joint field trips.

There was Lyn Heinz, a high-cheekboned, androgynous, feather-cut Ziggy lookalike, Sandra 'Whatname' Campbell, who had a big heart and often served as an agony aunt for the others, and Caroline Burns, with her long, straight blonde hair and consistently good manners. Her family lived across the street from Musky.

Caroline was teased relentlessly about her older brother, Jackie (Jake), who fronted the covers band Highway Star. A talented guitarist with ambitions to be the next Rory Gallagher, his long hair, loons[6] and cheesecloth shirts

'Pastures not greener but meaner'

rendered him a figure of fun for the Debs. He was in Sixth Form and the Drama Society and wore thick-lensed glasses. But secretly we coveted his undoubted talent and stage persona. Standing well back in the shadows of local community halls, we even mimicked air guitar to the Black Sabbath and Lynyrd Skynyrd songs that his band (later to become Stiff Little Fingers) reproduced faultlessly.

'D'ya wanna slug?' Giffin asked the girls.

'Aye, dead on!' they called back sarcastically. 'Does yer ma know yer out?'

'Suit yerselves. See youse at the disco.'

'I'm drunk already,' Stinkleroot said, his words slurring.

'Give us another welt of that,' TC said, reaching for the flagon.

I crinkled my nose. 'You've gone a bit heavy on the oul Brut aftershave there, Root. Are you chasing yer hole the night or what?'

'Aye', Musky said, 'you reek of the stuff. What else did ye get for Christmas?'

Stinkleroot looked confused. 'I thought it was the Jap.'

'Nah, nah ... that's the home brew,' Giffin helpfully explained. 'I put Brut in it for an edge.'

There was a moment's silent disbelief, then a chorus of outrage.

'*Aftershave* ... are ye mental!'

Giffin took another slug, virtually finishing the stuff off. 'Just for the taste. I prefer Blue Stratos ... or maybe Denim ... but my Da and our kid had used it all.'

'I think I'm going blind,' Lambsy said, reaching out to touch the graffiti on the wall in front of him.

'Right, tell Sledger I said he's a cunt! We'll see yez over there. Me and Burgess are away,' announced TC.

'Are we?' I said. 'Where are we goin'?'

'To see a man about a guitar.'

We should have stayed away and left them to it, for as it turned out it was not a night to be engaging in hand-to-hand combat. However, TC and I re-joined the gang later that evening to find it had been augmented by a classmate from the Shankill/Woodvale,[7] the son of a well-known senior UVF figure from that area. He was mild-mannered enough in school, but as we later learned, he was locked into some fucked-up rites-of-passage mission to prove himself worthy of his 'celebrity' father's status. And, terrifyingly, he had the motivation and the means to do it.

He recklessly announced that he would fight with our crew *against* the Bootboys, the gang from his own area (even though he had to return home there next day). To show he meant business, he produced from the folds of his coat what looked like a hand-cannon (I later learned it was a .45 semi-automatic pistol). Although we tried to feign cool indifference, we were all considerably unnerved. This went far beyond our usual rules of engagement and was allowing, by proxy, the paramilitaries into our sanctum sanctorum.

When all hell broke loose at the disco, participants tended to flood out into the streets, often locked together, grappling, throwing punches and scuffling back and forth for dear life. But nothing brought an end to that manic choreography like the production of a powerful handgun, brandished by a spotty, greasy-haired man-child.

So on this particular night, as the Bootboys scattered and ran in all directions, there he was at the head of the pursuing pack, waving the .45 around his head, occasionally dropping into the two-handed firing stance that he'd probably seen on *Starsky and Hutch* or *Kojak*. Mercifully, he never discharged a shot. But for TC and me, this was colouring dangerously outside the lines.

'Pastures not greener but meaner'

NOTES

1. The lyrics in the chapter title, 'Pastures not greener but meaner', are from 'I'm Tired Joey Boy', by Van Morrison. From the album *Avalon Sunset* (1989).
2. Norman McIlvenney – Heckle – is now a mechanical design specialist whose expertise is much sought after throughout UK and European industry.
3. Many of these young men were establishing a fledgling reputation for themselves as 'hard'. Tragically, this would inevitably lead to paramilitary membership, appallingly violent acts and premature death or jail time.
4. See Gareth Mulvenna, *Tartan Gangs and Paramilitaries: The Loyalist Backlash* (Liverpool: Liverpool University Press, 2017).
5. A style of jeans popular in the 70s with skinhead gangs.
6. Loons trousers were low-slung hipster trousers that hugged the backside and thighs before flaring out dramatically from the knee.
7. Not much later, he went to prison for the brutal shooting and murder of two Catholic civilians travelling on a Citybus. It was rumoured that he had turned himself in to police after 'finding God'.

3
Anderson, Kelly and Greene

Meanwhile, as 1977 progressed, word was starting to seep across the Irish Sea that something cataclysmic might be stirring in London. It wasn't just a new kind of music or some fresh bands; it was a groundswell of discontent with the established order; it was a new movement, a new dispensation. Most importantly, at its core was the reliance on a 'fuck you' attitude as a precursor to action and a DIY ethos to band formation, song writing and performance. The name 'punk' seemed to encapsulate it all perfectly.

If you were seventeen years old and music and politics were your defining raison d'etre, then this stirring of energy and defiant insolence – set to a three-chord, two-minute sonic pile-driver – was like mother's milk. And if you lived in a UK war zone ... well, suddenly you had a soundtrack to it all, and one that you yourself could perhaps contribute to.

It's difficult to convey *that* teenage energy, *that* excitement, the affirmation of *that* time. It was a *cause*, one that no one had to die for, a perfect storm of rebellion, belonging and purpose where none had existed before. I believe this unique set of circumstances is the reason why punk rock meant more to youth in Belfast than in any other city in Britain or Ireland.

Anderson, Kelly and Greene

On the ground, things in North Belfast began to happen fast. The Damned were at the vanguard of it all. TC was raving about their first album and the single from it, 'New Rose'.

Jackie Burns (Caroline Burns's brother, as he was to us) got a haircut, acquired some contact lenses and drainpipes, became known as Jake, and transformed Highway Star into Stiff Little Fingers, a name taken from a Vibrators' track. Covers of Lynyrd Skynyrd, Deep Purple and Zeppelin were out; from now on they would be writing their own material and were soon to acquire some one-piece industrial jumpsuits (à la The Clash).

By 1977 and following bruising scrapes with the law (in TC's case) and the school authorities (in my case), we had in all respects outgrown our street-gang love affair and retired the Debs. It was becoming too dangerous. There were no hardmen anymore, only gunmen. Local notoriety of any kind was likely to bring unwanted attention. And it was increasingly incongruous with our evolving self-image. At sixteen and seventeen, thoughts were turning to more grown-up pursuits, and concerns about qualifications, jobs and relationships began to crowd in.

To fill the vacuum left by the Debs, a new collective began to shape up, one that looked to drums, bass and guitar rather than boots, blades and belts. Anderson, Kelly and Greene might sound like a firm of solicitors ... or undertakers. They were, in fact, the first inductees into our nascent grand scheme of things.

Ivan Kelly was a whip-smart, wisecracking pain in the arse. But he was funny, and he was musically and politically sound. He hated hippies and advocated insurrection at every opportunity. We had met in Sixth Form and shared a passion for Samuel Beckett and French Revolutionary despots. When he asked me if I'd be interested in writing for a punk fanzine, we became best mates for a while. The fanzine was called *Complete Control*, partly in homage to The Clash classic. We wrote record reviews and screeds of vitriol and passionate denunciation of the system longhand and Kelly's mother, an office cleaner, would surreptitiously photocopy and staple together dozens of editions at night on the machines of the multinationals and major corporations where she cleaned. The delicious irony escaped neither of us. These we then sold in school and at gigs for pennies.

Kenny Anderson and Barry Greene were co-opted for no other reason than that they both owned guitars and practice amps. Neither of them had any serious interest in punk but they liked the idea of being in a band. Kenny owned a smart white Telecaster that his parents hoped would give him a reason to stay in at nights; Barry had a mustard Stratocaster copy. TC and I decided that we could 'bend them to our will' until such times as they were surplus to requirements.

By that time, we had a vision forming – of a four-piece, just like The Spiders from Mars or The Clash – and we were ruthless in exploiting any means to this end. We decided to start by performing punk covers anywhere we could: church halls, school discos, work dos – wherever they were stupid or trusting enough to let us in the door – and then graduate to playing our own songs.

I was already penning lyrics, but I discovered that I had considerable difficulty handing over my songs for interpretation to anyone else, and while I had a passable voice, I lacked the self-confidence to carry off the frontman role.

Kelly was no shrinking violet and became our lead singer (TC tried out for it but couldn't hold a note). While he wasn't a great vocalist, he took to it as to the manor born, interpreting each song's message intelligently and phrasing the words to good effect. He was also the 'punkiest' looking of the ensemble and enjoyed thrashing around in early rehearsals like an electric eel on speed.[1] However, it was only a matter of time before Kelly and I would clash over song writing roles and direction of the band.

TC decided to teach himself to play bass and perhaps through an innate ability arising from his total immersion in music and his sheer bloody mindedness, soon had the basics cracked. Kenny and Barry played rhythm and lead guitar respectively. Neither showed enthusiasm or initiative in their contributions, preferring to be guided by our single-minded vision and instruction.

I was a natural choice for drums, even though I didn't own any, for not only had I previous experience and training, but I also had a degree of proficiency. I'd been fortunate, when at Glenwood Primary School, to have been taught to read sheet music for percussion by George Chambers. George was some man for one man, as we say in Ireland. Trumpet player and frontman for the popular Apex Jazz Band, he was a lifelong socialist and a founder member of the much-respected Northern Ireland Labour Party. His family ran a small newsagents on the Shankill Road, while he taught the local children in school. George ensured we all learned an instrument (to the great vexation of many a suffering parent, this was usually violin or recorder), and we regularly performed in school concerts and the like. But he also took time to encourage my enthusiasm for drumming in both orchestral and military styles.

My very first performance – as a member of the Belfast Primary Schools' Choir and Orchestra – was memorable, if distressing. Stage lights fashioned from one-hundred-watt bulbs were burning bright in empty aluminium cake tins. An ensemble of seventy massed recorders had taken 'In the

Silver Moonlight' just about as far as it could go and it was time for the ranks of pubescent musicians to provide the denouement to the evening.

A hundred or more expectant parents packed the auditorium in a hushed silence as their offspring offered up some kind of validation of their parenting skills.

I was sweating profusely under the heat of the makeshift lights. Pressed into a woollen V-neck sweater knitted by my mother and strangled by an elasticated bow tie, I was one of only two side drummers in the orchestra. Whoever the other kid was, he was a model of expectancy, poise and purpose.

As we'd been taught, we held our drumsticks high, at eye level, in anticipation of the forthcoming trial. I was supposed to fix my gaze on the music stand in front of me. But I had eyes only for the spindly snare drum stand and the vast blackness of the auditorium ahead.

My moment came with a seemingly benign rendition of 'When the Saints Go Marching In'. Sweat was running into my eyes and they smarted in the lights. But I drew on the memory of the countless sessions practising on the living room furniture with my mother's knitting needles. There were four beats, just four beats, in the opening verse. 'Anyone can do that,' I told himself. Easy-peasy-lemon-squeezy.

My fellow drummer and I struck our small snare drums in perfect unison: *Oh when the saints ... diddle ... dit ... dit ... dit ... go marching in ... diddle ... dit ... dit ... dit ... Oh when the saints go marching in ...*

Suddenly, my drum lurched worryingly on its rickety tripod. I hit it again and the clamps holding it to the stand began to yawn open. With every strike, the drum leaned over a bit further and soon it was lurching alarmingly at a crazy angle. Another sound thwack and I faced the humiliating prospect of my drum leaving its mooring and rolling slowly across the wooden boards of the stage, leaving me standing exposed and drum-less.

But equally awful was the alternative: of standing immobile, arms by my sides, as the band played on, like some bozo who, presented with his moment in the sun, quite simply bottled it.

Faced with Hobson's choice, I opted for the latter. For what felt like an age of excruciating mortification, I stood stock still as all and sundry, puzzled, looked on.

A lifeless stooge under the expansive gaze of public judgement, I wilted and my eyes filled with tears. My teacher, George Chambers, stared at me, uncomprehending. My fellow drummer played twice as hard in an attempt to make up for my absence.

In that awful cauldron of indignity, illuminated in a sea of unforgiving electric light and with nowhere to hide, I vowed never again to stand immobile while others beat the drum on my behalf. So really, I had no choice but to play drums in our punk band ten years later.

Our rehearsals initially took place in Kenny Anderson's sitting room, thanks to his compliant parents, but graduated to TC's house, which had a basement big enough to just about accommodate us. It was an inhospitable space, a concrete bunker into which occasionally leached carbon monoxide fumes.

All the while, and much to our vexation, Stiff Little Fingers were making considerable headway. A couple of years older than us, they always seemed a step ahead. Undoubtedly, an emerging rivalry was forming. I knew rhythm guitarist Henry Cluney's younger brother, Ronnie, from school. And I was friendly with the Faloon family, drummer Brian being generous enough to let me have his cast-offs – a broken cymbal here, a battered bass drum (with large Mickey Mouse sticker on the skin) there.

After a while, I learned that shop floor machinists in Short Brothers, where I started working in 1978, often took their own cars into the aircraft hangers after hours for 'homers', especially bodywork repairs. So I made a few enquiries and discovered that, for a small fee, the machining of folding telescopic cymbal stands wasn't a stretch for them. Up until then, though, other more desperate measures were required.

I have always had a particularly heavy foot on the bass pedal and no amount of weighing the drum down with beer crates or breeze blocks seemed to stop the bloody thing from wandering off across the room or stage. TC's solution was to place the young brother of his then girlfriend with his back to the drum, feet braced against the breezeblock wall of the cellar, thus checking the movement of the drum. He served another purpose too: high in his right hand he held a broken drumstick which was pushed through the centre hole of a cracked cymbal. In effect, he was a human cymbal stand.

A more uncomfortable role it's difficult to imagine. As we thrashed through The Stooges / The Damned '1970', the poor lad looked like he was loading WWI artillery shells into a howitzer. Eventually, we took pity on him and suggested he put cotton wool in his ears and strap a pair of football shin pads around his hand and wrist to avoid bruising.

Punk rock!

There was only one place to go in order to be kept accurately apprised of this gobbing, pogoing, two-fingers-in-yer-face phenomenon – *The New Musical Express*. *Sounds* and *The Melody Maker* were clinging on desperately to the old order of prog and cock rock bands and virtually held their noses when reviewing live gigs from the emerging vanguard of The Adverts, The Sex Pistols, The Clash, The Vibrators, The Damned et al. So we devoured *NME* like wartime sweethearts awaiting news from the front.

Then armed with a Carlton Gaelic snare drum (used by pipe bands), various percussive bits and bobs, a small, hired PA system and mic, we went for it: 'Gary Gilmore's Eyes' by The Adverts; 'Do Anything You Wanna Do' by Eddie and the Hot Rods; '1 2 X U', 'Lowdown' and 'Ex Lion Tamer' by Wire (we particularly liked Wire); and a few early originals: 'Poppies', 'Communism', 'Don't Panic'.[2]

Next, we needed a name, a more challenging task than you might imagine. A few doozies made the shortlist. TC was particularly fond of 'Leather Ice-Cream' and the wilfully idiosyncratic 'Working Late Professor?' There was also a penchant at the time for smart-arse names, the crasser the better. 'Des and the Troys' and 'Dingle and the Berries' were typical of this.

I don't remember how we settled on 'Roofwrecks', but we must have thought it clever word play at the time. Sammy Ireland, an early devotee and sometime roadie, made badges with the band's name on them and passed them around. It was all DIY and spontaneous. He was so taken with one of our earliest songs, 'Poppies', a vitriolic anti-war anthem, that he set about mocking up a poster in the unlikely event that we would release it as a single. It featured the name of the band, the song title and a large red poppy pierced by an outsized safety pin, dripping blood. Hardly original now, but at the time we loved it.

I proudly showed the poster and the lyrics to my mother when she returned from her shift at the factory one day, expecting the positive affirmation she unfailingly offered. Instead, she stared at them for some time, saying nothing. Then, as the paper shook in her hand, her whole body quivered and her tears fell on it. When she spoke, her voice was a whisper.

'I had one brother, your uncle Jackie, who died in the war. Another, Bertie, was in the SAS, lost behind enemy lines for months before they found him. I remember the "killed in action" telegram brought to our door. Your own father fought in Burma ...'

Then she handed the now sodden lyrics back to me and, shaking her head, walked away.

I didn't know it then, but the intractable tension between rebellion and Loyalism that would challenge the ethos at the heart of our band and frame my own personal and political journey, had only just begun in earnest.

NOTES

1. Ivan Kelly later went on to front The Wall who recorded the debut LP *Personal Troubles and Public Issues*, released in December 1980.
2. See Appendix 1 for the lyrics.

4
The Pride of Ardoyne

Back in the day, there were a few good reasons – far removed from triumphalism and monarchy – why a young man in Northern Ireland might want to join an Orange marching band.

Firstly, parades were probably our best chance to be a musician or perform in front of an audience. There was undoubtedly kudos to be had from fellow band members, peers and the wider community if you excelled at playing your instrument in the semi-regular marches that were held throughout the year.

Secondly, it did not escape our notice that parades attracted young women.

So-called kick-the-pope bands (euphemistically called 'Blood and Thunder' bands in the post-peace process era) were catnip to 'millies'.[1] They would dance in a straight line behind the bandleader with his flailing mace and just ahead of us side drummers. They were tough young women, waving their mini Union Jacks and, in tartan trousers, swaying in time to the beat. For the drum corps, it was almost like having groupies.

As well as this, membership brought a positive sense of community and belonging. You were invested in the area that you represented and enjoyed the camaraderie engendered from being in competition with other bands from other parts of the city. And when fife and drum music is played well, with well-executed, accented passion, there is little more rousing and uplifting experience. I would go so far as to say that it is *soul* music of a kind, as real as Van Morrison's quasi-gospel hall fervour. It is no surprise that this music has led armies of men into battle for hundreds of years.

And so it was that when I turned fifteen, I became a side drummer for the Pride of Ardoyne Flute Band. My tenure was brief (18 months) but memorable. Although I ticked all the boxes required for membership of this loyal fraternity (family who were members of the Loyal orders and had served and died fighting for king and country in two world wars), I never felt any great need to express my loyalty to the Crown or fidelity to the flag. Moreover, I suspect many other band members felt the same way. It was wholly different in the late 70s, of course, when a sense of tribal affinity engendered a siege-like mentality, but it is interesting to reflect now on the changes that have taken place within the demographic profile of Orange Order membership and its subsequent decline. Interesting, too, is the simultaneous surge in popularity and membership of the flute bands that lead the loyal orders in parades.[2]

Then, as now, there remains a hierarchical structure to marching bands. Award-winning flute and brass ensembles kept their musical notations on stands mounted on their instruments, as did the better accordion bands. The best drummers were unfailingly in pipe bands. Unfortunately, most if not all of them have abandoned the Belfast circuit, preferring to parade in rural areas and at the demonstration at Rossnowlagh (Donegal) in the Republic of Ireland.

The Pride of Ardoyne

The Pride of Ardoyne Flute Band had always enjoyed a particular place in the hearts of the Loyalist crowds. At parades, it invariably drew applause as it passed. This was largely because Ardoyne is recognised as a PIRA/Republican/Nationalist stronghold in Belfast. The Protestant community there is almost exclusively limited to a small enclave on the fringes of the area called Glenbryn.[3] The two communities are affectively demarcated by a long residential road, Alliance Avenue, which acts as a peace line of sorts (that designation 'Alliance', another small residential area on the interface, allotted no doubt by some public official with wildly naive optimism or a twisted sense of humour). The very existence of an Orange band with the temerity to include the name 'Ardoyne' in its title was a definite two fingers to the other side.

108 Glenbryn Park was on the absolute front line of that Protestant enclave, and it was here – to escape the intolerable damp and cold of our Sunningdale maisonette – that the family Burgess moved. It was the very definition of leaping out of the frying pan. High walls of corrugated iron sheeting separated the two communities while British Army regiments took turns to man a small, fortified outpost, essentially offering themselves up to be shot at by the snipers of the Provisional IRA's Ardoyne Brigade. Occasionally, they would go one further and attach an explosive device on or near the observation post. At such times, RUC officers and soldiers would arrive at your door to instruct you to open all windows (otherwise the blast from the bomb would blow the glass right back into your home).

At times of imminent danger, our next-door neighbour Roy 'Spike' Milligan and I brokered a novel response. While others gathered bottles for petrol bomb manufacture or broke up paving stones for ammunition, Spike and I set up

Wild colonial boys

our respective stereo speakers outside on our adjoining bedroom windowsill ledges and on a 3-2-1 countdown, touched our styluses down on the vinyl in unison, with a full-volume bass woofer *thump*! It was always either 'Brainstorm' or 'Master of the Universe' from Hawkwind's live *Space Ritual* album, chosen for their uncompromising volume and electronic swell. A wall of guitar and synthesiser noise filled the street below and wafted across the barricades to the other side. To this day, I'm amazed that our sonic attack was ignored by the area's self-appointed UDA 'defenders'.

We became expert in identifying by sound the ballistics used by the Ardoyne Provos (Provisional IRA): the low wallop of the bolt-action 303; the high-pitched, fast action of a 9mm semi-automatic pistol, emptying a full mag in one go; the feared high-velocity staccato *crack-crack-crack* of their signature Armalite (AR-15) assault rifle.

Street invasion from the other side invariably meant looting and burning of homes and the fear of this was real, rooted deep in the Belfast working-class psyche of both communities and for good reason. The pogroms of 1969 were still fresh in the memory. Not surprisingly, then, the Glenbryn community has always had something of a siege mentality, emboldening them rather than allowing it to demoralise them.

The whole area amounted to three or four streets, radiating out from a squat, concrete pillbox community centre called The Jolly Roger, a UDA-affiliated establishment where locals watched horseracing and drank cheap pints. It was somewhere I tended to avoid due to its paramilitary associations and stories of afterhours 'romper rooms' where summary beatings and worse were handed out. There were few shops or facilities for children to play, although the area did back on to the municipal Ballysillan Playing Fields (often used as a dumping ground for bodies). Somehow, for better or worse, the Pride of Ardoyne Flute Band became the colourful, raucous, indomitable expression of all of this and more.

Fluters Bobby and Gerry Spence had a direct family link to one of Loyalism's great icons, Gusty Spence, incarcerated commander of the UVF. This essentially marked the band as a UVF one, with other members affiliated at one level or another. While there were UDA members who drifted in and out, the Pride of the Shankill Flute Band – our sworn rivals – were UDA through and through.

Murderous feuds between the two paramilitary organisations usually spilled over to the bands on parade, when confrontations took on the dimensions of a Liverpool vs Manchester United derby. The objective was to figuratively 'blow them off the road' with lung-busting volume, earthquake drumming and full-on chutzpah. The opportunity often came as the bands drew level with each other while marking time. At those times, band captain Spence would call a tune designed to feature the 'double fortes' (essentially a song with a strong chorus that would feature all the members in together, playing at full intensity).

Post-parade, in our cups, boasts would be made and individual performances praised, just like any team sporting event or performance-based endeavour. But it was the undeniably sectarian aspect to these parades, and the bitter triumphalist experiences arising from these, that ultimately soured my involvement with the whole thing.

On the Twelfth of July, the biggest day in the Orange calendar, word went around as the bands marched back from the field that the customary ritual baiting of the 'Taigs'[4] was imminent. In what was to become a common event, years later attracting notoriety, the band would come to a temporary halt outside Donegal Street Catholic Chapel, and while the police escort turned a blind eye, the lads would pump up the volume. The drum major would pass amongst the ranks of us drummer boys, his veins bulging and eyeballs popping, exhorting us through gritted teeth to 'play up! ... play up! ... Let the papist bastards hear ye in Rome!'

Further up the road, Nationalists and Republicans would be standing five hundred yards back from the procession, behind massive canvas screens that British soldiers had erected. Grateful for the advance notice of the procession, they always came well-armed, and as the band drew level with them, the old 'Belfast confetti' would rain down on us – bricks, bottles, razor and Stanley knife blades slipped into cakes of soap or dug into potatoes, like lethal porcupines. Then the drum core would respond by turning their drumsticks round to the fat end so as to batter the drums all the harder, despite the blisters and blood oozing from the friction burns.

And when it was all over and our drum skins were burst, we returned home, wearily standing for a final rendition of 'God Save the Queen' before dispersing for another year, drenched in sweat and the certainty of our own superiority: *We are the people!*

Band rookies like me and fellow side drummer Billy Fisher saw an opportunity, in the preambles to the traditional tunes the band played, to bring something new and imaginative to the table by introducing a 'call and response' sequence between the drums and flutes to kick the tune off. It wasn't much, but in a typically unadventurous and traditional medium, there was a creativity and originality to this that was satisfying for us.

The Pride of Ardoyne

Billy was a couple of years older than me and had taken me under his wing to some extent. He worked on the shop floor of Short Brothers and would have been well paid. He was an avid motor biker, and nothing seemed to give him more pleasure than to scare the bejaysus out of me on pillion as we raced up and down the motorway on his Kawasaki. Afterwards, he'd treat me to what was then considered an exotic Beef Curry and Fried Rice from one of the newly emerging Chinese takeaways.

I had arranged to meet him one Sunday afternoon outside The Jolly Roger. As he lived in Alliance Avenue, this was a convenient halfway point between both our houses. We were to catch a bus into town together where, over a pint, I planned to tell him about my intention to leave the Pride of Ardoyne, something I knew he would try to talk me out of. He moved in different circles from me and had only derision for the emerging punk rock scene and my own recent endeavours with Roofwrecks.

The Jolly Roger was only a three-minute walk away for me and, being fastidious about timekeeping, I would usually have left early for an agreed 1 p.m. rendezvous. But I had been working on a song to show TC and this had delayed me. Then, as I opened the front door to leave, I heard a familiar tune from the TV in the living room introducing the BBC's football highlights. I tarried on the doorstep, one foot in, one out, watching the week's goals through the open gap.

Just then, shots rang out, loud and in quick succession; they were nearby. Instinctively I ducked down. A few seconds later, men ran along the street, shouting and pointing. Two Jolly Roger members, a doorman and punter, had been shot dead. Five men had pulled up outside the club in a red Fiat, got out and shot the doorman instantly, then kicked open the door of the club and sprayed the inside with semi-automatics.

My first thought was that Billy Fisher would have been there, waiting outside for me.

My next thought caused my stomach to flip – I myself should have been there, standing outside, probably idly chatting to the now dead doorman.

By the time I'd mustered up the courage to go around there, ambulances had been and gone, the police were there and a small crowd had gathered.

I was relieved, to say the least, that Fisher was amongst the spectators, standing on tiptoe and craning his neck for a better view. We tentatively peered in through the open door, now swathed in yellow crime scene tape. Tables were overturned where drinkers had futilely sought cover, bullet holes punched into cheaply upholstered seating, leaving foam and splintered wood spilling out. Shards of glass littered the floor where rounds had ripped through pint glasses and beer bottles; pools of lager and blood were coagulating on the linoleum.

As we walked away, I told Billy Fisher then and there that none of it made sense anymore, that I felt ridiculous in my blue cap with orange plume and black trousers with red stripes down the side, 'like some fuckin' clown'. I had another band now, I said, a very different one, and as we had our first gig coming up, I was going home to write songs for it.

Things were never the same after that. I handed back the uniform and equipment at the next band meeting much as I had done earlier to Harry Half-a-head, the UDA 'corporal'. No one seemed too concerned.

The Pride of Ardoyne

NOTES

1 'Millie', a term used to describe young female linen mill workers in the north of Ireland in the nineteenth century. It has come to be used in a largely derogatory way to mean a working-class girl or woman with a broad Belfast accent.
2 See Sam McCready and Neil Symington, 'To the Beat of a Different Drum: Loyalist Youth and the Culture of Marching Bands', in *The Contested Identities of Ulster Protestants*, ed. T.P. Burgess and G. Mulvenna (London: Palgrave Macmillan, 2015), pp. 177–90.
3 The area became notorious through the national and international press coverage of the Holy Cross Dispute of 2001–2.
4 Primarily in Northern Ireland, a derogatory term for a Catholic or Irish nationalist.

5
Bad vibrations

Stiff Little Fingers, Roofwrecks arch-rivals (at least in our minds), were moving on apace. Word had it that they had teamed up with two English journalists, Colin McClelland and Gordon Ogilvie, who had assumed something of a management role and there was already talk of recording time booked in via their new contacts in the media. Then, as now, it was becoming clear that, to get that all-important break, it was all about who you knew.

SLF personnel changes saw Ali McMordie replace Gordy Blair (who would play in a number of other Belfast bands before eventually joining Ruefrex). Both Ali and Gordy fitted the emerging trend of the lean, mean punk bassist pin-up, with low-slung guitar, spiked hair and looking elegantly wasted in drainpipe jeans and biker jacket à la Paul Simonon (The Clash), Jean-Jacques Burnel (The Stranglers), Dee Dee Ramone (Ramones) and Sid Vicious (Sex Pistols).

'Image' was important, yes, but to us it smacked of style over substance. Something that we, as a band, consciously disparaged, probably at the cost of greater popularity or commercial success, even in those early days. We were passionate about upholding the purity of the punk aesthetic, the nihilism at the core of the ideologies

Bad vibrations

that drove songs like 'Anarchy in the UK'[1] and 'Career Opportunities' and were scathing of those who seemed to spend more time on their appearance than on their music (or politics). Roofwrecks threw itself into the new order of things with a righteous, almost religious zeal, and we were determined not to sacrifice our principles for commercial considerations. As an example of this, we wouldn't give The Stranglers the time of day simply because they had a keyboard player. (Dave Greenfield, their keyboardist, also sported a dubious moustache, but then so did I.) To us, keyboards harked back to a techno era that predated punk and seemed superfluous. Bass, drums, guitar, vocals was the stripped-back, streamlined prerequisite for punk. We were young and idealistic and had no idea that Joe Strummer was actually someone called John Graham Mellor. Nor were we aware of the machinations of Messrs Malcolm McLaren and Bernie Rhodes behind the scenes, or the inevitability of commercial enterprise sullying this new, pristine religion and its means of testifying.

Collectives and allegiances had already formed in the Belfast punk scene, and schisms were starting to appear. Much has been made, retrospectively, of the success of punk in Northern Ireland as a means of transcending sectarian divisions. While this remains a matter for conjecture, other rifts were playing out between participants.

Divisions that were represented in musical form, attitude and fashion were key indicators of something seminal. There were clear fissures between those keen to embrace a developing orthodoxy of belonging, shown through the use of uniforms, appearance and group allegiance, and those who embraced literally the nihilistic mantle of punk – the misanthropic separatism and rejection of the conformity of collectives and movements.

Wild colonial boys

In addition to this, voices were emerging from some of the most disadvantaged and marginalised areas of Northern Ireland that sought to articulate the anger of the dispossessed. They represented, through their songs, aspects of working-class experience that transcended (in our case anyway) traditional cultural orthodoxies of Unionism and Loyalism.

This heartfelt dissent existed uneasily alongside the multicoloured Mohicans and safety-pinned drainpipes of the rapidly emerging punk 'yoof-culture' and its ever-faster commercialisation by the Svengalis of Oxford Street and the King's Road.

For many cultural, political and societal reasons, Northern Ireland is often viewed through the prism of dichotomies, simple dualities that confine the complexities of belonging and identification within the straitjacketed stereotypes of Protestant/Unionist/Loyalist and Catholic/Republican/Nationalist.[2] The unwillingness or inability of the mainstream press, and the music industry generally, to see beyond these easy polarities would later come to stymie and frustrate the efforts of our band throughout our entire performing and recording career. The narrative we promoted did not easily fit into socio-religious pigeonholes, and so their reporting often took the form of lazy indifference or wilful misrepresentation. Easy clichés were just too compelling and made for better copy.

In the face of this, we malcontents focused on the absolute certainty of our music and musical influences, our fiercely independent vision and our complete contempt for those who followed the herd. And this provided a resolute, galvanising energy, albeit one completely fuelled by fury and one that rendered us the pariahs of the Belfast punk scene.

So it will come as no surprise, then, that Roofwrecks, with our Spiderman attire, our Spiderman following, our

Bad vibrations

working-class Loyalist background and our prodigious capacity for arrogance and sarcasm, made few friends among other Belfast punk bands. Rudi and The Outcasts at best tolerated, at worst despised us. Stiff Little Fingers, either because of our common schooling and North Belfast location, or simply out of a sense of guilt arising from our (self-appointed) role as their 'punk conscience', extended us courtesies we neither earned nor deserved. We rarely crossed paths with The Undertones since they were from Derry. When we did, I found them refreshingly grounded following their rapid success and elevation with 'Teenage Kicks' and Sire Records. When we played on the same bill, drummer Billy Doherty in particular was most accommodating in allowing me to use his brand new red Premier drum kit (an uncommon courtesy at the time). It didn't escape our attention either that they eschewed the punk uniform in favour of ordinary corner-boy garb, much like ourselves.

Bearing all this in mind, it's easy to see how our relationship with Terri Hooley and his Good Vibrations record shop and label was doomed to failure from the get-go. We were coruscating about his clientele's increasingly elaborate Mohicans and body piercings and let it be known that we saw his developing 'scene' as little more than a youth club. We dismissed him as a hippie and called him 'Cyclops' due to his glass eye, all the while berating him for not having the courage to release a song by us. It's a wonder he let us over the threshold of his shop in the first place, much less acquiesce to us bringing out a record on his label (and for this I remain eternally grateful, despite our differences).

His enduring ire against us may originate from those early days in his shop on Great Victoria Street. The man himself, when asked about the band, has been consistently dismissive, even aggressively offensive, 'Ruefrex are shite!' being a common response.

He has suggested that our antipathy towards him is because we believe he owes us money from record sales of the *One by One* EP. While we never received one red cent for sales or licensing from Good Vibrations, I can categorically say it was never about the money. Rather it was the fact that he clearly had his favourites on the label, and promoted and celebrated them at every turn. Conversely, he gave Ruefrex little or no credit or recognition for our successes. This became particularly spiteful when, in later years, Ruefrex were effectively written out of the Good Vibes history by a small cabal of devotees, well placed in broadcasting, film making and journalism. For us, our enduring antipathy toward the Good Vibrations myth was about the lack of love and respect shown to the band (and I appreciate how cringeworthy that sounds.)

We couldn't have known then, of course, about the eventual (and dubious) beatification of Terri Hooley. Not that it was entirely surprising. Thanks to a concerted (and perhaps heretical) retelling by a coterie of Belfast's music and film establishment, punk rock in the city is now forever intrinsically linked with the Good Vibrations record store, label and owner (blue plaque and all). I was bemused, to say the least, when I heard that the 'Godfather of Belfast Punk' had been added to the pantheon of my hometown's greatest figures and now shares a pedestal with other luminaries of that era – John Peel, Malcolm McLaren, Bernie Rhodes, Geoff Travis, Alan McGee, and so on.

I have written elsewhere in this book about my memories of this early period and of relations with Good Vibrations. In my experience, Terri has two undeniable talents: firstly, he is one of the most opportunistic self-starters I have ever come across (and I've met some wheekers), and secondly, he has a specific talent for taking half-truths and manufacturing noteworthy legends from them. These two talents are particularly in evidence when they help to further the narrative that all around him seem eager to promote of him as a 'lovable scoundrel'.

Revisionist musicologists and sociologists have often cited the apparently non-sectarian Belfast punk scene of the late 70s/early 80s as representing an alternative youth/cultural environment that transcended ethno-religious divisions. The film *Good Vibrations* (2013) tells the story of the Belfast impresario and his record store and the influence he had on youth culture at that time. The film posits the idea that Hooley's (questionable) predisposition for socialism created, in the record shop, a religiously and culturally neutral venue in which young people could comfortably find commonality through non-sectarian punk music. But for those of us who were there, we know that if such an environment did evolve, it was purely by accident, not design. However, the movie – like the man himself – doesn't let the truth get in the way of a good story. It presents a wonderfully affirming, hopeful account for a province where, cinematically, so many awful tales have gone before, and I completely understand the appetite for wanting to move on and accentuating the positive.

In my opinion, the *re*-writing of history in Northern Ireland, be it sanitised reflections on the atrocities of our troubled past or anodyne accounts of cultural rebellion, should be approached with some sense of responsibility to the facts. As I see it, there is a core dichotomy at the heart of the Good Vibrations/Terri Hooley 'legend'. On the one hand is the story that music sought to create an alternative space within an intolerable reality, to generate an environment of apparent indifference through the manufacture of a pseudo-normal, counter-cultural punk 'scene'. On the other hand is the suggestion that music should play a role in contextually reflecting or challenging the dysfunctional society that has spawned it and, by so doing, affect change therein.

Put more simply, one could adopt a *non*-sectarian stance, as Terri and Good Vibrations did, by opting out, burying one's head in the sand and creating a neutral, escapist bubble. Or one could embrace the challenge of an *anti*-sectarian remit, as Ruefrex did, accept the inherent dangers intrinsic in that stance and work actively through art/music toward peace and an end to sectarianism. To my mind, the latter is the better story and more deserving to be told.

So despite, and not because of, Terri and Good Vibrations, we forged on.

Our first gig of note was supporting Stiff Little Fingers in The Trident in Bangor, Co. Down on Wednesday 14 December 1977. That gig is immortalised by the reference to it in their anthemic song, 'Alternative Ulster'. Despite our continual haranguing of them for having English journalists write their lyrics, they showed surprising patience in giving us opportunities like this. That was soon to change.

We didn't make much effort for our stage appearances. Kelly wore my father's GPO peaked cap in an attempt, I think, to look like a Nazi. I had my long-suffering mother remove zips from old trousers and sew them onto the legs on my best jeans in an effort to replicate bondage trousers.

By the time we started to pester Hooley for a single, we'd moved up the pecking order from church halls and community centres to dedicated music venues: the Pound, the Harp Bar, the Glenmachan and the Trident. And, of course, the more we played, the tighter and better we got, as did the quality and arrangement of the songs.

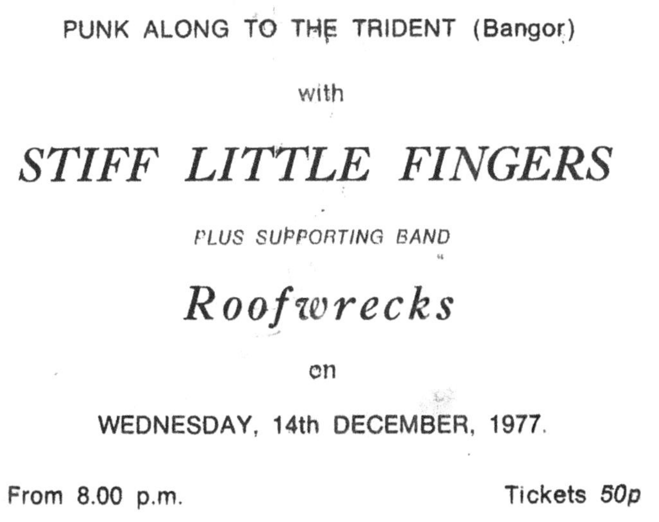

Bad vibrations

PUNK ALONG TO THE TRIDENT (Bangor)

with

STIFF LITTLE FINGERS

PLUS SUPPORTING BAND

Roofwrecks

on

WEDNESDAY, 14th DECEMBER, 1977.

From 8.00 p.m.   Tickets **50p**

Illustration S1.1 'Okay, so there's the Trident in Bangor ...'. Only 50p! Ad for debut gig at the Trident in Bangor, 14 December 1977. Photo by the author

TC took to bass guitar immediately and it became clear that, just as he had assumed the leadership role in our earlier gang manifestation, he was determined to master the instrument and the music writing brief. I typically brought him lyrics that he would compose to, but often he would arrange songs solo, fitting my lyrics around them later.

His playing style became the source of some humour. His need to assert himself in performance, as in everything else, meant that he would stray further and further up the fret board, playing higher and louder as he felt necessary. It resembled the bravura of Gene Simmons from Kiss, a guilty pleasure he liked to indulge from time to time. Later, his style was more like Peter Hook's (Joy Division). When drink rendered him incapable, he claimed to be playing jazz.

Wild colonial boys

It was at this point that TC and I decided to revise some key personnel. We had always viewed Anderson and Greene as a means to an end and had been looking for another guitarist who could subsume both their roles. And unbeknownst to Ivan Kelly, his days were numbered too. Kelly, all mouthy attitude and in-your-face antagonism, might easily have been mistaken for The Boomtown Rats frontman Bob Geldof. So Kelly's removal was put down to ideological differences as well as the well-worn musical ones. We used to joke that he was Trotsky to my Lenin and TC's Stalin and would be required to vacate the role with good grace or face the ice-pick.

As we improved and tightened as a unit, the band's name began to seem inappropriate – facetious, insubstantial, out of step somehow with how we saw ourselves and our place in the order of things. A change of name was required to herald our second coming of sorts. But we had steadily built up a decent following as Roofwrecks, and we were loath to abandon it completely. I felt that the solution was to keep the name but change the spelling. Maybe something with a X in it. It had worked for T. Rex, X-Ray Spex, XTC, Siouxsie Sioux, Generation X. Something more angular, more jagged, more raw-boned maybe, and so in 1979 Ruefrex was born.

It was not without its initial problems. Ads announcing forthcoming gigs in local newspapers, the *Irish News*, *Belfast Telegraph* and *News Letter*, went variously with 'Reufrx', 'Rufux' and, my particular favourite, 'Ruf and Rex' (which made us sound like a dog act or a ventriloquist and his dummy).

Ever since, and despite these purely pragmatic motives for changing the name, I have consistently fielded questions about it, 'So, what does it mean?' being the most common. In response, and for mischief, I've found myself offering

Bad vibrations

the following explanation: 'rue' is French for street, 'rex' is Latin for king. Et voila – Kings of the Street or Street Kings. In truth, this was an afterthought, but to my impish delight, English journalists, American musicologists and Japanese archivists all later came to embrace it enthusiastically.

NOTES

1. Johnny Rotten had pondered 'is this the UDA? Or is this the IRA? I thought it was the UK' and at once sent out a clarion call that immediately registered. It was as if he was speaking to us personally.
2. See my books *The Contested Identities of Ulster Protestants* (with G. Mulvenna; Palgrave Macmillan, 2015) and *The Contested Identities of Ulster Catholics* (Palgrave Macmillan, 2018).

6
The boy looked at Clarkey

It remains a conviction, held by the other members of the band, and indeed anyone else who knows him, that when Allan Clarke looks in the mirror, he sees Ziggy Stardust looking back. Or perhaps not Ziggy alone. Over many years, as Bowie's look changed, we can confidently say that this was also the case with Clarkey's alter-ego. Aladdin Sane, Major Tom, The Thin White Duke – all shared the looking glass at one time or another with the Ruefrex frontman.

I can only speculate that the changes in the rest of us down the years – receding hairline, extra pounds around the middle, the stresses and strains of family life – have not in fact impinged one iota on Clarkey's unshakeable belief that he is somehow hardwired into the Bowie psyche. As Kraftwerk famously observed,

> He made up the person he wanted to be
> And changed into a new personality
> Even the greatest stars
> Change themselves in the looking glass.[1]

The *Cross the Line* documentary made by BBC Northern Ireland in 1980 offers an insight into his thinking around this. As wife number one draws an Aladdin Sane lightning

The boy looked at Clarkey

bolt across his face with her own Max Factor products, Clarkey ruminates on the appeal of donning 'the mask': 'It does something else for me when I'm actually onstage.'[2]

Allan Clarke was (and remains) infatuated by all things David Bowie. He religiously catalogues the most obscure bootlegs and Japanese releases, owns all the T-shirts, has photos taken in *that* phone booth, and under the K-West sign in Heddon Street, London. His lifelong worship of the late, great Bowie is almost childlike in its devotion.

But despite this and his great longing to inhabit the shapeshifting, lizard-hipped, uber-cool façade of his hero, it was with two other iconic figures that his stage persona could be more accurately compared. Stripped to the waist, covered in sweat and tattoos, he was as likely to scamper up the PA speakers as to launch himself into the middle of the audience and thrust a mic in their faces so they could join in with the chanted refrain of 'One by One' or 'Capital Letters'. In this respect, he was like Iggy Pop in full flight. However, his enthusiasm for stage props – rubber knives, fake blood, replica guns – was reminiscent of Alice Cooper.

These stage theatrics caused the band quite a bit of discomfort, and yet while these antics often seemed cringeworthy to us, we were also acutely aware that the crowd, in the main, seemed to adore them. Indeed, over time, they came to be accepted as part of a Ruefrex gig and were anticipated by our audience. In addition, his photogenic persona and strong stage presence, coupled with his high-octane performance came to be synonymous with the visceral musical signature of the band.

Nonetheless, as the band's lyricist, I lamented that all this was detracting from the crucial anti-sectarian message of the group and the songs. It was certainly detrimental to the quality of his vocal performance. By this time we had established ourselves as a band whose songs almost always contained a message. The crowd expected there to be something activist-orientated, even cerebral at times, about our central mission and ethos. As fine a voice as he had, subtle word plays or coruscating denunciations were somewhat undermined when they were delivered hanging upside down from the stanchion.

You might think that such political sensibilities would be ridiculed by the pogoing, gobbing punks of the Harp Bar, but in my experience, punters who loved The Clash and The Pistols placed considerable emphasis on 'the message' of our songs. Some bands wrote about 'chocolate and girls', as The Undertones, in their brilliantly perverse and contrarian manner, claimed.[3] But Ruefrex, amongst others, was unashamedly political in outlook and expression, and we made no apology for this.

It is difficult to convey the feeling of handing over lyrics that you are deeply invested in, to someone who doesn't fully engage with what you are trying to do or say. It's worse still when that person wilfully or clumsily misrepresents you in onstage comments, press interviews or politically questionable behaviour.[4] It's a bit like leaving your kids with Hannibal Lector as their babysitter, or putting them up for adoption by Tommy Robinson.

The tensions arising from Clarkey's central role in the band were evident from the outset and were pivotal both to our progress and, ultimately, our demise.

I had been vaguely aware of Clarkey many years before inviting him to join Ruefrex. His older brother Roy moved in the same circles on the Shankill as my brother David did, and a few years later Clarkey resurfaced in North Belfast, resettled like so many others. He went to the same school as the rest of us, worked as a shop assistant in a hardware

The boy looked at Clarkey

store and was known for his Bowie obsession in particular and his passion for music in general. But it was his reputation as an exhibitionist and well-known 'header' that first brought him to our attention.

A typical stunt illustrates this. While we were walking around our patch one day, someone pointed out that a new security grill had been put over the front window of a corner furniture shop. Without prompting, Clarkey scaled the metal grill in two bounds and head-butted the one unprotected pane of glass at the top until it cracked.

In local parlance, he was 'game as a badger', a characteristic held in high regard, as Henry McDonald's novel *Two Souls*, set during this period, so ably conveys.

A babysitter of his once told me that, as a child, Clarkey had chased a fellow playmate until she slammed a glass door shut and locked it in order to escape him. But that didn't deter Clarkey, who just jumped headfirst through it. It's a story he would proudly relate himself and happily show you the scar.

Offstage he had a knockabout, arms-flailing, feet-tripping, wind-milling gait, reminiscent of the comedian Norman Wisdom. He attempted to make this appear endearing and klutz-like, but these prat-fall theatrics were practised and easy to see through. Onstage, he was continually tripping over mic stands, guitar leads and bass drum legs, so much so that TC and I secretly nicknamed him 'Bepo' and rather cruelly imitated circus pipe-organ music when he appeared.

To this day, he possesses the most outrageous capacity for *im*plausible deniability in anyone I've ever met. In rehearsal, you might ask him to come in at a prearranged point in the song and he would repeatedly fuck it up. When you pointed out his error to him, he would deny ever having been given the instruction in the first place, despite there being other band members in the room and a producer at the recording desk willing to play the conversation back again. Then, after much debate, he would magnanimously consent to try again, as if for the first time, to see if it worked. If it did, he would insist, with no sense of irony, that it had been his idea all along. On several occasions I have recounted stories to him, only to have him tell them back to me weeks later, with him as the chief protagonist instead of me.

So if manic, force-of-nature unpredictability with a fluid take on reality were prerequisites for a frontman, he had them in spades. It was a considerable relief to learn that he could sing as well. The stage outfits and make-up followed shortly thereafter. Then came the props based on his interpretation of my lyrics, sometimes apt, sometimes mystifyingly outlandish.

But the machismo was never far away. Where I may have celebrated our working-class roots onstage, inspired by the power of the collective or the dignity of labour, Clarkey took this as an opportunity to assert the persona of a no-nonsense hardman. The tattooed torso helped with this, of course. All this meant that he was closer to TC, who he revered in terms of his past street reputation and shared musical enthusiasms. So it was TC who invariably coaxed the best performances from him.

Yet all of this is not to sell Clarkey short. He was a hardman with an incredible set of pipes on him. At his best, he could bring genuine feeling to a ballad, and blistering energy to a three-minute heads-down, see-you-at-the-finish, power-punk anthem. Clarkey could take a lyric and, in collaboration with TC and me, show real talent in developing harmonies, hooks and catchy vocal refrains. But live, he was not blessed with witty repartee or the ability to deliver pearls of wisdom between songs. We'd given him a mic and

The boy looked at Clarkey

PA, for chrissakes, and we lived in apprehension of what he might say next to the crowd.

In short, he was no Bono ... he was Clarkey, and we had our replacement for Ivan Kelly.

NOTES

1. Lyrics from Kraftwerk, 'The Hall of Mirrors', from the album *Trans Europa Express* (1977).
2. *Cross the Line*, BBC documentary, 1980. www.youtube.com/watch?v=6AVVDopBZOY&t=1034s.
3. The Undertones, 'More Songs About Chocolate and Girls', from the *Hypnotised* album (1980).
4. Clarkey also had a penchant for wearing military/army clothes. When you place this in the context of efforts by a band from a Loyalist background to promote cross-community tolerance in a Northern Irish setting, you can understand the problem. It later transpired that he had served in the British Army for a while and saw no contradiction between this and the broadly pacifist stance of Ruefrex. Latterly, I have had a number of fans from the nationalist community express their unease regarding his social media persona and enthusiasm for populist right-wing causes.

7
Lousy body

John Hepburn Forgie was an enigma. And that's exactly how he liked it.

To say he was conflicted is something of an understatement. He grew up right around the corner from me, on Charleville Street, in a house just beside a popular corner shop, Archie Adam's grocery store. It was an important hub for the community as it housed a public telephone, a rarity on the Shankill Road in the 1960s. My family and I would have visited it countless times.

Despite his proximity, and the fact that we attended the same secondary school, I have no memory of him during that period. He didn't play sports or engage in any of the rough-and-tumble backstreet high jinks that might have endeared him to his peers or a wider constituency. As a young man, he was spindly, short-sighted and wore Coke-bottle glasses, perched on a prodigious schnozzle. He grew up as a self-conscious, insecure and introspective teenager. Despite this, or perhaps because of it, he concealed vast reservoirs of anger beneath a placid and self-effacing persona. A beta male in a world of alphas, he possessed a sharp mind and an able intellect, but was clearly frustrated, which

Lousy body

further fuelled his ire. It came as no surprise, then, that he embraced the dynamic liberation of punk rock, where losers were winners, wholeheartedly and with gusto.

Forgie first came to our attention through Ivan Kelly, who had been prompting us to invite him to rehearsals. At that time he worked as a clerk in Rediffusion television rentals, leasing coin operated TV sets to hard-up punters. As might be expected of a friend of Kelly's, Forgie had a strong interest in social issues, music and politics. Perhaps because of this – and our shared love of books and movies – he was to emerge as the intellectual ally who most closely shared my personal vision for the band.

However, his proficiency on guitar was limited. Unlike, say, Jake Burns, Forgie couldn't master the 'noodling' bag of tricks that guitarists often employed to set out their stall. But ten-minute solos were a thing of the past, we reckoned. He could play a solid, three-power-chord rhythm and a shared sense of who we were and where we were going.

It is said that bands work best as benign dictatorships, not democracies, and crucially, Forgie was able to take instruction and guidance on song arrangements without recourse to ego and artifice. He grasped immediately that all-important overdriven, sustained guitar sound that TC and I were looking for and did it as if he were channelling all that internalised anger through his instrument.

As his confidence on his guitar grew, so too did his willingness to self-deprecatingly celebrate his difference. Soft spoken and styling himself as the odd, alternative, introvert of the band, he welcomed teasing at his expense and happily embraced the pseudonym 'Lousy Body' before settling on 'ArtRat', which he emblazoned on his first guitar. Unlike

Wild colonial boys

Jake Burns, who self-consciously swopped his glasses for contacts, Forgie wore his thick-lensed specs as a perverse badge of honour. He looked the part, with his high cheekbones, sallow complexion and mop of spiky jet-black hair, and was, for us, the last piece of the puzzle.

8
If you go down to the Harp today ...

The Harp Bar in Hill Street, Belfast, was a dingy, heavily fortified pub in a dimly lit, narrow, cobblestone street in a run-down part of the city. Frequented by dockers, horse racing punters and winos, it was an unlikely venue to establish itself as the mecca for punk in the city.

Even seedier than The Pound, the established music venue and haunt of hippies and bluesmen, the Harp offered a small bar on the ground floor, patronised by a varied clientele, and a performance space upstairs that became the number one live venue for the growing number of punk acts emerging at that time.

If you timed it right, you could be setting up your band equipment at the back of the stage for a sound check – late afternoon, early evening – when the strippers from the matinee were still finishing their show, right there in front of us teenage boys. Within touching distance. A single gold-lacquered metal chair with a heart-shaped cushioned back sat centre stage and the working girls sometimes incorporated this into their gyrations. I remember that the dark burgundy-coloured fabric sported a dubious stain in the shape of South America.

Then, when the girls quit their shift, the punters cleared out and the bar staff went off for a fag break or to change kegs for the evening, one band member would keep watch while the others reached across the bar to pull pints, which were urgently downed in one. It was a fraught business as detection attracted a harsh penalty.

Our Harp Bar gigs were always notable for the many members of other bands in attendance. We knew they were there to see what we were up to with new material, rather than out of any sense of unambiguous fandom. Nevertheless, we liked to believe that we commanded respect from our rivals – for our songs, our performance or maybe even our uncompromising musical and political integrity.

Despite the popular myth that the Harp offered an open-armed, no-questions-asked sanctuary for punks seeking to escape the sectarian divisions of the city, that was not always the case. The pub had a reputation for its hard-drinking, hard-living clientele who did not suffer fools gladly. The politics of the management, bar and door staff was predominately nationalist, likely with a socialist/Official IRA leaning. Punk music and its followers were more likely to be indulged for the revenue they generated at the bar than for any high-minded aspiration to create a cross-community neutral space. One story perhaps illustrates this.

We were rounding off a solid Friday night set and were on to our encore. The floor in front of the stage was awash with writhing, pogoing, body-slamming punks. Thankfully, gobbing had been at a minimum, something I attributed to Clarkey's menacing scowl when the phlegm began to fly. But hurling the contents of pint glasses toward the stage was de rigueur. By the end of a good night you could count on being soaked in beer and sweat.

If you go down to the Harp today ...

For the encore we had chosen to cover Sham 69's 'Ulster Boy'. We weren't particularly fans of Jimmy Pursey, his band or his cockney sensibilities, but the lyrics (inane as they are) are about our patch. If you know the song, there is a repeated refrain of 'Ulster ... Ulster ...',[1] delivered with chant-like, air-punching monotony and easily comparable with popular Loyalist songs. I would be lying if I said that the ambiguity did not appeal to some sense of mischief on our part (although Clarkey and TC might have harboured darker intent).

During the performance I noticed an urgent confab taking place amongst some huddled figures at the back of the room, and when I played the final cymbal crash to end the song, the applause was quite muted. Despite this, we quickly got in tune and tightened cymbal wing nuts for a rendition of '1 2 X U' by Wire to cap off the night.

As we did so, a small, heavy-set man in his mid-fifties wearing a suit and open-neck shirt approached the stage front, smiling and nodding as he made his way through the crowd. But his expression changed to a scowl as he came to the lip of the stage. With his back to the crowd, he unbuttoned his jacket and held it wide open to reveal the butt of a semi-automatic pistol stuffed into the waistband of his trousers.

'Play one more note and yer fuckin' dead men!' he growled.

We looked at him in shock. We'd heard of nothing like this in the Harp before. It was as if we had overstepped some invisible line and our punk rock protections had been revoked, with extreme prejudice.

'Pack up yer gear and get the fuck out of here ... NOW!'

TC and Forgie were playing through amps borrowed from the support act, so they only had their guitars to worry

Illustration S1.2 A small libation to help with the creative process! Recording the *One by One* EP in 1979. L–R Coulter, Forgie, Burgess, Clarke.
Photo by Norman Creaney

If you go down to the Harp today ...

about. A house PA system, shared with the other acts on the bill, meant that Clarkey was also untrammelled. I, however, was not so lucky. Imagine trying to walk, very quickly, carrying two stands and a hi-hat with cymbals still attached, a snare drum on its stand, a bass drum with tom and pedal attached, and a floor tom.

Somehow we managed it through a combination of adrenaline and chutzpah. But it was the last time *that* song featured in our repertoire ... and the end of quaffing illicit pints.

We later heard stories that backed up our experience, that the Harp Bar was not always the neutral, non-sectarian idyl it was lionised as in later years. For example, Joe Zero of The Androids claimed he had had a gun pulled on him in the toilets when they played their debut show there, supporting Rhesus Negative, but that the 'harder' punks in attendance had stood up for them and chased the gunman away.[2]

But there was to be redemption. Next day we travelled to the Good Vibrations shop to learn that Terri Hooley had finally given way to our petitions to make a record. A date was set at Wizard Studios to record our first single, 'One by One'. However, we intended to maximise the opportunity, as The Undertones had done, by releasing an EP of three songs. After all, we might never get the chance again. As predicted, and despite the EP's success, it was the one and only disc we were asked to record for the label.

NOTES

1 'Ulster Boy', from the album *Tell Us The Truth* (1978). Written by Dave Parsons and Jimmy Pursey.
2 The Androids' Facebook page and Garth Cartwright, 'Belfast and the Furious: How punk rock made its mark on Northern Ireland', *The New European*, 10 September 2020, www.theneweuropean.co.uk/brexit-news-punk-in-troubles-torn-northern-ireland-91176.

9
GOT-8

The EP appeared in the Good Vibrations catalogue as GOT-8, and was preceded in the series by Rudi, Victim, The Outcasts, The Undertones, Xdreamysts, Protex and a compilation disc.

The old Wizard Studios in Donegall Street, Belfast, was located behind an unmarked door, down a side alley. To say it was unremarkable was an understatement. Sound Engineer Davy Smith largely earned a living recording radio jingles and Irish country-and-western songs. The décor was fairly grim and the equipment basic, but we were thrilled to be there, nonetheless.

It had been impressed upon us that time was money, always the case when someone else is paying for the studio and all the more so when that someone is Terri Hooley. So I immediately made for the drum booth, but my heart sank when I saw it. Without a decent kit of my own, I was reliant on what the studio would provide – an old Premier four-piece. Nothing wrong with that per se, but the skins were loose and gaffer-taped to dampen them. So too the cymbals, which clunked rather than splashed. The bass drum had had cuts of carpet and underlay jammed into it to deaden the sound. I was horrified. We knew the cutting, high-octane 'live' sound we were after but lacked both the technical knowledge and the confidence to produce it. We would have to make the best of the situation.

While an old acoustic screen was being set up in the corner for vocal purposes, we gathered conspiratorially around the portable Superser gas heater to vent our concerns and stave off the biting Belfast cold that had followed us in off the street. We slagged off Forgie for his lack of technical nous, accusing him of trying to plug his guitar into the Superser. But the humour was short-lived.

Was Hooley trying to fuck with us? we wondered. It was already clear that he disliked us. Might this have been an act of sabotage? I decided to strip the tape off the drums and remove the carpet.

We'd asked an old school friend, Norman Creaney, to join us and record the event with a DIY photoshoot. He had borrowed his brother's Pentax and was firing off shots in all directions. Disillusioned and uncertain as we were, we had come to play.

After a while, our enthusiasm, and the material, grew on the sound engineer and he started to warm to the task in hand. We began with our most alternative, off-the-wall song, 'Don't Panic (in a Siberian climate, cuz the pendulum swings both ways)'. It abandoned any traditional four-four time or verse-chorus sequence, using instead a staccato guitar stab backed by a low rumbling bass and 'mummy-daddy' beat played out on the toms. Just when it might have become repetitive, the song exploded into a fast middle-eight section. The lyrics were a jumble of alliteration, suitably surreal to complement the essential oddness of the track. The song could easily have sat on the *Pink Flag* album by Wire. We had inadvertently recorded a homage to one of our favourite bands, although it was not our intention at the time.

'Cross the Line' was solely a Forgie creation.[1] Structurally, it fell into a fairly 'rockist' arrangement and was, on reflection, overlong and bordering on the ponderous. The lyrics were a call to challenge prejudice against difference and were perhaps drawn more from Forgie's personal feelings of alienation than from any particular community or movement. Clarkey's vocal went a long way to carry this off.[2]

Undoubtedly, the strongest song of the three was 'One by One'; indeed, it was always intended as the featured track. The lyrics draw on literary sources (James Plunkett's *Strumpet City*) and formulate a dystopian nightmare careering toward chaos and anarchy. At over four minutes, the track is long for a punk song, and features an atmospheric preamble that, via a feedback guitar flourish, builds into a scorcher.

Despite the challenges we faced with the studio equipment to help us produce our preferred sound, the final mix began to adopt a character and individuality all its own. Perhaps more Cure than Pistols, the enforced stripped-back ambience added something to the song in one of those fortuitous alignments of style and substance.

That night, we virtually skipped out into the Belfast darkness, clutching our demo cassette tapes that would be endlessly played to all and sundry. The songs could now also be played in the sanctuary of our own teenage bedrooms, where we were free to fantasise about what might be before us. We'd arrived! We'd done it! Or so we thought.

Over the coming weeks, it became apparent that recording a record was only one step in the process. The master tapes would not be released from the studios until Hooley had paid the bill. After that, the records needed to be pressed, a sleeve designed and distribution to be organised. It was clear that we hadn't thought this record lark through at all,

Illustration S1.3 'ArtRat'.
Photo by the author

and the frustrations that followed, as Hooley took his own sweet time in moving things along, only fuelled our rancour with him and the label. Imagine having a record that no one could hear! The more we cornered him for a release date, the more he seemed to enjoy stringing us along and the more frustrated we became with each other.

This became evident when we played a gig in Omagh, Co. Tyrone. For kids in rural communities, away-day gigs by Belfast bands were a serious affair. Organised by Tony McGartland (aka Ernie Badness), friend of the band and local punk, we had been instructed by Hooley to be at a prearranged location in Belfast to join him and The Outcasts for transportation to Omagh, seventy miles away. But unsurprisingly, when we reached the rendezvous point we discovered that they had gone without us. Stranded with our sparse equipment, we mused on what the 'punk' thing to do would be. So we hailed a cab and instructed the driver that he would be handsomely recompensed on our arrival by Mr Hooley. Well, Mr Good Vibes was incandescent. We left him negotiating with the cab driver and set up our gear onstage.

Earlier that week, we had arrived unannounced at his door in Belfast's Holy Land to enquire again about a release date for our EP. He answered the door looking somewhat dishevelled in a threadbare candy-striped dressing gown and slippers. In a blur of movement behind him, a young man in an electric blue silk kimono shimmied across the hallway. We tried hard not to smirk but ... No one had ever speculated on Terri's sexuality before. Or perhaps this was simply a glimpse into a south Belfast bohemia that we knew nothing about.

It was clear that an already strained relationship was now completely down the toilet. So that night in Omagh, when

GOT-8

I approached him for the umpteenth time to ask about the single, I shouldn't have been surprised when, ranting and raving at the top of his voice, he grabbed a nearby stool and brandished it above his head, screaming *'Fucking Ruefrex! Fucking Ruefrex!'* He was a big man made even more intimidating by his evident rage.

To my great relief, Clarkey stepped between us, glaring at Terri and daring him to attack – wanting him to. But Hooley was no hardman and quickly lowered the stool and walked away.

Unsurprisingly, there was no imminent release of GOT-8. Nor was it a shock, post-gig, for us to carry guitar cases and cymbal stands into an empty rain-lashed car park only to find our transport back to Belfast long gone.

NOTES

1 Indeed, it holds the dubious honour of being the only Ruefrex lyric not written by me.
2 The song's title and lyrics were often later used for a number of press articles and the title of a BBC documentary about the band. It became emblematic of the band's cross-community mission.

10

Cross the Line

Amongst some of my teenage peers I became known by several derisive names that would follow me into adulthood. It wasn't unusual in these circles and it would be unwise to read too much into it. 'Jap' I have already mentioned; it was mostly a school yard taunt, apparently encouraged by the shape of my eyes. Later, I got called 'Commie', more often than not as a pejorative but it was one I wore with honour. It stuck simply because I saw the principle of redistribution of wealth and the inevitability of resource exhaustion, due to insatiable capitalism, as axiomatic. And as a mouthy, adolescent ideologue, I spread the word with evangelical zeal to anyone who would listen (although perhaps not in those terms).

However, the intended slur 'Fenian-lover', also ascribed to me, seemed to be in an altogether different category. It has resonances with that other crass insult, born in the southern states of America and aimed at inter-racial relationships.

Perhaps it had something to do with my propensity for meeting and falling in love with girls from across the religious divide. During the Twelfth of July celebrations in Belfast, when the town was almost exclusively full of partying uber-prods, I would somehow manage to meet, and leave with, the only Catholic girl amongst the red, white and blue throng. It wasn't necessarily by design, but as these incidents increased, there was some merit in calling it a definite trend. That 'tortured romantic' tendency, so popular amongst a certain type of young man, perfectly played into the 'forbidden love' of 'mixed' relationships in the warzone. Montagues and Capulets predestined for tragedy. I was a sucker for all that.

One such doomed affair involved a gentle and generous soul called Jacqueline, a trainee dental hygienist at the Royal Hospital in Belfast. It was the first serious relationship for both of us, and my memory of it now is coloured by her trust and generosity of affection, ultimately thwarted by my own selfishness, petulance and penchant for drama. However, the challenges and differences I obsessed over were less to do with 'barbed wire love' and more about class war.[1]

Jacqueline came from an upper middle-class family who lived in a large, detached house in the affluent suburb of Bangor West, Co. Down. Her brother was a trainee architect at Queen's University Belfast and her father was captain of the local golf club. So the impediments to our harmonious union had little to do with holy icons, transubstantiation, or what religion our kids might be brought up in. The real stumbling block was my raw sense of inadequacy regarding our difference in social status.

All my life, I had accepted the civil rights mantra that Catholics in Northern Ireland were second-class citizens, deprived and excluded from basic freedoms and opportunities. Yet here was a Catholic family – one of several I would subsequently meet – that enjoyed a superior standard of living to me and my family and friends in every aspect of their lives.

It was confusing, to say the least, and did not fit the narrative I had been spun, the lie perpetuated by 'big house' unionism when hoodwinking the proles with assurances of Protestant 'exceptionalism'. It seemed that the words of UVF icon Gusty Spence had never rung so true: 'We may have got a slum quicker than a Catholic, but it was still a slum'. Clearly there were poor Protestants and Catholics ... and affluent ones as well. This 'we are the people' malarkey evidently wasn't all it was cracked up to be.

Either way, put the two together – social *and* religious injustice – and it gives some insight into the ideology that underpinned Ruefrex's philosophy and the politics of the songs and the band. As the years passed, this perspective developed into a more nuanced mission to contest social inequality and challenge the evil of sectarianism.

It was perhaps not surprising, then, that I identified, at an early stage, the fundamental necessity for integrated education at nursery, primary and secondary level in Northern Ireland, and supported and promoted initiatives to further that goal. It wasn't long before I was in contact with Joanne McKenna, then Development Officer for All Children Together, enquiring how the band might provide support to this fledgling enterprise.[2]

Some parents had made tentative inroads, despite fierce opposition from churches, politicians and segregated schools, by establishing Lagan Integrated College, the first integrated school of its kind in Northern Ireland. Ruefrex offered its support in whatever way was deemed appropriate. In practical terms this meant fundraisers and promoting the school in newspapers, radio and through any media opportunity that presented itself. This in turn led us to become involved in other ventures dedicated to furthering anti-sectarian work. Later, perhaps most notably, we collaborated with the Dublin-based activist group behind the Peace Train Movement and later New Consensus.[3]

While this espousing of good causes may seem like some bourgeois, anodyne exercise in salving our consciences from a safe distance, let me assure you, nothing could be further from the truth. For Ruefrex it meant 'walking the walk' as well.

Martin Lynch is an internationally respected playwright, but it was his brother, Seamus, who I most looked up to. From North Belfast, Seamus became a republican activist around the start of the Troubles and sided with the official wing of Sinn Féin in the split of 1970. He was a strong supporter of the Official IRA's ceasefire in 1972 and official Sinn Féin's vocal socialism. As a result, he became active in the republican clubs movement. Somehow, Seamus and Martin (already active in community arts) had heard of the work and the message that Ruefrex had been promoting and contacted me with an interesting, if daunting, proposition: come and play for the kids of the fiercely nationalist Turf Lodge housing estate in West Belfast, with the promise that our pint glasses would never run dry.

Turf Lodge lies in the shadow of Belfast's Black Mountain, and for most of its history it has been a place of poverty and social unrest. The estate was originally built to house people from the overcrowded terraced housing of the Lower Falls Road. With no shops, schools, public transport or roads infrastructure, life for the population of largely young families with children was challenging to say the least. Poorly constructed flats exacerbated the problems. To further aggravate an already set of dire circumstances, the impact of the Troubles on the area was immediate and calamitous.

It was something of a minor miracle, then – and to the enduring credit of the Lynch brothers and other activists like them – that an unbreakable sense of community identity and spirit prevailed there.

When I discussed the proposition of the gig with the others, there was a considerable amount of trepidation. Sectarian murders were happening daily, committed *by* young working-class men *on* young working-class men. For a band from the Shankill Road to venture into the area to perform was unheard of at the time. The risks were just too great. But Martin had given us a guarantee of safe passage (and there was that offer of unlimited free drink!). So after some discussion, we agreed that, as this kind of gig was the band's core mission, we would play.

A rusty tan-coloured Nissan car with some heavy-looking older men in it met our hire van on the fringes of the estate. We usually transported our gear to gigs by any means possible – sometimes by black cab – but that was out of the question here.[4] When the community centre came into view, we were both reassured and unnerved all at once. It looked exactly the same as the facilities in *our* area: a concrete block of a building, pebble-dashed and set on a sea of tarmac, sprinkled with broken glass, bottle tops and crushed cigarette boxes, the kind of place, we thought, from which bad men ventured abroad to spread carnage and waste lives.

Around this time we were working with a film crew from BBC Northern Ireland on *Cross the Line*, a documentary about the band that featured live performances in the now notorious Tyndale Community Centre. Unbeknownst to us, the infamous Shankill Butchers gang were operating out of there at the time, a truly distressing revelation when we learned of it later. Here, in Turf Lodge, was a similar venue, but one associated with the IRA (albeit the Official IRA or 'Stickies').

Martin met us at the door, and his effusive welcome and generosity helped steady our nerves somewhat. The interior, too, bore a striking resemblance to Loyalist clubs we had been in, the key difference being the photographs and flags on the walls – the Starry Plough, James Connolly, Che Guevara.

The locals soon began to arrive and file in. They were predominantly men our own age or younger, and they dressed and carried themselves much like us. They danced wildly to the upbeat, frenetic songs and bled into the shadows on the slower numbers, just as the kids in the Loyalist estates had done. They faced the same problems daily and sought refuge and escape in the same ways. If ever there was an affirmation of cross-communal affinity, it was here.

The gig culminated with much backslapping and handshaking. Pints were quaffed and jokes told. It was a moment of epiphany for everyone there. Most of those kids would never venture out to The Pound or the Harp; it just wasn't their scene. They were 'Spidermen', just like us. If they were to hear the message, it had to be *taken* to them. For a brief window in time, there was no difference between Prods and Taigs or Spides and punks.

It was the first of many cross-community ventures that Ruefrex was to play around the province. But it was Turf Lodge that steeled our resolve not to dilute or shy away from our mission to challenge the scourge of sectarianism.

NOTES

1 See 'Barbed Wire Love' from the album *Inflammable Material* (1979) by Stiff Little Fingers.
2 Since 1974, All Children Together (ACT) had been lobbying the churches and government to take the initiative in educating Protestant and Catholic children together. By 1981, there had been virtually no movement from either the churches or the government toward integrated education.

Wild colonial boys

3   New Consensus, founded in 1988, was an activist pressure group that called for the revision of the Republic's territorial claim on the North and encouraged the development of a devolved government for the people of Northern Ireland based on 'mutual respect, civil liberty and freely given allegiance'. Founding members included Michael Nugent, Michael Fitzpatrick, Ken McCue and the late Anne Holliday.
4   Throughout the Troubles, black taxi cabs, often overseen by paramilitaries from both sides, provided a community transport service in North and West Belfast.

11

'Wasted Life'

'Musky is dead.'
'What!'
'Jim Mawhinney ... he's dead.'

TC couldn't hold my gaze as he gave me this news. His eyes looked teary, confused and angry all at once. He glanced anywhere other than at me – down at the iron gratings near the kerb, at black car tyres squashed against the pavement, at the traffic passing, at the children kicking a burst football up and down the road.

When he did look up, it was to say, 'The funeral's on Wednesday. We should go up to the house before that ... to see him ... to see his Ma.' He looked away again.

'Are you sure?' I asked, my doubt nothing more than a coping mechanism.

TC looked like he might punch me. 'No, I'm fucking making it up!' he spat sarcastically.

It had been some time since the Debs had met. The collective had splintered in many different directions, growing up, moving on. TC and I still had the band and so a gang of sorts, but school was out for most of the others and we rarely saw them.

Musky had been our roadie for a few early gigs but had drifted away to a new circle of friends and acquaintances. Croucher had tried out for the role of roadie too, but his tendency to walk off with expensive items belonging to other bands, then present them to us as a show of allegiance meant that this could not continue. Having to return a stolen white Aria bass guitar to Greg Cowen of the Outcasts, following a gig at Queen's University, was the final straw.[1]

'What the hell happened?' I asked.
'You won't believe it. It's too fucked up.'

He was right about that. It transpired that Musky and Croucher had ventured together into the city centre security zone in search of pints and craic. I felt the air drain from me and must have visibly winced because TC raised his eyebrows and offered an involuntary 'I know' in response. Croucher had a famously short fuse and was prone to action, rather than reflection, and it seemed unlikely that he and Musky would befriend each other without the calming presence of TC. Croucher was almost never in our company without TC's authority to hold him in check.

Anyway, they had made their way back to North Belfast, taking the number 57 Ligoniel bus. This wouldn't have been their first preference, as the 39 (Silverstream) or 61 (Carr's Glen) would have more safely delivered them back into their own Loyalist community. Ligoniel was a staunchly nationalist/republican enclave at the end of the line. Failure to get off at the stop before last would carry you right into the heart of it.

It seems that, somewhat the worse for wear, they failed to alight in time and remonstrated with the driver as the bus picked up speed toward Ligoniel, insisting that he stop and allow them off. The driver refused and it was suggested that Croucher lashed out at him.

Still the bus rolled on.

Observers say that Musky engaged the emergency button, causing the concertina doors to flap open. He gestured to Croucher to jump off, which he did. But by the time Musky was jumping off, the driver had manually overridden the emergency instructions and the doors closed, trapping Musky's heel and pulling him under the back wheels of the twelve-ton double decker bus. He was crushed and died soon afterward. He was not quite eighteen.

Adding insult to injury, the driver, fearful of retribution and recrimination, claimed that Musky and Croucher had been attempting to rob him of his fares. To this day, no corroborating evidence has been offered. None of us believed it for a second.

The days leading up to Musky's funeral were agonising. Young men in such circumstances are more comfortable with anger than loss and we were no different. I had never seen a dead body before and didn't expect that when I did, it would be someone of my own age. We speculated in whispers as to whether, given the nature of his demise, the casket would be closed. In the event, he was laid out in the living room of his parents' home in the customary way, but with only his head and shoulders visible. We filed by the coffin, pale-faced, dry-mouthed and with little to offer his mother in terms of condolence.

I kept re-running in my mind the time when he had bent down to tie the laces of my Doc Martens.

In some bizarre, perverse, roundabout way, the sectarian hatred and violence that, in the main, we had managed to avoid up to that point, had prevailed enough to pull Musky under those wheels. Sectarianism manifested not in the way we might have feared – by gunshot or explosion or brutal gang beating – but as a result of trying to avoid all those possible scenarios.

I felt that I too wanted to get off the bus before its terminus, get off and run far away, leave the hatred and the carnage far behind. It seemed inconceivable at that point that the band would provide me with an opportunity to do just that.

Some months later, Jake Burns of Stiff Little Fingers invited me to attend a rehearsal at practice rooms in the city centre. SLF were preparing for a tour and had signed to Rough Trade Records in London. There was little doubt that they were destined for great things. I felt somewhat conflicted by his invitation: I was flattered to be asked by the hottest act around but I was also resentful and envious that it wasn't us. However, there was talk of a support slot on an Irish tour and for that I was deferentially grateful.

I was still disdainful of SLF's use of outside journo-lyricists, but the set now seemed to be featuring more original material written by Burns and the band themselves. Two of the newer tracks stood out and I tried not to be overawed as they burned through a blistering version of 'Johnny Was', the lyrics adapted for a Belfast street scene. At the time, I didn't realise 'Johnny Was' was a Bob Marley and the Wailers song, and believed it to be a tour de force of song writing by SLF.[2] But where Bob Marley's lyrics drew on poignant lived experience, I thought then, as now, that SLF's lyrical style was essentially sloganeering, lacking any of the subtlety or imagery I tried to bring to my own writing.

The second new song caught my attention for different reasons. 'Wasted Life' has become a much-loved standard in the SLF canon. Cited by many as an anthem for youth

'Wasted Life'

seeking to escape the suffocating attentions of paramilitaries, the simplicity of its message seemed appealing:

> Be a people's soldier
> Paramilitary gun in hand
> I won't be a soldier
> I won't take no orders from no one[3]

Sometime later we learned that Burns, in a music press interview, had stated that the inspiration and dedication for the song had been 'a friend' who had joined the paramilitaries and tragically died in the Troubles, someone who had lived in the same street as him. Eventually, the penny dropped. He was talking about our mate ... our *brother*, Musky.

Burns did indeed live in the same street as Musky, but that was as far as it went. He was an older 'hippy' muso, and we Debs, including Musky, ridiculed his crushed velvet loons and cheesecloth shirts, his ten-minute 'Free Bird' guitar solos and his membership of the school Amateur Dramatic society.

Our outrage was palpable, and some of the others had to be dissuaded from violence. To falsely suggest that someone was involved with a paramilitary organisation, and to misappropriate their life (and death) for artistic credibility, was simply beyond contempt. The sleight was one that remains hard to take, and went way beyond healthy band rivalry. It was naked opportunism beyond the pale, and was consistent with some of the questionable ethics that SLF rushed to embrace in pursuit of their own success. (For example, 'Suspect Device' was self-released on tape by the band's management, packaged as a cassette firebomb and sent around Belfast newsrooms and radio stations. Commercial premises in Belfast were being destroyed on an almost weekly basis by the real thing.)

But it made us all the more resolved to beat them at their own game. To do that, we had to get better, better at everything – song writing, stage craft and performance.

NOTES

1. His reasoning, when questioned, was that – as TC had pointed out to him, and Ziggy himself had counselled – 'The bitter came out better on a stolen guitar'.
2. Its adaptation was timely and opportunistic, while the aping of The Clash's reggae-themed 'Police and Thieves' was perhaps indicative of what was to come from SLF.
3. Stiff Little Fingers, 'Wasted Life', from the album *Inflammable Material* (1979). Written by Jake Burns.

12

The fly and the dandelion

By 1978, a hierarchy of bands had already formed in Belfast. Posturing and ego were nipping around the edges of what we had all assumed punk was supposed to be about. Preening and strutting rock gods were a thing of the past now as far as we were concerned. But The Stranglers were wrong when they announced that there were 'no more heroes anymore'.[1] In truth we all still had our heroes.

I had no compunction in wearing a 'Red Army' armband over my crappy leather jacket, in honour of my guitar hero, Mick Jones. Worse still, secretly, we all wanted to *be* heroes ourselves. The promise of recording, performing, a music mag cover, it was all so compelling, so seductive when it started to come into view.

To rub shoulders with the big boys from the capital was perhaps the greatest validation of all. So when The Adverts came to play Queen's University, Belfast, I was elated to blag a backstage pass (probably off the back of the SLF support for the evening).

Bass player Gaye Advert was every sixth former's wet dream – all fishnets, biker jacket and heavy mascara. QUB security were not prepared for the level of adoration that would be visited upon her, and subsequently they overreacted by clearing the dressing room of people who weren't supposed to be there, accidently locking me inside with the band and their entourage. In short, I was sealed in a room with Gaye Advert, the singer-songwriter T. V. Smith and a particularly annoying, mouthy hanger-on who turned out to be a seventeen-year-old Julie Burchill, then a staff writer for the *NME*. I wanted to tell them how much I loved 'Gary Gilmore's Eyes',[2] to ask for an autograph, a photograph ... but I didn't as that wouldn't have been 'punk'.

During the gig, I watched from the wings. The crowd of Belfast punks were going absolutely apeshit. I caught a glance from Gaye and noticed that she was unquestionably terrified. This level of mayhem was clearly something they were not used to. At one point, she got too close to the edge of the stage and grasping hands latched onto her leg, almost pulling her down into the maelstrom of the mob. The gig was stopped and the audience told that the band would not resume until there was (relative) calm. When they did return, she played from behind the PA stack for the remainder of the gig. It seemed that Belfast punks were serious about this whole anarchy business.

Later, in 1980, John Peel came to town to present the Battle of the Bands gig at the Ulster Hall. Ruefrex played at the behest of Good Vibrations and Terri Hooley, which meant we had a spot well down the ranking, behind Rudi, The Outcasts and others,[3] and our allocated time onstage was strictly curtailed.[4] But we got our photograph with John Peel – drunken, cheesy grins, all of us demonstrably in awe of him. It's deeply embarrassing now, and probably was for the great man himself at the time.

Throughout all this, we were becoming a bigger fish in a very small pond. We had enjoyed a play on John Peel's radio show and a Gavin Martin *NME* article. Consequently,

The fly and the dandelion

Illustration S1.4 Clearly starstruck. With the late John Peel at *that* Good Vibrations gig.
Photo by the author

I was pleased when, after having played a particularly strong Saturday night set at the Harp, support band The Androids suggested that I travel down with them the next day to Dandelion Market, Dublin, for a gig. The Androids heavily referenced The Velvet Underground in style and content and were none the worse for that. Their planned support act, Ask Mother, an art-rock outfit that had jumped on the punk bandwagon, had somehow misplaced their drummer and they wondered if I'd like to sit in with them for their set.

Now, my hands tended to blister quite badly after a gig and that Saturday had been a belter, with four encores requested and granted. Nevertheless, The Androids' flattery was just too much to turn down. I loved the idea of interchanging band personnel. It echoed the London and New York scenes – Bowie, Iggy, Lou. So, having applied swathes of sticking plaster and tape over raw digits, I was in.

We set off for Dublin at an unholy hour, so there was little point in going to bed, and we squeezed into a rickety transit van, drinking and toking en route as you do. The driver, the late Robin Holmes, was the bassist for both The Androids and Ask Mother. He was six foot six, a punk Herman Munster, who deliberately augmented his striking appearance with extreme make-up and hairstyle. Edgy androgyny was The Androids thing. Even when they weren't trying, they looked like extras from *The Rocky Horror Picture Show* on tour, with me as their sensible, straight cousin.

As we throttled headlong toward Strumpet City, I had no sense of trepidation. Ruefrex were in the ascendant and my companions on this trip had enough front for all of us. I was going to let this take me wherever Herman Munster wanted it to go.

When we arrived in Dublin we headed straight to Dandelion Market. Fevered discussions began about the traffic, the one-way system and parking. I had no concept of the city's geography and, liberated from the usual tyranny of these organisational concerns with my own band, was happy to leave this to others. I grinned inanely, stoned, behind a pair of 60s black Polaroid sunglasses borrowed from my mother: 'I'm just here to play, mannnnn!' I thought they made me look like John Cale, but a photograph from that day, taken in the mid-afternoon Dublin sunshine, suggested that I more closely resembled a butch Jackie Onassis on acid.

The bohemian buzz around the market seemed a million miles away from the open wound of urban decay and raw violence associated with Belfast at that time. Vintage clothing, accessories, furniture, music, Dandelion Market evoked

The fly and the dandelion

childhood memories of Smithfield Market at home. It was also where you could find buskers entertaining shoppers as they browsed the stalls.

A little unsteady on my feet, I negotiated a slow pace through the crush of punks, hippies, punters and tourists until I felt a hand on my shoulder. I turned around but could see no one in my immediate line of sight.

'You're Paul Burgess, right?' said someone with a Dublin accent.

I looked down. A shortish guy, sporting a bad mullet, leather trousers and a wide grin seemed pleased to see me. I was searching my memory for a name but was fairly sure I didn't know any Dubliners. I played for time.

'Don't tell me … I owe you money, right?'

It was a weak rejoinder and, believing it to be self-deprecating and witty, one I employed on the very rare occasions when I was treated like a minor celebrity by someone who had liked our single.

He was still grinning. 'Paul Burgess from Ruefrex. I heard your record on the John Peel Show … on the BBC.'

'That's great! Thanks!' Unused to this kind of interest from strangers, I was genuinely disarmed by the attention.

I looked over my shoulder to see the others walk off into the distance, being swallowed up by the crowds. I hadn't a clue about Dublin or where we'd left the van and I made to follow them.

The hand was on my shoulder again. 'I have the record … "One by One" … love it!'

'Brilliant … listen, I need to catch up with my mates …'

The hand stayed on my shoulder. For the first time, I noticed his blue eyes – the intensity, the earnestness, the urgency, the burning need to share something he clearly deemed of huge importance.

'I'm in a band,' he announced. 'We're playing here today!'

There it was. 'Oh yeah ... what are you called then?'

He squeezed my shoulder hard, locked on my eyes and with an almost devout vocation said, 'U2 ... we're called U2.'

I was to see them perform in Belfast, at Queen's University, sharing the stage with Stiff Little Fingers on 23 January 1981. They were well on the way to becoming a wholly different entity by then. And my enduring memory of that night in Queen's was of Bono in an oversized Romantic poet-style white shirt and Adam Clayton, wearing Michael Caine glasses and clutching a bottle of Hennessey, bellowing with public-school enunciation, 'Oh for fuck sake, Bono!' when displeased about something.

Later, in subsequent interviews, Bono had complimentary things to say about Ruefrex and we obviously shared some common ground on music as a force for social change. Višnja Cogan wrote in *U2: An Irish Phenomenon*, 'U2 have more in common with bands like Stiff Little Fingers or Ruefrex, who advocated the surrender of violence and the bringing together of the Catholic and Protestant communities ...'[5]

I again saw them at the King's Hall, Belfast, in 1987, on the Joshua Tree tour. By that time they were close to the established franchise we all recognise today and the 'rockist' shapes thrown by them were several removes from any so-called punk origins. I had been picking up occasional journalism assignments for the music press then, and as the band were supported on the tour by Lou Reed, I was delighted to secure a press pass from the *Record Mirror*.

I dined out on the Dandelion Market story for years afterwards, rather churlishly boasting that Bono had more records of my band than I did of his (untrue, as *Achtung Baby* is an unadulterated classic). But now when I think

The fly and the dandelion

back on that day, I see how we were both playing out a scene in which – unbeknownst to both of us, of course – our roles were to be utterly reversed. I would go back to my job in the aircraft factory and he would go on to London, ultimately to be signed by Chris Blackwell and Island Records. The rest, as they say, is history.

Punk could do that – make everyone a star and a fan at the same time.

NOTES

1   The Stranglers, 'No More Heroes', from the album *No More Heroes* (1977).
2   The Adverts, 'Gary Gilmore's Eyes', from the album *Crossing the Red Sea with The Adverts* (1978).
3   The Battle of the Bands gig was immortalised by John T. Davis's movie *Self-Conscious Over You* (1980) and was essentially a vehicle for The Outcasts. It later became fêted as the dénouement to *Good Vibrations* (2013). In both films – and despite playing at the gig – Ruefrex were overlooked completely.
4   Hooley liked to boast that he'd had Hells Angels remove us from the stage during a gig at Queen's University because we overran our allotted time.
5   Višnja Cogan, *U2: An Irish Phenomenon* (Cork: Collins Press, 2006).

13
The indignity of labour

Working in Short Brothers had become unbearable. The work in the Sub-Contracts department was mind-numbingly boring. Aeroplane parts – engine cowl sheaves, wing flaps, tail fins, fuselages, for Boeing and Fokker – were all designated by an obscure code. Parts A49764000 or BE0006767-543 might translate into a heavy metal component that had come off the production line, was sent out to a contractor for some chemical treatment or other, and had to be returned in time to meet assembly deadlines.

These manufacturing targets were mapped out on elaborate and labyrinthine 'Ready Reckoners' (this predated the extensive use of computers). Massive documents, running to hundreds of pages of graph paper with small annotations, were pored over by draftsmen, fitters and humble clerks like yours truly. Woe betide any hiccup in the supply chain that held up assembly, particularly on Boeing. It seemed to us that those fucking Yanks never went home! They were on the phone around the clock, wanting an update on this or that. When under intense pressure, senior management thought little of throwing juniors like me under the bus.

Sub-Contracts supremo Ronnie Lennox was an early devotee of the new sunbed fad. He complemented this with

The indignity of labour

coiffured grey hair, Italian suits, chunky gold jewellery and membership at one of the more prestigious County Down golf clubs. When an all-important part was held up at the Inwards Bay, pending inspection, and so holding up assembly, I was called to his office.

'Paul, nip down to the bay and you'll see a part just like this one here.' He gestured to a metal engine rod on his desk about a foot long. I had always taken it for a paperweight. 'It will have a tag attached, BE843672-000. Pick it up and bring it back to me, there's a good lad'.

He seemed more anxious than usual, and it was obvious that this wasn't one of those rookie hazing errands you heard about, when some apprentice would be humiliated by asking shop floor workers for 'a left-handed screwdriver' or 'a gallon of tartan paint'.

The Inwards Bay was its usual hub of activity. Forklifts and trolleys whizzed around the cavernous space, brakes screeched and horns echoed a warning, while men in overalls clanged hefty metal parts onto pallets. The air was thick with petrol and diesel fumes from the heavier lorries that were dropping off and picking up. I knew where to look and in no time had the engine part in my hand.

'Where are you going with that, son?' asked a small, bald man with a bull-dog demeanour, wearing tan-coloured, oil-stained overalls. It was Billy Blackstock, famed union shop steward and scourge of the management classes. He was sitting at a work bench covered with tools.

'Ronnie Lennox sent me down to pick it up and bring it back to Sub-Contracts.'

'Oh, did he now!' Billy said, reaching into his shirt pocket for the makings of a roll-up. He pointed as an electric cart whined by. 'See that man driving that cart?' Then he nodded in the opposite direction. 'See those lads loadin' those pallets?'

He stood up, scratching the tip of his nose with his thumb like a street fighter. 'When you come down here carrying away parts with ye, you're doing all those men out of their job. Understand?'

Before I could fire off any appeal blaming my callow youth and naive gullibility, he had crossed to some industrial shelving. On the wall beside it was a scarily ominous red button, which he pushed with the flat of one hand while holding the other in the air in proclamation.

What sounded like an air raid siren blared around the huge hangar. Stevedores everywhere stopped what they were doing and looked in my direction. Engines were switched off and tools laid down. Billy removed his hand and the siren faded to a pin-drop silence.

In a matter of seconds, I had closed down the whole Inwards Bay and so stopped assembly and production in the entire complex.

Billy Blackstock walked toward me and, taking the rod from my hand, said, 'Next time, tell Ronnie Lennox to come down here and do his own dirty work.'

It was becoming abundantly clear to everyone in the production offices on Airport Road that I was both a liability and someone who increasingly didn't give a toss. My timekeeping was poor, and my sick leave close to maxing out. I would arrive in, badly hungover from the gig the night before, my hands heavily bandaged from bashing them off drum rims and cymbal edges and because of friction burns from the sticks.

I found sanctuary from the soul-crushing boredom in the toilet cubicles, reading novels that I'd secreted down the front of my trousers. Adding insult to injury, I'd write 'Ruefrex' on the walls in ballpoint pen. Ill-advised, really, for who else could have written it. It was only a matter of time before a formal reprimand was forthcoming.

The indignity of labour

When I did come under uncomfortable scrutiny, I simply announced that I was off down to the shop floor or Goods Inwards bay in search of some missing part or other, and once there, I'd hang out with the working guys, some my own age, enjoying the noises and smells of heavy industry and negotiating the illicit assembly of drum kit parts from raw materials.

Many of those I'd kept in touch with from school had left to study at the New University of Ulster, a glass and steel cathedral located in the middle of a field outside Coleraine, near the north Antrim coast.[1] They seemed to do little else but drink beer, read books and play *Space Invaders*. Stories of drunken parties, sexually frustrated convent girls and reefer madness were beginning to filter down from Portrush, Portstewart and the north-west. There was also a burgeoning live music scene that was of considerable interest to me. At that time, too, there were government grants to be had. It all seemed a million miles away from troubled, late 1970s Belfast. It wasn't long before watching my peers embark on a variety of university courses became too much for me.

So at twenty years of age, I hatched my masterplan: I would go to university, get a professional teaching qualification and begin a career in education (back in the system that had served me so badly). I would need to finish my earlier abandoned A levels to get into university, but I could do that at night school.

However, one major impediment stood in the way – O level Mathematics at 'C' grade or above was a mandatory entry requirement for a teacher training degree course. I initially considered a radical fast-track approach, which involved employing the talents of two good friends, one a gifted graphic artist (and latterly Ruefrex's record sleeve designer) who good-naturedly offered to doctor my CSE examination certificate to show a top grade in Maths, and the other, an exceptional mathematician (subsequently a pioneer AI wizard) who agreed – for a fee and armed with my identity card – to sit my Maths O level exam for me. It was great to have friends! All this presented me with an ethical quandary, the resolution to which I will leave to your imagination. Suffice to say, a pass grade was secured.

But hatred of the hamster-wheel grind of heavy manufacturing was prompting me to do more than improve my education. The band's stock was climbing, and fast. If I put more effort into my musical career, who knew where it might take me. I thought that by doing both – teaching *and* music – I could cover all the bases.

The *One by One* EP had been picking up favourable attention. The twin bastions of 'cool' had been stormed and breached. John Peel had played it on his show and Gavin Martin had written a feature about us in the *New Musical Express*.[2] To say we were excited by this recognition was an understatement.

And in 1980, BBC Northern Ireland broadcast *Cross the Line*, its gritty Ken Loach-esque social documentary about Ruefrex. Disappointingly, but perhaps not surprisingly for TC and me, the production team chose to feature in-depth personal portraits of Clarkey (the extrovert/hardman) and Forgie (the tortured/sensitive loner). TC and I appeared briefly in a couple of straight-to-camera interviews and in the live performance footage, but an outsider might be forgiven for thinking it was the Clarkey and Forgie show! The musical performances were rough and ready, genuinely live with no opportunity to clean up a dodgy 'One by One' guitar solo in any post-production remix.[3] Nevertheless, the documentary was well received and provided another tangible staging post on the journey.

The indignity of labour

Illustration S1.5 Still from the BBC documentary *Cross the Line*, 1980.

Meanwhile, two invitations opened up the tantalising prospect of going on the road properly for the first time and, we assumed, all the hijinks of sex, drugs and rock n' roll that went along with that.

NOTES

1. The decision-making process to choose the site at Coleraine, rather than in Derry City, was manipulated by the usual unionist gerrymandering. It rankles nationalists to this day.
2. Gavin Martin, 'The Problem with Being Ernest', *New Musical Express*, 5 May 1979. p. 22.
3. The documentary has held up surprisingly well, despite a rather pedestrian voice over by then local jazz impresario, Jackie Flavelle. Its longevity is in part due to its value as a social record of a Shankill community under the twin pressures of political conflict and savage redevelopment. Many of the buildings featured have long since been replaced. It also offers a charming vox pop of locals' attitudes toward the new punk rock phenomenon.

14
A sense of Ireland

The first invitation was for Ruefrex to take part in the Sense of Ireland Festival in London that year. It comprised over ninety events covering all things Irish – music, theatre, dance, literature, the visual arts, crafts, film, photography, architecture and archaeology. The festival's finale, The Sounds of Ireland, was a musical extravaganza that purportedly included the best of the island's punk and new wave bands, such as U2, the Virgin Prunes and The Atrix, and headlined (on St Patrick's Day) by Rory Gallagher.

The ethos of the event was primarily to promote talent from the Republic – indeed, the whole festival presented a distinctly green-tinged hue, but Northern Irish bands – The Moondogs, The Tearjerkers, Rudi – did get a look in. It was when Derry band The Moondogs pulled out that someone, somewhere threw us a scrap from the table and offered us their slot.

It was the latest indication that we were being noticed and attracting respect from a number of sources. This stimulated a new confidence among the band, which in turn fed into our song writing and performing chops. Not surprisingly, time spent together (and the investment of hard-earned money in new and second-hand equipment) was engendering a stronger shared purpose, a collegiality born of common aspirational goals and collaborative artistic endeavours. Each band member was improving individually, as was the band collectively. Songs were getting better; arrangements were getting tighter.

Song writing alliances were forming and a degree of competition to produce something that would best the song that went before proved healthy and fruitful. While TC was my natural ally in this (we spent long periods of time at each other's homes working on material), there had been notable successes working with Forgie too, and the unpolished drafts were brought back to TC's cellar for collective embellishment, arrangement and rehearsal.

Through incremental payments, I had bought a small but adequate drum kit and cymbals. It had an orange sparkle laminate finish that might have been better suited to a showband. The larger ride cymbal I had 'liberated' from the support act of reggae band Prince Far-I and the Arabs when they played the New University's Student's Union. Much the worse for cider and home brew, I had brazenly climbed up onstage and simply unattached it from the stand during the changeover. The crowd didn't seem to notice or care, but the last bus back to Portstewart, where we were staying, drew some disapproving looks. To us, it was a punk rock thing to do, and we told ourselves that our humble beginnings and meagre means somehow justified this redistribution of wealth from those better off than ourselves.

Clarkey's stage outfits, usually festooned with Bowie badges, and his antics were becoming more outlandish, but his commitment to his vocal range and performance was undoubted. We had secured for him an HH PA amp and two high-quality Shure mics (don't ask!).

Wild colonial boys

Forgie found a small valve amp that resembled a bread bin, but its appearance belied an overdriven, sustained sound that was just right for us. This he mic'd up and played through the PA system for greater heft. (He soon swopped it for a transistor HH combo favoured by bands like The Skids and Buzzcocks.)

TC, too, invested in an HH bass combo and decorated the body of his guitar with a logo taken from the cover of Mott the Hoople's *The Hoople* album. This guitar was held up by a leather strap tooled for him by the father of his then girlfriend, Sharon, while serving time in Long Kesh. The motif simply read 'Coulter' and was embellished with a red heart.

These HH amps and PA featured signature displays lit up by an ethereal green electroluminescence, and pre-gig, we would lounge in the semi-darkness at the back of the venue and indulge ourselves in the sheer filmic efficacy of it all.

We now looked the part and noted how the punters immediately clocked our little shrine, responding accordingly by staking their place in front of the stage. It fed our egos and undoubtedly helped us with any lingering 'imposter syndrome'.

Such was the camaraderie we enjoyed at that time that it came as something of a shock when, at a rehearsal a week before the London gig, TC informed Clarkey and me that he had unilaterally thrown Forgie out of the band. His patience had been tested one too many times, by Forgie's whingy, faux bohemian posing, he explained. While I may have known exactly what he was getting at – sympathised, even – I was dumbstruck by the predicament he had left us in.

The English music press would be there en masse; so too, the A&R reps from major record companies. On the eve of such an important staging post in our progress, this cavalier act would surely set us back disastrously.

A sense of Ireland

Not to fear, he assured us. He had lined up a replacement: Willie Foster, who had been assiduously learning off the set. Willie was a sometime acquaintance of TC's whom neither Clarkey nor I had met before.

It was the first, but not the last, of TC's muscle flexing / taking 'executive action' without consultation, and it made me wonder whether he was as invested in the band's success as I was. I was aware that he had often flirted with a self-destructive arbitrariness. Despite this, of the four of us, he was the only one who had something that resembled a career (as opposed to a job) outside of the band. The more successful the band became, the more likely that TC would have a difficult choice to make. And it made me realise something else for the first time: the band might have been my lyrical platform, my political soap box, but in TC's mind, it sure as hell was *his* band.

Final rehearsals were unpromising. Willie's guitar sound seemed anaemic in comparison to Forgie's and his style was incongruous, and all this was before we struggled with any sound check in south-west London's Venue club. Perhaps most damagingly, that esprit de corps that had galvanised us and brought us to this point had disappeared.

Despite this setback, we were not going to walk away.

Transport was by ferry and we travelled light with only guitars and drumsticks, as the backline would be provided at the venue. We were staying at the London Tara Hotel in Kensington, and £150 had been granted to cover fuel expenses from Liverpool to London with a per diem of £5 allowed. It all seemed impossibly rock 'n roll.[1]

The gig itself was underwhelming. A smallish crowd were present, and our performance lacked any of the panache and passion we had become known for. To make matters worse, Paul Morley, an *NME* journalist we all admired, could find little to enthuse about. His review remarked on Clarkey's powder blue Bowie suit and how our sound was 'punily underweight'. Lamenting the southern Ireland prominence, he noted that 'the Ulster bands had been relegated to an afterthought'. He nonetheless feted a (then) new song in the set, 'The Wild Colonial Boy', remarking, '[it's] the first indication that Ruefrex may be the explorers they are touted to be, and I realise I'll be back again.'[2] It was enough to hang on to. Just.

We returned to Belfast with our tails between our legs and I immediately began petitioning TC – not for the last time – for the return of Forgie to the ranks. This was granted under sufferance, and so with him back on board, we set about learning from our mistakes in time for the upcoming support slot on Stiff Little Finger's Irish tour, the second invitation we received that year.

NOTES

1. It became obvious to me that the band badly lacked a manager or indeed anyone outside the band to simply deal with publicists, bookers, sound engineers and others. Our failure to retain anyone in this capacity can be put down to naivety, a mistrust of business people and a reticence to see ourselves as a going concern. In the absence of representation, these tasks fell, in the main, to TC and me (latterly to me alone), something that both I and the other band members would come to resent for different reasons.
2. Paul Morley, 'Live: Tearjerkers, Rudi, Ruefrex', *New Musical Express*.

15
The Black Catholics

By 1980, Stiff Little Fingers' star was truly in the ascendent. They had a successful first album via Rough Trade Records under their belt and, as Northern Ireland's sole ambassadors on the mainland, a place at the top table with the punk elite. So it was the stuff of dreams when Ruefrex were offered the support slot on their Irish tour featuring Dublin, Cork and Belfast.

SLF would be assured of full houses all the way, so a captive audience was guaranteed. And the tour was to culminate at Belfast's iconic Ulster Hall, a Grade A listed building with acoustics to die for, historically, the venue for pivotal political rallies leading to the very formation of the state, and the scene of legendary gigs by the Stones, Led Zeppelin, AC/DC and Rory Gallagher. NYC had Radio City, LA, the Hollywood Bowl, but the Ulster Hall was the holy of holies for any Belfast music fan. So to be performing there in front of our hometown friends and fans – well, it just didn't get any better.

Jake Burns kindly sent me a copy of their live album, *Hanx!* (1980). They had moved seamlessly from indie to mainstream. Now they had a bloody live album! Could *Top of the Pops* be far behind? In his note, written on Chrysalis

Records headed notepaper, Jake said he would see us at the Mansion House, Dublin, for the first leg of the tour. It was on!

By this time SLF were a well-oiled machine with all the associated paraphernalia of a successful touring band. We were minnows from the provinces by comparison and their decision to take us on tour with them was both principled and generous (as Chrysalis would have had a support act of its own that they wished to showcase). But it would be a mistake to assume that this placed us in thrall to them. Quite the opposite in fact – we were determined to 'blow them off the stage'!

The Mansion House on Dublin's Dawson Street is a prestigious venue by any measure. Built in 1710, Dublin Corporation purchased the house in 1715 as the official residence of the Lord Mayor. It retains that purpose to this day and, much like the Ulster Hall north of the border, it has hosted some seminal events in Irish history. But this eminent venue meant little to the throngs of Dublin punks filing into the empty hall and racing to the front of the stage. Amongst them was a gang who were making a dubious name for themselves. The Black Catholics had a reputation for disrupting gigs and were in situ early that evening. Meanwhile, backstage, we had arrived early to drink in the atmosphere ... and several slabs of lager that had been provided on SLF's rider by the promoters. Only Jim Reilly was present from the headliners.

Jim had replaced original drummer Brian Faloon, who was a personal friend of mine. He seemed a genial enough guy and joined us in a libation. As the hall filled up and the lights went down, the heady mixture of adrenaline and alcohol was taking hold. I was back and forth from the stage to the dressing room, scoping the crowd and watching it swell in size. The vibe was tangible and undeniable: heightened

The Black Catholics

expectation shot through with the threat of mayhem, possibly violence. It was wonderfully intoxicating to be part of it and I just couldn't resist.

I made my way alone out onto the stage and sat down behind the kit. No one in the crowd paid much attention; they probably assumed I was a roadie carrying out final checks. Without warning, I blazed into an uptempo Ramones-like beat. The crowd exploded into a pogoing, beer-throwing sea of pandemonium. I'm still not sure if they assumed that the gig proper had begun. But as quickly as I set this firework off, I stood up, waved at the crowd and sauntered back to the dressing room sipping a can. What a drug this all was!

Things were becoming unhinged backstage as well. TC was nibbling at some triangle-shaped sandwiches with the crusts removed while crew and hangers-on with backstage passes milled around. Jim Reilly, who had been talking to Forgie, ducked as a tuna and onion sandwich bounced off the side of his head. He looked around to see TC arming himself for another volley, so Jim scooped up a handful of ham and cheese baps and fired a sortie in reply.

Bedlam ensued. Sandwiches and pieces of fruit were being hurled across the room. Clarkey took to shaking up cans of Harp lager and spraying all and sundry with the contents. Complete strangers appeared and joined in. By the time Jake, Henry Cluney and Ali McMordie arrived, the dressing room was awash with beer and cola and the floor covered in upturned food trays and snacks. If they had planned on a pre- or post-gig drink or bite to eat, then the support band (and their own drummer) had put paid to that. They were not amused.

The gig itself was electrifying. Ruefrex were tight and on form, and Clarkey was at his demonstrative, boisterous best: 'Biceps like bison, shoulders like cabers and – most intimidatingly – huge, glistening tattoos', as *Melody Maker* journo Colin Irwin would later write.[1] Stripped to the waist and sporting some new tattoos (there always seemed to be new tattoos) it wasn't long before – mic in hand – Clarkey was scaling the PA stacks while belting out the songs. There had been an unrelenting stream of gob and crushed beer cans aimed at the stage for much of the show. Generally we accepted this as par for the course, but some of the Black Catholics gang had become more vocal and threatening at the front: 'Fuck off back to Belfast!' Clarkey ran a few passes, feigning to strike but holding back.

As we moved toward the end of the performance, Clarkey returned to stage centre for a ballad, 'Even in the Dark Hours'.[2] The Black Catholics' behaviour grew worse, and one of the gang, noticing that Clarkey had reverted from his manic, all-action style to stand still and deliver a love song, saw his chance.

He had been grabbing at Clarkey's ankles all night, trying to trip him up or stub out cigarette butts on his shins. Now he produced a lighter and attempted to set fire to his trouser bottoms and the laces of his DMs. Anyone familiar with Clarkey could have told him that this behaviour was reckless in the extreme and sure to end badly. Clarkey unbuckled his large, studded belt, wrapped a length of it around his fist and sliced it through the air. *Thwack!* It caught the arsonist full on the side of the head, sending him to the floor like the proverbial bag of spuds.

Chaos kicked off again. TC moved stage front to discourage any of his compatriots from climbing onto the performance area. His menace was real. Throughout it all, we never missed a beat and returned for a well-deserved encore. SLF looked on rather sheepishly from the wings and

The Black Catholics

were doubtless unimpressed when we left for Jury's Hotel without staying to watch their set.

Once there, things only got worse. At the London Tara Hotel we had been on our best behaviour, perhaps straitened by the change in our band personnel and the lacklustre performance. But in Jury's, high on booze and adrenaline, we were determined to have a night to remember. Sure, weren't we on tour, for fuck's sake!

The first indication that something might be awry was the black smoke that started billowing from a chair in the lobby. It was hard to say who might be the guilty party – several people had travelled south with both bands and then there was the stage crew, record company people, promoters and Dublin liggers.

As SLF arrived back at the hotel, stories were circulating that the PA stacks Clarkey had navigated later collapsed during a surge from the crowd. A young girl had apparently sustained quite a bad cut to the head and was now back at the hotel being sweet-talked out of any potential litigation by Fingers and Chrysalis officials – signed albums, T-shirts, photos with the band. She looked quite bemused by it all.

The entire troupe was booked in for a late supper at the hotel restaurant. I drew withering looks from the waiters, and from TC and Clarkey, when I skinned up and smoked a reefer at the table – several, in fact – assuring someone sitting next to me that it wasn't a problem.[3]

It was late as we moved back through the lobby to the residents' bar in search of more drink. Someone had decanted industrial quantities of soap powder into the foyer's ornamental fountain, and splashing around in the mounds of suds that ensued was a Dublin punk in motorcycle jacket and tartan bondage trousers, declaring it 'fuckin' bubblicious'.

When everyone else had retired, TC – in one final act of unnecessary carnage – eyed up all the used pint, spirits and wine glasses that had been gathered by the saloon staff and placed on the long, polished counter and ran the length of the bar, arm outstretched, sending them all crashing on to the floor. Grinning, he looked at me for approval. All I could think to say was 'punk rock!'

When we arrived at Cork City Hall the next evening, somewhat the worse for wear, it escaped no one's attention that we had been relegated to a small cloakroom with barely enough space to turn around in. No rider, no fellow musicians' affability from Fingers, or anyone else for that matter. We were just left to our own devices to think about our previous night's indiscretions. It was clear we were being punished. Indeed, SLF didn't speak to us again for the remainder of the tour.

For a while I railed against the injustice and hypocrisy of it all, but I knew we had it coming. As we waited in our shoebox to go onstage, Forgie sat with a half-smile on his face. 'What's so funny, cunty-bollox?' TC asked him, looking around the gunmetal-grey, municipal compartment. 'It's incredible what you can get away with when you *truly* don't give a fuck,' he replied.

The Cork gig was notable only for the enthusiasm of the audience. It was also a salutary lesson in hubris pre-empting a chastening fall from grace. Getting gobbed on or being right in the line of fire from a lager can were de rigueur. For the drummer, who cannot duck and weave as effectively as the others, that could be quite a challenge. But as we got deeper into the set, it was encouraging to see the crowd switch their attention to the music and away from the hijinks.

The stage at Cork City Hall was old-school – elevated and deep, so much so that, sitting a fair way back on the drum

The Black Catholics

riser, I felt that I was at a safe distance from the flak of hardcore fans. Or so I thought.

A single stream of liquid emerged from deep in the darkness and, cutting a high silver arc in the stage lights, it flew over the heads of the others and landed on me and the drums again ... and again. How was it possible?

After a couple of well received encores featuring Wire covers ('Ex Lion Tamer' and '1 2 X U') we exited stage left, exhausted but happy.

'You've gotta hand it to those guys in the crowd,' I said to TC. 'Somebody out there had a fucking water pistol. I'm soaked!'

'How do you know it was water?' TC asked, wiping the grin from my face as I stood there, sodden (probably) by some stranger's bodily fluids.

Then, at gig's end, having lingered under the stage lights, luxuriating in the applause and cat calls, playing the rock god before exiting, I was suddenly mortified that I would have to slouch out onto the stage again to dismantle and remove my own drum kit. No roadie privileges here. The house lights had gone up between our set and SLF's and the all-conquering hero (in my mind, anyhow) was revealed to the Cork crowd as a phoney wannabe. Worse, a pretender, a part-time performer. That said, it was the punk DIY ethos at its best. No more heroes and all that.

But despite the highs and lows of Dublin and Cork, no one was going to deprive us of a valiant and triumphant performance in our native city at the iconic Ulster Hall. We had played there at the Battle of the Bands in April, when we were treated as also-rans by Hooley. This time, though, it would be different. We were there as the sole support act and the Belfast punk Good Vibrations mafia had no say in proceedings.

We opened with 'The Perfect Crime', an Alice Cooper-esque slow-burner that builds to an overdriven power-chord anthem. The place erupted. From my vantage point behind the drums, all I could see, in the dazzling stage lights, were tidal waves of faces as the crowd, surging from the back, came into view, then retreated from the footlights. It was a mesmerising sight, all the more so as I began to recognise a face here and there. Lads from the Shankill, Ballysillan, the turn of the road at Ligoniel, all punching the air, singing along, and in their expressions, nothing short of abounding pride and wild celebration to see their mates up there, representing them and the lives they lived. It felt important to give them a voice, to do it for them. It felt like how a working-class hero might feel, and it felt intoxicating and addictive.

I was close to tears as we trooped off, but not before thanking everyone I could think of. Hooley would have been apoplectic ... and that was good too.

NOTES

1 Colin Irwin, 'Look Back in Anger', *Melody Maker*, 15 March 1986, pp. 24, 25.
2 Bizarrely, 'Even in the Dark Hours' was recorded and released by Page 3 model Samantha Fox in 1987 (under the title 'Even in the Darkest Hours').
3 Interestingly, in common with many working-class young men of the time, the use of drugs of any kind was frowned upon. I was asked more than once, 'Aren't you frightened you'll turn into a junkie?' when enjoying a joint. Hard to believe now, in a society where working-class communities are devastated by Class A drugs.

16

Of giants and sandcastles

By 1983, things were reaching a crescendo and the end of a self-imposed hiatus. We had just released our second single, thanks to the generosity and good graces of Davy Simms, a local DJ at Downtown Radio. One of the many unsung heroes of the period, Davy had broadcast a studio session featuring four songs and essentially provided us with the masters for a subsequent release. This we did via a London-based indie label, Kabuki Records, set up by members of the Maghera band Kissed Air (previously Know Authority), with whom we'd become friends, and Gareth Ryan, a Dubliner who worked for Rough Trade distribution.

With typical Ruefrex elan, we remastered the original and, being unable to decide which was the better track, declared it a double A side. 'Capital Letters'/'April Fool' entered the charts in *Sounds*, stayed six weeks and peaked at number thirty-one. 'Capital Letters' was a heads-down-see-you-at-the-finish stomper about the perils of nuclear warfare, while 'April Fool' was a tune with power-pop sensibilities and a tale about how simple pranks can lead to misunderstandings in Belfast, the then murder capital of Europe: 'There's a man with a mask in the hall ...'

Wild colonial boys

Illustration S1.6 'Gang of Four'. L–R Coulter, Clarke, Forgie, Burgess.
Photo by Colm Henry

So in many respects we were ticking all the right boxes, achieving cherished dreams that only a short time ago seemed fantastical. Singles released, check. Plays on the John Peel Show, check. Respectable positions in the UK Indies Charts, check. A BBC TV documentary, check. Support slot on national tour, check. Write ups in *New Musical Express*, *Sounds*, *Melody Maker*, *Hot Press*, check, check, check!

We were still in our early twenties, and had achieved these things while maintaining a fierce independence and a healthy mistrust of 'the industry'. It was full-on DIY. It was punk rock.

But if we had been pretending to be indifferent, to not take things seriously, to just be ourselves and see where this whole thing took us, then that wasn't going to pass muster any more. Natural progression indicated that a record deal with a major label, an album and UK and US tours were in

Of giants and sandcastles

the cross hairs. I sure as hell still had a lot to say and I was certain the others did as well. We were much more confident now. It was a swagger born of better song writing and tighter performances, a genuine belief in ourselves, gained through hard work and solid progress.

Each of us had become better players, having practised both on our own and in rehearsals together. And Clarkey had made himself virtually indispensable, ostensibly as an angry singer of angry songs. His threat was indisputable, authentic and box-office; he was the raging, gyrating, menacing face of the band (albeit one who could bring the entire edifice crashing down on an unhinged whim).

However, we were still a wholly amateur undertaking. We had no management, no financial backing and no stage crew. Everything was done on the cheap but on our own terms. While this appealed to our sense of independence

Illustration S1.7 Angry Clarkey.
Photo by Andrew Catlin

and idiosyncrasy, it became increasingly clear that to reach the next level, relocation to London or Dublin was a prerequisite. And that remained the unspoken elephant in the room.

Other Northern Irish bands had crossed the water with much less going for them than we had at that time. Kissed Air had left Maghera, first for Coleraine, then Dublin. When I visited them in Dublin, I was shocked by the relative squalor they were living in and the 'cold-shouldering' they experienced from the insular, back-biting Dublin scene. If we could avoid that kind of suffering for our art, it would be just fine by me. But for now, the members of our band were looking no further than the immediate future.

TC had been making steady progress in his job as a Housing Officer at the Northern Ireland Housing Executive. Both Clarkey and Forgie were in settled relationships and holding down a succession of unskilled jobs.

With the help of a government-sponsored maintenance grant (and no fees), I had secured a third-level education at the New University of Ulster in Coleraine, which required me to relocate from Belfast to the north coast. I had originally opted for a combined English and Education degree (a four-year course), reasoning that there would be a guaranteed teaching job at the end of it. However, I soon converted to a three-year BA English Literature degree.

During this period, it became apparent that Ruefrex was more like a social club than a band. While we did play the occasional gig in my new home from home (the Students' Union bar), the necessary momentum for advancement that we'd accrued had been lost. I didn't realise it then, but somehow a decision had been taken – subliminally and without discussion – that Ruefrex was to be a band made up of part-timers. The privations, relocations and career risks

Of giants and sandcastles

necessary to follow the dream were just too great to do anything else.

The main engineer of this mindset was TC. It turned out that he perceived the band as nothing more than a glorified hobby that could be enjoyed on the weekends and evenings without compromising hearth and home. As this dawned on me, I began to lament the loss of all we had and might yet achieve, for it seemed inconceivable that the band could continue without my co-founding member, my song writing partner and my best mate.

TC had been instrumental in forging the can-do, self-confident bluster that underwrote everything we had done up to that point. His appreciation and appetite for music, both as a fan and a creative collaborator, was inspirational – life-changing, even. And we had been inseparable since school days.

The socio-political crusade I was on personally, via the band, was interrupted, perhaps permanently terminated. But we were to have a parting flourish before 'cryosleep'.

In 1983 we returned to Dublin to record a radio session for Dave Fanning at RTÉ. Ironically, it took place on 12 July, the most important date in the Orange Order's calendar. I couldn't help but reflect that not that long ago, I would have been marching to the field, playing side drum with the Pride of Ardoyne Flute Band. Yet here I was, recording music in the capital of the Republic of Ireland, for its national broadcaster.

We all felt a little ill at ease with this and so marinated our doubts in vodka. This unsurprisingly led to an underwhelming recording session, when we roundly mocked the archaic nature of a station that still featured tape operators, decked out in white lab coats and armed with clip boards. We were never asked back again.

Wild colonial boys

Not long after this, TC's patience with Forgie snapped again, and once again I arrived at rehearsal to find Ruefrex sans guitarist.[1] Yet again, TC had acted alone at a key time for the band and in doing so indicated that his aspirations for the band deviated fundamentally from my own.

Ruefrex had just made a tentative deal with One by One Records, a new Northern Irish label, and we were due in the studio imminently.[2] Just like last time, TC urged me not to worry; Gary Ferris, who lived just around the corner from him, could do the job just fine. So TC and I turned up on Gary's doorstep and asked him if he'd like to make a record.

Gary was a skinny, hippy muso type with blonde hair, coiffured and piled high like a golden bouffant, and a liking for Telecaster guitars. The usual mandatory precondition of sharing our adoration of our musical gods was waived due to the urgency of the situation. His sound and style of playing was markedly different to Forgie's. He preferred Dean Markley guitar strings and carried vast quantities of them around with him, as if always ready for any emergency. The irony was that his playing style was unlikely to break a fingernail much less a guitar string. But he was an amiable guy who was soon accepted and given the nickname 'The Dean'.

The subsequent session at One by One saw the release of 'Paid in Kind'/'The Perfect Crime' (1984). Stylistically, 'Paid in Kind' was an attempt to create a kind of cinematic panoply within a song. To do this I employed a succession of vivid images that, as they progressed, told a fictitious short story from the Troubles that ended in lost lives. I was listening to a lot of Tom Waits at the time and the lyrical influence is obvious.

However, the song received little publicity and John Peel would not play it (for whatever reason).[3] Distribution problems in Great Britain also hindered the release, the

Of giants and sandcastles

Illustration S1.8 'Enter The Dean' – the peroxide days.
L–R Clarkey, The Dean, me, TC, Forgie.
Photo by Alastair Graham

prevailing feeling in the music press being that this was a noble attempt to implant contemporary folk quality inside hard rock dialects. I think that, just like at the Sounds of Ireland gig, our performance and the recording suffered from the absence of Forgie's distinctive guitar sound and his understanding of the band's musical ethos.

Soon afterward, TC suggested that 'the oul rhythm section' – he and I – meet up for a pint or two. We hadn't seen much of each other lately due to my university studies, he said, and he wanted to catch up. During that time, he and Clarkey, missing live music, had put together a band with Willie Foster called Eden Way. While they included some Ruefrex songs in a set of originals, I was somewhat relieved that TC hadn't tried to reconfigure the band without Forgie and me in our absence. He was certainly capable of doing just that.

So we met up in Lavery's Bar on a weeknight. As the evening wore on, we laughed about the underage drinking we'd indulged in as kids while in the Debs and the lengths we'd go to, to be served in the bars and pubs of city centre Belfast. We grimaced at the memory of our preferred tipple – copious pints of Harp followed by Pernod, Green Chartreuse, crème de menthe. It was no wonder we spent so much of that period throwing up.

'Remember we used to wonder what you'd prefer, given the opportunity, if you had to choose?' I asked him.

TC smiled. 'Yeah, walking back out onto the stage for an encore at a packed Albert Hall or scoring the winning goal in the last minute of extra time in the European Cup Final. For Man United of course.'

'And ...?'

'Depends on the goal.'

I smiled. 'The long ball is played over the top. You spring the off-side trap, take one look over your left shoulder and catch it full on the volley as it falls. Top corner. You keep running into the arms of the adoring supporters behind the goal.'

'That's it then. That's gotta be it.'

'You're sure?'

'Yeah, absolutely. Instant legend. George Best, Norman Whiteside.'

'Did I mention that the Albert Hall gig was with the reformed Ziggy Stardust and The Spiders from Mars?'

'Bastard!'

'Yeah, Trevor Bolder couldn't make it and you were in. Too late now though!'

Of giants and sandcastles

We both fell about laughing.

'Do your Sid James laugh for me,' I said.

TC obliged. He could replicate the Carry On star's distinctive cackle perfectly. Cracked me up every time.

But as we got deeper into our cups, TC grew more sombre. He leaned in close and said, 'There's something you should understand ... about me ... and the band, I mean.'

'Shoot.'

'I see it like this,' he said. 'You're on a beach and you're building a sandcastle. And it's the best sandcastle you could possibly make – tall turrets, drawbridge, moat – the works.'

I drained my glass and rose. 'You want another pint?'

'No, listen. Listen to me!' he insisted with urgency and grabbed my arm. 'Suddenly there's a racket from further up the beach. A giant is making his way down, slowly wrecking all the other sandcastles, one by one.'

'A giant?'

'Stay with me here. So before he reaches mine' – he looked me straight in the eyes – '*I wreck it myself!*'

It was a cautionary tale and one that perhaps I should have seen coming. My card had been well and truly marked.

NOTES

1 Forgie moved on for a period to Belfast band Colenso Parade.
2 Established in 1984 by Keith McCormack, an engineer and friend of TC's, the new record label took its name from our Good Vibrations-produced EP.
3 It may be that the portrayal of the IRA man 'MacLaverty' as perpetrator, and the subsequent deaths of the British soldier and young local boy 'Eamon Duffy' irked the sensibilities of the liberal left at a time when the Troops Out Movement was at its height.

Side 2

Second coming: London and Manchester (1985–87)

17
'The Wild Colonial Boy'

By 1984, Ruefrex had reached what seemed like an insurmountable impasse. I was approaching the completion of my studies and hoping to earn some much-needed coin. TC had made it abundantly clear that he would not be leaving his job under any circumstances. Clarkey, as always, looked to both of us to provide him with opportunities to perform. And Forgie, newly peroxide blond, consistently burned his bridges with TC, then rebuilt them again if an offer of rapprochement came from me. The Dean simply reverted to his role as nice-guy telephone engineer with British Telecom; his emotional investment in the band was close to zero.

Despite three well-received singles releases, there was little prospect of the band kicking on to the next level. That would require relocation, management and hard work. And no one seemed particularly enamoured of the upheaval and application required to sustain this. So against this unpromising backdrop, I decided that we should make one last grand, defiant gesture, a bold flourish to sign off with, before consigning our brief flowering to the indie bargain bin of history.

Martin J. Galvin was an Irish American lawyer and activist notable for his role in the formation and promotion of

Wild colonial boys

NORAID (the Irish Northern Aid Committee).[1] The organisation became known for raising funds for the Provisional IRA and other nationalist groups during the Troubles. Although banned from Northern Ireland for espousing terrorism, Galvin entered the country in 1984, attending high-profile gatherings, flouting his presence to the security forces and providing Sinn Féin with a press coup.

This flurry of activity provided the catalyst for Ruefrex to record and release a song that we'd finished a year earlier

Illustration S2.1 'They think it's all over!'. 'The Wild Colonial Boy' cover.
Original cover by David Pentland

'The Wild Colonial Boy'

and that had become a staple of our set. 'The Wild Colonial Boy' borrowed its title from the well-known Irish ballad of the same name. A favourite of Irish exiles the world over, it tells the story of Jack Duggan, an Irish rebel and native of Castlemaine, County Kerry, who became a convict, then a bushranger in nineteenth-century Australia.

The title is where the similarity ends, though. I wrote the narrative from the perspective of an Irish American, residing in Wisconsin, who is providing funds for IRA terrorism. The song has him ruminating that 'it really gives me quite a thrill to kill from far away' and accuses Irish Americans of perpetuating Irish stereotypes of British oppression while hypocritically mistreating the African American population. I was influenced by Randy Newman's 'Rednecks' which takes the perspective of a southern racist. Irish people everywhere would undoubtedly balk at a song with the line 'I know that if I get my chance, that I can jig and reel and dance, cuz in between the killing, that's what all us Irish do'. The finer points of employing a 'false narrator' would be lost on them, and there was a danger of gross misinterpretation and misrepresentation.

TC had shaped a killer tune to augment the lyrics and together we fashioned an arrangement that took it to the next level. It was clearly our best song, based on feedback from live performances, and also our most pertinent for the time and place in which we found ourselves. If one song could quintessentially represent the band, this was it. We simply had to get it out there before admitting defeat and leaving the stage forever.

We scraped some money together and called in a few favours in order to secure recording time. I was determined that the message of the song wouldn't be lost. So I commissioned artwork from Davy Pentland, an old school friend. I explained that I wanted a drawing of an

Armalite AR-18 rifle wrapped in brown paper and string, festooned with postage stamps and lying on a doormat as if it had just been delivered in the mail. On the reverse was to be the song lyrics and a still photo of TC and me taken from a performance on *Channel One*, BBC NI's live music show at the time. And in keeping with our intention to retire the band, we would thank those who had helped us along the way: DJ Davy Simms; photographer Alastair Graham; journalist Gavin Martin; the TOR (Turn-o-the-Road street gang) where we had many friends, and cryptically 'Blue Eyes', a spoof credit that TC thought would be intriguing in a Roxy-esque way.

In short, we would be committing commercial and political suicide with this release, and it was unlikely that any mainstream broadcaster would touch it with two bargepoles tied together!

Not that any of this overly mattered to us. It hadn't done up to that point, so why begin now? At least we would be in absolutely no doubt that our message would be out there, undiluted and undiminished, right in their fucking faces. It was to be a last beautiful act of self- immolation.

The recording took place in a glorified chicken shack in rural Aghadowey, Co. Antrim. Reasoning that beggars can't be choosers, we leapt at an offer from local recording artist Paul Lerwill. He had had some success as a guitarist with boyband outfit Rosetta Stone, an effort to exploit the 70s success of the Bay City Rollers by their ex-manager – and Paul's lover – Tam Paton. Paul later changed his name to Gregory Gray in an attempt to distance himself from that part of his life, and later formed the punk band Perfect Crime before embarking on a high-profile solo career.[2] CBS record label had signed him along the way, choosing to invest in his undeniable talent and irrepressible impudence,

'The Wild Colonial Boy'

by kitting out the modest studio for him in Aghadowey. There, he had the talented Hugh Matier in situ as producer/engineer.

From the off, Gregory took an instant dislike to me, or rather to my non-negotiable vision for the recording. Wonderfully camp, he would dance around the studio, sarcastically imitating my requests for reverb here, an overdub there. The others uncharacteristically kept their heads down and got on with the task, somewhat intimidated, I think, by his seemingly indestructible self-belief and larger than life exhibitionism.

The drum booth could barely be described as a 'booth' at all. The kit, surrounded by plaster and breeze-block walls, had virtually no sound proofing. This had the fortuitous effect of rendering an incredibly 'live' snare sound, like a gunshot, ricocheting off the naked surfaces. Unintentionally perfect!

The number of tracks/channels for recording were limited as we insisted on double-tracking at every opportunity. Electric guitar was piled atop electric guitar, intentionally creating a sonic wall of power chords. Almost every twelve bars we would introduce another guitar, heavier and more overdriven than the last, building and building to a climax.

Clarkey and I shared backing vocal duties, as had become the norm by this time, both live and in the studio, and when we had something approximating The Damned's 'Play loud at low volume' maxim, we knew that it was done. Or almost.

The problem was that I had neglected to double-track the snare drum. As the technology to duplicate it automatically was not available deep in the verdant hills of Aghadowey, I had to do it manually.

With so many guitar overdubs threatening to wash over the song's structure, it was vital to maintain the clarity of the rhythm and arrangement, or it would get lost in a formless mess. Again, fortune was smiling on us. I was sent back to the drum booth with instructions to play exactly on the original beat and the song was fed back to me through headphones. The others, having finished their parts and pleased with how things had gone, hit the beers and attempted to put me off by acting the eejit through the separating glass panel.

After a couple of takes, I returned for playback and was unexpectedly delighted. Anyone familiar with the 2014 Hollywood film *Whiplash* will know that it is possible for a drummer to either 'rush' or 'drag' the beat. This speeding up or slowing down is virtually imperceptible except to the keenest ear. (The late Charlie Watts famously held the beat back just a smidgen to give The Rolling Stones their distinctive R&B groove.) When the final mix of the evening was played back, I realised that not only had the snare beat been substantially beefed up – as was the original intention – but that I had inadvertently played just behind the original track. It was a nano-second really, but enough to fill out the sound even more and render it distinctive in a way that I couldn't have achieved if I'd tried.

We rounded things off with a shimmering guitar effect that served as an intro-outro for the song proper. All seemed well with the world.

Gregory announced that he had some ideas for the B side. These involved an electronic version of the song, featuring synthesiser and drum machine. 'You won't be needed for this Paul,' he announced with some glee and went on to produce a swelling strings arrangement and quasi-dance rhythm, accompanied by a similarly bombastic treatment

'The Wild Colonial Boy'

of Clarkey's vocal. It wasn't really Ruefrex, but as Joy Division/New Order devotees, it was fun for us to muck around with these unfamiliar sounds.

By the end of the session, we were all agreed – we'd got it down on tape and could now die happy.

Following an idea through from conception to fruition in the recording studio is a rare and unique privilege, and one that even to this day I truly miss. It provides a sense of fulfilment like no other I can think of, not least because it is a collaborative artistic undertaking that harnesses disparate personalities and interpretations to realise a common, shared goal.

But that was the fun part. Afterwards was the pain-in-the-ass business of pressing the recording to vinyl, printing the covers and distributing (not to mention promoting) the bloody thing. None of this seemed to us to have anything to do with being a musician, much less a rock star, and so the others returned to their day jobs and spouses, keen to be kept informed 'should anything happen'.

NOTES

1. NORAID, an Irish American membership organisation, was founded in 1969 by Michael Flannery (1903–94) with the aim of creating a United Ireland.
2. Gregory was a talented and dedicated artist who later emerged in another inimitable personae, 'Mary Cigarettes'. His devotion to his craft and to gay activism made him an unlikely confederate of both boy bands and Ruefrex. He tragically died in 2019.

18

'Change of Attention'

By this time, Kissed Air, the band from Maghera, were well ensconced in the leafy suburbs of North London. While struggling to command attention for their own music, like so many Irish exiles who went to London before them, each of the members had secured both accommodation and gainful employment, holding down sometimes quite menial jobs (the singer cleaned the large houses of North London's wealthy for a while). But eventually their efforts and interests brought them work and contacts on the periphery of the music/entertainments business.

While I was studying at Coleraine I had become friendly with Kissed Air's drummer, Larry Cudden, singer Cormac Tohill, bass player Norman Johnston (Jonty, a left-wing historian from North Belfast working a 'Citizen Smith' chic), who I knew from the Boy's Model School, and guitarist John (John-Boy/ 'Youth') Watt, a shy, self-effacing childlike lad whose comic book/fart joke humour belied a prodigious musical talent.[1] They had stayed in contact with Gareth Ryan (who had been instrumental in the release of our single 'Capital Letters'/ 'April Fool'), and who was also in London, working in distribution for Rough Trade Records and on his own independent music projects. All were fans and supporters of Ruefrex.

'Change of Attention'

Meanwhile, that summer in Belfast was dragging interminably for me. Lack of money saw me, and a few other university students, sign away our holidays doing temporary work with the security firm Securicor. From when I was young I'd worked in a variety of menial jobs for badly needed cash – loading furniture vans with piles of brush poles, reupholstered chairs and mattresses for Workshops for the Blind, for example, or rising at 3 a.m. to push freshly baked loaves of bread through an automatic slicer (which also wrapped them in wax paper) for O'Hara's Home Bakery (the smell of bread and melting wax, after a heavy night's drinking, was gut churning). But the most soulless and dangerous job of them all was doing Cash in Transit (CIT) work for Securicor.

Banks had to be replenished with cash on a weekly basis, but in Belfast, a city in thrall to paramilitary crime and heavily armed gangs, moving large sums of money around in fortified vans was terrifying; the (wild) West Belfast run was the most hair-raising.

Securicor gave us training as to what to do in any heist situation. Through our observation slit, if we saw the driver, weighed down with canvas money sacks, being accosted by armed men on his short journey from the van to the bank, we had procedures to follow. All dead bolts were to be sprung on the vehicle, a loud alarm siren was to be engaged and we were to get on the radio immediately with a Mayday.

The older senior drivers viewed this rather differently from management and instructed us accordingly: 'Listen ye wee shite ye, never mind what them wankers tell ye. If you see anybody put a gun to my head, you open up the van and give them what they want, no questions asked. D'ya hear me!'

Other tasks involved the 'Money run' from central bank vaults to clearing houses. Here, huge amounts of newly minted notes were bound into clear cellophane slabs and loaded by forklift onto pallets, then into our vans. I might at any given time have easily had a million pounds sterling in the back with me.

Of course, some of us students in temporary posts turned our creativity and imagination toward how we might swipe the lot and get away with it. We fledgling mathematicians, biologists and poets perfected a scheme, predicated on tight timelines and pre-planning, whereby we would be at Aldergrove airport boarding flights, the money sent separately as cargo, before any alarm was raised. The senior man on board the robbed van would be confined but not injured in order to prevent premature disclosure. By the end of our deliberations, we were convinced it could be done. The only downside was that we could never again return home to family or friends. Laughing, we consigned the ruse to the stuff of fiction. Who knew?[2]

'Static' duties involved being marooned, unaccompanied, in a factory with a caged attack dog. To deter sleeping on the job during the night, you were required to tour the factory perimeter at pre-set periods, clocking in on a device at fixed points. Although we were assured that the guard dog was 'trained to recognise the uniform', I was inclined not to remove the slavering 'Satan' from his pen to accompany me, as procedure required.

It was a temporary means to an end for us students; at least we had prospects of escape. But it was an altogether different proposition for the older men trapped within the company. Often troubled, sometimes violent (with minor infringements on their records), they couldn't access the better paying, more secure protection-orientated careers

'Change of Attention'

within the security forces and were thus marooned in a kind of thug's Foreign Legion.

One such nutjob chose to break a pool cue across my back during an overly competitive game in the recreational area back at base. Management, perhaps fearful that I would report the matter to the police – or maybe it was just good luck – sent me in my final week on the job to a posting at the Rowntree Mackintosh warehouses on the outskirts of Belfast.

Having something a sweet tooth, I needed no encouragement and my insipid lemon-coloured, beat-up Vauxhall Chevette was considerably lower on its axles by the end of the week, as I loaded up with boxes of Quality Street, Yorkie Bars, Rolo, Kit Kats and Smarties.

All the while, I was carrying around a cassette tape of 'Wild Colonial Boy', pressing it upon anyone who would listen. While I knew that the band had effectively broken up, I couldn't bring myself to say those words to the many fans who routinely asked when they might see or hear us play again.

I had been picking up short-term supply teaching posts in some of the toughest schools in the city.[3] Teaching English literature to kids, sometimes not much younger than myself, was certainly a challenge.

Cairnmartin Secondary School fell within the Greater Shankill catchment area, where I came from. Control in the classroom had to take priority, for no learning could take place without it. In order to build credibility with the older boys, I encouraged the notion that I was a hardman from the mean streets that they themselves hailed from. This was a dubious tactic and one that was unlikely to end well. Like a Wild West gunslinger, sooner or later, someone faster would call you out. 'My da's coming up here to shoot you!' was a not uncommon or entirely risible threat.

But over time, I secured breakthroughs and successes with the kids. This was largely achieved by bonding over those fail-safe, go-to twin passions of working-class male youths – football and popular music. I unapologetically constructed teaching plans around Ruefrex and other songs, inviting discussion and deconstruction of the lyrics, much in the way that some of my own teachers had done.

Meanwhile, there had been no real let up in the violence in the province. In 1985, a Provisional IRA mortar attack on an RUC base in Newry killed nine officers and wounded thirty-seven. This was the RUC's highest death toll from a single attack during the Troubles.

In the background, tension had been ratcheted up by the signing of the Anglo-Irish Agreement by British prime minister Margaret Thatcher and Irish Taoiseach Garret FitzGerald. This galvanised resistance to what was perceived by my community as a further move toward sell-out and a united Ireland. It seemed that terrorist violence was being rewarded, and that ramped up the urgency of getting 'Wild Colonial Boy', Ruefrex's paean against American funding for IRA bombs and bullets, out there and heard.

While I was at university, I had been bombarding the Kissed Air boys in London with plaintive and pathetic letters, bemoaning my lot as a penniless English lit student, trapped in a rural seaside town. The rugged beauty of the north coast of Ireland was sadly wasted on me, and I longed for the bright lights and big city. To their credit, they regularly responded but it was often to taunt and tease – I was a 'big jessie' with all my whining, later becoming 'Bur-gessie', a handle that stuck.

Back in 1982, and rather milking Ruefrex's relative success on the John Peel Show and our *NME* reviews, I had

'Change of Attention'

grandiosely offered my services as producer for Kissed Air's second single, 'Out of the Night'/'Change of Attention'.[4] While not ostensibly appearing on the credits for whatever meagre services I had rendered on these recordings, it allowed me to add valuable studio craft to a steadily growing skill set.

I also learned for the first time about 'Porky prime cuts'.[5] This practice took its name from the legendary vinyl engineer of the 1960s and 70s George 'Porky' Peckham who engraved messages into the run-out groove of the records he was pressing in order to show their authenticity. While many of his messages simply read 'Another Porky Prime Cut', others were humorous or insulting and have become collectors' items in themselves. And so taking their cue from Porky, Kissed Air inscribed their single with 'Burgess is a student Tee Hee!'[6]

The Kissed Air crew and Gareth Ryan expressed an interest in paying for the pressing, cover and distribution of 'The Wild Colonial Boy'. They were not particularly flush themselves, but they had fallen in with someone who was: Neil Cuthbertson. Neil was a white South African 'Del Boy' of sorts – more of an opportunist than an entrepreneur. His toothy smile, yellow-gold feather-cut hair style and perma-tan evoked *Let's Dance*-era Bowie. As manager of the Video Palace in London's West End, Neil oversaw the hottest movie rental store in the country at that time.[7] The large open-plan premises became the place to be seen and hang out with a host of celebrities from the music and film industries who dropped in to acquire the latest flicks and classics on VHS cassette.[8]

The Kissed Air boys had secured jobs working on the front desk and in the warehouses. More importantly, they had been spending a lot of time socially with Cuthbertson who enjoyed the live music scene and quite fancied playing a role as indie record executive. He set up Kasper Records, fronted the money needed to press 'The Wild Colonial Boy' and utilised the video rental chain's infrastructure to store, stock and distribute it.

It was a complete win-win for me, but I was keen to keep the demise of our group from them. I grasped the offer with both hands, figuring I would worry about little details like fellow band members, gigs and promotional responsibilities later.

So off to London went the master tapes and back came the finished product – fifty copies in a cardboard box. I duly doled out the singles to the other band members, friends and family and waited for the response.

While the others were delighted by these developments, their reactions were varied. Clarkey immediately sniffed the possibility of the limelight again and a revival ... but, fatefully, on his own terms. Forgie was unabashedly enthusiastic. Despite facing both his impending wedding day and the birth of his first child, he was excited about promoting the record in the UK.

Crucially, however, while TC welcomed the disc as a fitting monument to the band, he rejected any prospect of taking things to the next level and refused to leave his comfort zone. Yes, perhaps we might play at the occasional community centre bash or a gig at the Harp Bar, but it would only be on a casual roster that fitted in with his other commitments. In short, the other major creative influence in the band – my chief co-songwriter and founder member – intended to sit this one out.

I pleaded with him to keep an open mind and await critical reaction to the single. It was not long in coming.

'Change of Attention'

NOTES

1. John Watt would later go on to write the theme tune for the popular BBC TV show *Dragon's Den*.
2. In 2004, the Provisional IRA carried out a robbery at the Northern Bank. They seized £26.5 million in mostly used notes. Much of it was never recovered and no one has been held responsible for the heist.
3. At that time, it was possible to secure temporary teaching work in schools on the strength of a primary degree and without a teaching qualification. I didn't know it then, but the experience I secured at that time would later provide opportunities in higher education beyond all my expectations.
4. This and their first single, 'Kariba' (1982), were released on the Kabuki label, along with Ruefrex's 'Capital Letters' (1983).
5. George Peckham – 'Porky' – reportedly began this practice in the late 1960s while working at Apple Studios. Beatles singles were being illegally produced in large numbers and sold abroad 'off the books'. Porky's run-out inscription sought to address this by proving authenticity.
6. We had our own hidden message on the 'Capital Letters' single: 'Another Generation's Young', which was a line taken from the unrecorded song 'Poppies', and 'Slap the oul head skipper', a popular Belfast saying at the time, signifying instant retribution for behaviour that warranted it.
7. This was before the advent of Blockbuster and other national franchises that eventually drove smaller video rental stores out of business.
8. His fiancée, Sophie, was the sister of Peter Richardson, impresario of the emerging TV comedy hit series *The Comic Strip Presents...* which initially ran from 1982 to 1988 on Channel 4. Its founding members were Adrian Edmondson, Dawn French, Rik Mayall, Nigel Planer and Jennifer Saunders, with guest appearances by others such as Keith Allen, Robbie Coltrane and Alexei Sayle.

19
Our Tune

Refreshing to hear somebody voice anything about Northern Ireland beyond dogmatic sloganeering and strident rhetoric and while Ruefrex run a colossal risk of bitter misinterpretation, their articulate combination of the ethics that inspire Noraid surely deserves to straddle creeds and frontiers. Single of the Week. *Melody Maker.*

Ruefrex are everything that punk should be in '85. No preaching, just ably cropped verbals digging at Americans who 'kill from far away' with donations to terrorist causes. Lyrics that are pertinent instead of merely impertinent. As Mishima wrote, 'A line of poetry written in a splash of blood.' Buy!' Single of the Week. *Sounds.*

[W]ithin the Trad rock mould, they are undoubtedly the superior animal type. The guitar drones, the lyrics are quite simply wonderful and Allan Clarke's voice is better than any other on this page. Single of the Week. *New Musical Express.*

[A]n intelligent comment on our American cousins and the dollars that find their way into extremism across the Irish Sea ... also a great record, with descending bass lines, stinging guitars and lyrics you just know they mean. Single of the Week. *Record Mirror.*

Our Tune

'The Wild Colonial Boy' reached No. 30 in the UK charts, sandwiched between Bruce Springsteen and Sister Sledge, and the telephone started to ring ... and ring ... and ring.

'You've to get the fuck over here ... like yesterday!' exclaimed Jonty. 'We've got to build on this ... catch the tide ... get out there and let people see you live!'

I held the phone away from my ear and swallowed hard. No one, but no one, had anticipated this. The idea had been to go out with a bang, pull no punches and sign off bloodied, but unbowed and unbroken. I truly believed that the incendiary lyrics and sleeve would to be too hot to handle for the English media. Pride, adrenaline and dread rose up in equal measure and parched my mouth. Should I tell him now?

'Jonty, about that ...'

'Let me put Neil on.'

I had just started explaining when Neil came on the phone.

25	(—)	LOVE IS THE SEVENTH WAVE	Sting (A&M)	1	25
26	16	CRAZY FOR YOU	Madonna (Geffen)	13	1
27	(—)	DON'T MESS WITH MR DREAM	Thompson Twins (Arista)	1	27
28	20	RASPBERRY BERET	Prince (Paisley Park)	5	20
29	19	GLORY DAYS	Bruce Springsteen (CBS)	5	9
30	49	WILD COLONIAL BOY	Ruefrex (Kaspar)	2	30
31	14	FRANKIE	Sister Sledge (Atlantic)	13	1
32	(—)	I CAN DEAM ABOUT YOU	Dan Hartman (MCA)	1	32
33	22	AXEL F	Harold Faltermeyer (MCA)	12	2
34	(—)	DIRTY OLD TOWN	The Pogues (Stiff)	1	34
35	(—)	DO NOT DISTURB	Bananarama (London)	1	35

Illustration S2.2 Illustrious company. UK Chart. Straight in at No. 30 ... then straight out again!
Photo by the author

Wild colonial boys

'Paul? Look, if you don't believe what's happening here, listen to Radio One tomorrow morning around eleven. I'll call you again then.'

'That's fucking Simon Bates!'

'Exactly!'

Simon Bates was the quintessential middle-of-the-road, Home Counties DJ. His weekday mid-morning show had a listenership of eleven million, many of them housewives. The pinnacle of his show, a segment called Our Tune, had become something of a national institution. It typically featured a personal story submitted by a listener, together with a song that was significant to them. Many of the stories, read out over Nino Rota's 'Love Theme' from *Romeo and Juliet*, had a tragic ending, such as serious illness or premature death.

So it was with complete incredulity that I listened to the opening refrain of 'The Wild Colonial Boy' drift out of my tiny transistor radio. Ruefrex had somehow stormed the bastion of peak daytime radio for the silent majority!

> A people cannot live that way,
> or so the songs and leaflets say,
> and all this while we're trying hard,
> to keep the black man down.

'Un-fucking-believable!' was all I could manage.

I could hear Neil Cuthbertson's manic cackle at the other end of the line. 'I know, *I know*!'

In a daze, I didn't register what Simon Bate's comments were or his reasons for playing the song in this context. It didn't matter. Incredibly, we were on the daytime Radio One heavy rotation playlist. I had to tell the others.

By this time, imaginations were running amok – record deals, American tours, an album. Suddenly, all those years of teenage, thwarted dreams and harsh disappointments seemed to be turning around. Everything we had hoped for could be ours if we wanted it badly enough. To listen to Neil and Jonty, we just had to reach out and take them.

When I met with TC, I was reminded that we tended to be a band that was accomplished at snatching defeat from the jaws of victory.

'Let's see what happens,' he pronounced.

'What? No! We have to *make it* happen!' I pleaded.

'The Undertones never left Derry and they did okay,' he countered.

'They did leave. They toured so they could come back and stay there on their own terms. Besides, they're a pop band. They had *Top of the Pops* to sell themselves. This is different.'

He looked at the floor and his face grew dark. I knew what that meant.

'Wise the fuck up!' I shouted. 'Think about all that we set out to do – all the things we wanted. You're going to ruin this for all of us. *For me!*'

Then he raised his eyes. They had a hard look in them that took me back to the street life we'd shared as kids, to the gangs.

'You're not too big for a slap!' he shot back.

He meant it. It harked back to an earlier time, and now, like then, it felt like a personal betrayal. We were in our mid-twenties but he was still the alpha male, still Top Cat. And he clearly believed it was still *his* band.

There was a tense silence.

'I'm going to London,' I said. 'I don't know about the others, but I'm going.'

'Do what you have to do.'

I turned in the doorway of the bedroom he shared with his younger brother, Colin, where we had written so many songs together and dreamed of a moment such as this that we now found ourselves daggers drawn over.[1]

'If they pay for it – travel, hotel, I mean – will you at least play a couple of showcase gigs,' I asked, steeling myself to say what we had both been thinking. 'Till we get someone else to take your place.'

There was another long silence.

'I'll think about it.'

And so it was on Saturday 13 July 1985 that I arrived at Heathrow airport, clutching a suitcase and a box of singles. Electricity was coursing around the place as VIP artists arrived from all over the world to take part in the Live Aid gig at Wembley stadium later that day. It seemed like an auspicious time to be starting something. London was awash with high-summer sunlight and I was there to join the great extravaganza.

I had been promised bed and board by the Video Palace/Kasper Record crowd, while they organised a series of live showcase performances for Ruefrex. The principal motivation for them was to have their label licensed by a major record company; our band was to be the bait for this. It would mean both a financial settlement and the opportunity for them to expand their label with other artists.

Of course, this was never broached with me. Rather, they flattered my ego with whoops of wild excitement and professions of undying love for the band and the single, and as many of the people behind the label were friends and acquaintances from home, I was content that this was in some part true, that we were in safe hands.

Treading a well-worn path taken by generations of Irish before me, I headed to North London, to the Murphia/Paddylands of Willesden, Neasden, Cricklewood and Kilburn High Road, an established hub for the ebb and flow of Irish exiles just like me. The members of Kissed Air had made the same trip and been able to take advantage of the good offices of Irish men and women who had gone before them. It was practically a tradition. Newcomers got to sleep on spare beds, mattresses on floors and sofas and learn the ropes regarding benefits, cheap cafes and Tube travel, before earning a living and graduating to kips of their own. From there, they often took over the role of host, teacher and guide for the next intake of exiles and acolytes. It was a foot up, a word-of-mouth system of recommendations that worked very well and one that didn't seem to be fettered by the political and religious boundaries of home or any reservations about cross-border issues. We all mixed in along with the native English (many of whom seemed to be claiming Celtic heritage) and a variety of multi-ethnic minorities. It was new, liberating and exhilarating.

For the foreseeable future, 55 Olive Road, Cricklewood, was to be my home. It was similar to the many other large, detached houses crammed together in this typical leafy suburb of North London. Most of the properties were let out by absentee landlords who benefitted from the government rent allowances claimed by the half dozen or more tenants who occupied each of them. In this manner, expats enjoyed reasonably comfortable shared accommodation, which even had a decent-sized back garden and some greenery for recreational purposes. Most importantly of all, of course, it was a London base, offering all the infrastructure, transport links, opportunities and temptations of one of the world's great cities.

But the mock Elizabethan façade and shrubbery was where the normality and convention of 55 Olive Road, Cricklewood ended. Once you passed through the front door, it was like entering into an alternative reality; a surreal bohemia assailed the senses immediately.

Wild colonial boys

The residents, Cormac, Jonty, John-Boy and Sean O'Hagan, were joined by Frank Toner, another exile from rural Northern Ireland. A stout, quiet, unobtrusive character, Frank might have been taken for a cattle farmer under different circumstances. Instead, he fixed photocopiers by day and was responsible for sound-mixing at live gigs by night (for this reason he was invariably referred to as a 'sound man', and because of his generally avuncular disposition)

Sean was not a member of Kissed Air; he was the guitarist/founder member with Cork outfit Microdisney. Originally from Luton, he too was an orphan in the London music business; he had washed up there, seeking out gigs and label interest with his musical partner Cathal Coughlan.

Between them, the residents kept a menagerie of pets. There were two adult ducks named Fa-Duck and Ha-Duck who made sorties between rooms as the mood took them and resided in a cardboard box under the dining table. Tramp, the mongrel rescue dog, possessed the sweetest nature of a canine imaginable and seemed only able to move in circles, bouncing joyously forward by degrees, mouth open, tongue lolling, as if smiling broadly. Finally, there were two black cats, Kasper and Kabuki, named after the independent labels that had issued Kissed Air's singles.

Music of all kinds provided an almost 24/7 soundtrack. Nothing was off limits, as John-Boy compiled eclectic mix tapes featuring reggae, punk, glam, disco, power pop, indie, dance, R&B classics and obscure 12-inch mixes that no one else paid any attention to. For me, it was the beginning of a serious schooling in bands that I hadn't previously heard but would come to love.

Shouts of exasperation and screams of triumph came constantly from the sitting room, which was given over to round-the-clock bouts of mortal combat, thanks to whatever martial arts video game, requisitioned from the Video Palace, was in vogue. We also watched an endless supply of cult movies 'borrowed' from the store – *The Blues Brothers* (1980), *Once Upon a Time in America* (1984), *Blood Simple* (1984). *The Big Chill* (1983) was a favourite amongst flatmates and we dutifully learned off the key dialogue by heart, adoring William Hurt's damaged drug dealer persona and lusting after ingénue, Meg Tilly.

The kitchen (and the house in general) would easily have fallen into chaos were it not for the regimented control-freak tendencies of our 'Mother Superior', Cormac. They bordered on obsessive-compulsive traits, but they somehow kept the bedlam from swallowing up everything else. I can still recall the smell of his cooking intermingled with the tang of hashish, duck shit and wet dog.

Companionship with Cormac came at a price. While living in Northern Ireland, he'd had a long-term relationship with a local girl, Mary McGlinchey. As she was the sister of Dominic 'Mad Dog' McGlinchey, an Irish republican paramilitary leader who become head of the Irish National Liberation Army (INLA) in the 1980s, the attentions of Special Branch were never far away. He was in hiding then and had earned himself the sobriquet, emblazoned on tabloid front pages: 'The most wanted man in Britain'. A dark blue Ford Granada, with two occupants sporting squaddie haircuts, sat parked across from 55 Olive Road around the clock. You could run from the conflict at home, but you couldn't hide from it.

Cuisine took an exotic turn for me. For the first time, all the takeaway treats of the former colonies were available. The local family-run Indian restaurant provided new culinary adventures, and I became addicted to their unfeasibly large onion bhajis, the size of tennis balls, smothered in mango chutney. Even convenience food from the local M&S seemed wildly glamorous. Marinated Chinese chicken wings and Jamaican jerk recipes. All of this was countered by John-Boy's penchant for what he called 'brain food' – for example, baked beans mixed in with eggs – named so not because it offered cerebral stimulus but because it resembled, he thought, the contents of a spilled cranium.

Bed was a mattress on a bedroom floor, the room sometimes shared with two or three others. The next stage in elevation was from the floor to a divan base and then – if you stuck around long enough – the Holy Grail: a room of your own.

John-Boy and Jonty had just discovered *Le Pétomane* (1979), the British humorous film based on the life of Le Pétomane, the stage name of Joseph Pujol, the late nineteenth-century French flatulist (farter) and entertainer. He was famous for being able to fart at will, a feat with which he delighted large audiences at the Moulin Rouge. Musical farts were where it was at when I arrived at Olive Road and the night air hung heavy with the noxious odours of those who sought the illustrious title of 'Trumpetbum!' On any given day, random adolescent pronouncements could be heard – 'Drink!', 'Arse!', 'Shite!', 'Drawers ... drop 'em!' – so much so that I'm convinced a young Graham Linehan and Arthur Matthews must have been in attendance at some point to harvest ideas for a future *Father Ted* (not unfeasible, given the amount of human traffic passing through).

All in all, I cannot think of a more welcoming haven for emotionally immature young men in the big city for the first time and hell-bent on adventure. It was heaven.

My new home saw an unrelenting stream of visitors, mostly fascinating to me, post-punk pretenders to the throne, who came to plot the next phase of world domination or simply to hang out, get pissed and stoned, listen to music and play video games. They were variously Irish Catholics, Ulster Protestants, English Anglicans, and Scots Presbyterians, people of all creeds and none.

Politics were rarely mentioned, unless it was to roundly harangue Margaret Thatcher and the Tory government, particularly in the aftermath of the miners' strike led by Arthur Scargill, the failure of which weakened the power of most British trade unions. The conflict in Northern Ireland seemed in the main, a taboo topic (at least around me).

All were music fans and knew of Ruefrex from what we'd achieved to date in the indie scene. But my stock was exponentially rising, and I detected as much from the cache of enthusiasm, respect and mounting buzz for 'The Wild Colonial Boy' and the band themselves. The only problem was, there was no longer a band. The time had clearly come for me to do something about it or miss the bus entirely.

Back in Belfast, TC and Clarkey had been spending more time together and my instincts told me this didn't augur well for our chances. TC was well aware of our growing popularity and, as a skilful manipulator, he began priming Clarkey to be his eyes and ears in the band – a fifth columnist, if you will – since TC couldn't be there himself. It was only later that I came to understand how far they'd take this betrayal.

NOTE

1. Professor Colin Coulter went on to attain his doctorate in sociology and is a prominent scholar in higher education in Ireland. He has published seminal works on The Clash and The Smiths.

20
Home thoughts from abroad

By August 1985, I personally had a full-page spread in *Melody Maker*. Staff photographer Andy Catlin shot some moody close-up portraits of me with a beard, which lent themselves to a general mood of troubled intellectual or 'poet warrior', and journalist Barry McIlheney wrote the article.

Barry hailed from the lower Oldpark Road area of Belfast that skirted the Shankill, and his childhood experiences and reference points would have been broadly similar to my own. Indeed, I had known him a little from his time fronting Belfast band Shock Treatment some years before. The *Melody Maker* piece ran with the headline 'The Wild Colonial Boy', and a quotation, pulled from the interview, appeared in bold at the bottom of the page:

> Some people might tell you that once we get a 32-county Ireland then all the Provos will dig a big hole in their back gardens and bury all the armalites. That's bollocks.[1]

As this was 1985, I will leave it to you, dear reader, to decide whether this pronouncement was prescient or not. In the article, I went off on a rant about how Sinn Féin/IRA were the common enemy of all Irish citizens, north and south

Home thoughts from abroad

of the border, and about how the Provos had targeted the southern state for insurrection and political change once Northern Ireland had been subjugated. But it was what I later said that seemingly rattled some cages at home.

In trying to establish that my community – the Loyalist working class – were neither dupes nor right-wing stereotypes – I perhaps overstretched. Citing a proud tradition of Northern Protestant dissent – that of McCracken and Orr – I suggested that a 'new' thirty-two-county federal Ireland might be possible, one where those who identified as British might have privileges and rights protected. This new entity could then turn its attention to eradicating Sinn Féin/IRA. In effect, I deftly managed to offend *everyone* in a few short sentences.

One thing was certain. The band's politics were now fully front and centre ... and people were listening, not all of them sympathetically.

When I rang home that weekend, I was upset and disturbed to learn that my parents' house in a North Belfast council estate had been targeted. First, several snooker balls were thrown through the living room window (fortunately, no one was hurt), then the following evening, anonymous reports of a fire at the premises, then a stabbing, brought a succession of fire brigade, ambulance and police to the address repeatedly throughout the night and into the early hours. My parents, who were getting on in years, were of course distraught. While *they* didn't make the connection between my press pronouncements and these events (they weren't avid music press devotees!), it certainly gave me pause for thought.

I was happy to take responsibility for my words and actions, but I was not the one at the sharp end. I reasoned that this could simply have been mischief-making by local youths who resented the band's growing success and wanted to take me down a peg or two, but I couldn't escape the unsettling anxiety that it was something more sinister. I knew from my own experience of living in that housing estate that a subtle scent of intimidation hung in the air, an undertow of bullying that made ordinary people feel powerless and afraid. Tragically, it remains to this day.

What was happening to my parents was all too familiar to me from the past. When I'd arrived home from my first job aged 18, pay packet in hip pocket, a rite of passage realised, I'd frozen at the garden gate. There, halfway up a ladder, a pair of puffy, white, hairy-arse cheeks cracked over a denim jeans waistband. Some tattooed thug was tying red, white and blue bunting to the drainpipe outside my bedroom window. It was the Loyalist marching season and this wanker hadn't even asked permission. Instead, he had just planted his ladder in the middle of my mother's begonias and was peering into my room, gawking at my 'Kung Fu' pyjamas, my 'Charlie's Angels' poster. I wanted to scream at this usurper, 'You don't know me … I'm not one of you. Take it down … take it all fucking DOWN!' I wanted to grab the ladder and shake it until the fat fuck crashed to the ground.

But of course, that didn't happen. You couldn't do or say anything, not if you wanted to keep your windows intact. Later that year, I watched wretchedly from my bedroom window, as the same fat fuck, the son of a well-known paramilitary figure, bounced up and down on the bonnet and roof of my first car. His intention was to lure a squad of young RUC officers into the area for a confrontation. The little second-hand Simca hatchback stove in like a metal eggshell.

Home thoughts from abroad

Those memories and feelings returned in spades – the frustration and impotence in the face of armed threat. I resolved to press on regardless. In London, no one knew, much less cared.

NOTE

1   Barry McIlheney, 'The Wild Colonial Boy', *Melody Maker*, 31 August 1985, p.14.

21

Hot to trot

Sean O'Hagan, Microdisney co-founder and my new flatmate, thought it was time to take me in hand. He was an unlikely member of an ostensibly (post) punk rock band, for his influences were The Beach Boys, The Band and Van Dyke Parks. He was an accomplished player who took his craft very seriously, although his playing style and sound seemed weedy and thin to my ears. However, he was perfectly juxtaposed by bandmate Cathal Coughlan, an inspired lyricist and frontman, whose withering wit and scathing delivery ticked all the right boxes.

One day, he suggested that we take Tramp for a walk in the local park, and while the lovable mutt spun in circles until he wore himself out, Sean sagely counselled me to plan my next musical steps very carefully.

We walked through the leafy thoroughfares of North London, past Dollis Hill Tube Station (our Jubilee Line jumping off point for the rest of the city) toward Gladstone Park. On any given day, ordinary office commuters mingled with Hasidic Jews, Rastafarians and Sikhs, punks, navvies and school children. Compared with the meagre cultural dichotomy of the two warring tribes back home, it was a joyous kaleidoscope of philosophies for me.

Hot to trot

We passed the house in Melrose Avenue where the lads told me about the skinny man with glasses who used to hang over the end of his garden gate and regularly bid them good day. This man was none other than Dennis Nilsen, a serial killer who had murdered several young men and boys in North London. Police had caught him in 1983 when the dissected remains of his victims, having been flushed down his toilet, blocked the drains in the area. People may have been shot and maimed in explosions in Northern Ireland, but hearing about Nilsen somehow made me miss the dubious certainties and reassurances of back home.

Sean knitted his eyebrows and looked at me with concern. 'They've presented you as a sort of Dylanesqe character,' he said. 'That's the angle to go for. It's so important, what you do right now.'

I was a little taken aback. I didn't have a basic plan, or even a functioning band, much less a sense of a public persona. I felt pressured and uncomfortable. Suddenly something became apparent to me. Other musicians like Sean were trying to cultivate a public profile themselves. It was a dog-eat-dog environment, irrespective of common purpose, so their advice had to be taken with a pinch of salt. In essence, there was an unspoken resentment, a belief that they had paid their dues and deserved your new-found success more than you did. But there was also a premium to staying on your good side in case you opened up opportunities for them. After all, they might be able to ride on your coat-tails to greater things. I would have felt the same myself if the roles were reversed.

One way or another, the pressure was subtly ramping up. Strangely, people were treating me differently now – with a kind of deference – due to the currency of emerging celebrity. And to be honest, I was loving it. Things were taking shape.

Forgie arrived, with his guitar, new bride Marlene and just-born son, Leigh, and moved into a small room that became available in Olive Road. Looking back, I can see how it took a lot of bottle for them to pitch up in London in such a fashion, ready to make a new start with a baby in tow. Marlene, however, was salt-of-the-earth Shankill stock and took things in hand from the get-go, redeeming and reorganising Forgie's shambolic lifestyle.

Gary 'The Dean' Ferris also arrived with his guitar and girlfriend Nancy, who already had some contacts in the capital. This time, instead of being left high and dry when Forgie inevitably departed or was kicked out of the band, we decided we'd play as a five-piece. It wasn't ideal for that perfect symmetry seen in The Clash, The Sex Pistols, or even The Beatles, but the additional band member offered fresh permutations in writing, recording and performing, as well as that insurance policy against Forgie's brooding petulance.

Clarkey was hedging his bets, but when he learned that TC was prepared to travel for a couple of showcase promo gigs, he couldn't resist the draw of the limelight. He was, after all, the focal point for the band, and his performances and vocal chops were attracting a lot of column inches. The band was as central to his sense of identity as it was mine, and being recognised on the streets of his hometown proved a heady drug. He wanted more.

I knew only too well that TC standing in for a couple of gigs would not address the long-term problem. He made it clear that his appearance was a considerable imposition, as his absence from work was to be taken out of his holiday allocation. So, unpalatable to me as it was, I pushed the others to see the problem for what it was: 'nothing personal,

Hot to trot

just business you understand. We need a new bass player sooner rather than later.'

Hunkered down in Herne Hill, SE 24, Gordy Blair had lineage stretching back to the Debs days in 70s Belfast. An accomplished musician, he had variously been a member of (pre-punk SLF outfit) Highway Star, Rudi and The Outcasts. He was, in fact, Belfast punk royalty, who whilst in London had been double-jobbing, playing bass fiddle in a jazz band while managing The Ritzy Cinema in Brixton (where a patron might comfortably flop on the back row, spark up a spliff and watch the feature uninterrupted, and where, occasionally, you might catch a live performance from an artist such as John Cale, if you were lucky).

Gordy was uber-cool. Over six feet tall, with a cherubic countenance under a shock of spiky blonde hair, he favoured old 1940s second-hand, three-piece tweed suits with braces and boots, and ankle-length leather trench coats. He had the look, he had the attitude and he played bass in the style of those gods of punk Simonon, Burnel and Ramone. He had also been on the London scene for a while and was able to offer insights into music business challenges and conventions that I had routinely overlooked.

As I had known him from way back in the day, I was confident I could talk him into coming on board. He would instantly boost the visual appeal of our band by one thousand per cent.

Calling at his flat one morning, I found him wreathed in clouds of marijuana smoke with a copy of *The Guardian* spread out in front of him. He was wearing a tweed waistcoat, complete with brass pocket watch and chain, and collarless shirt. I thought he could easily have walked straight out of the pages of a D. H. Lawrence novel. He could be mistaken for taciturn, but his relative silence only fuelled his mystique and disguised a wicked sense of humour. It was the start of a beautiful friendship.

We were dependant on our fellow housemates for the backline – amps, PA, drums, and so on – and what we couldn't borrow we hired. Neil Cuthbertson fronted the money required and Jonty, the bass player from Kissed Air, made the phone calls and did the legwork. Both of them protested against taking on these essentially management roles, but to see them bask in the reflected glory of what was unfolding suggested they were more than happy to be involved. Indeed, more than once they enthusiastically went well beyond any requests from me on the band's behalf, especially when talk turned to record contracts from major labels and advance payments.

I was relieved and grateful to have them involved, for they possessed more nous, had more contacts and were more familiar with the geography of the place than this young Irish schoolteacher literally 'just off the boat'. So Neil, Jonty and I became the Ruefrex management team, a role I genuinely didn't want and one that would almost completely overshadow any of the unbridled enjoyment that should have gone with being a successful artist and performer.

BBC Radio One's *Roundtable* was a long-running, singles review programme broadcast every Friday evening. It typically featured two 'special' guests who discussed the week's new releases with the host DJ. Only a matter of hours before it was due to air, Neil excitedly phoned us to say that 'The Wild Colonial Boy' was one of the singles to be reviewed in the show that week. This was considered a major coup and added to the growing momentum behind the band.

So he invited a few of us over to his place to listen to the *Roundtable* broadcast that evening. Neil lived in a stylish flat conversion in Kilburn, perfect for an upwardly mobile young entertainment executive, full of cool furnishings, music and film paraphernalia. When we got there, we found that he had a 'roundtable' of his own.

The show was already broadcasting through his Bang & Olufsen wall-mounted speakers, and in the centre of the room was a round, glass table on which Neil had lovingly laid out a regiment of finely chopped white lines, four heavy-cut glass tumblers, replete with ice and Jack Daniels, and an ornate Thai bowl filled with pre-rolled spliffs. Beside this was a bottle of amyl nitrite, popular with the gay community. This man knew how to entertain!

Neil passed me a glass and the joint he was already smoking.

'To the man of the hour!' he pronounced in his unmistakable Afrikaans brogue.

Regarding the coke and amyl, I was well out of my depth and hesitant at first, figuring anything that went up your nose (or in a vein, for that matter) was off limits. Back in Northern Ireland, recreational drugs of *any* kind were considered taboo. You could rot your liver and your prospects in lakes of alcohol, but there was an almost existential reaction to drugs, the reasoning being that one toot would ensnare your soul in mindless addiction from which there was no escape. But after a few tokes on the joint, I jumped right on in with the others. The drill went in rotation around the table: coke snort – drink – toke – drink – amyl snort – fall back in a swoon – drink. We were having so much fun that we almost missed the record review.

Midge Ure of Ultravox was the star guest. He was riding high on his association with Bob Geldof and the hugely successful Band Aid single 'Do They Know It's Christmas?'. He damned our single with faint praise, complaining that the guitar mix was muddled and lacked clarity. The verbal abuse hurled by us at Neil's sound system regarding Ure's sexual preferences and parentage suggested that we begged to differ.

> 'Slik ... he was frontman for fucking SLIK! Bubble-gum boyband SHITE!'
> 'Aye, "Ohhh Vienna" my arse! Ultravox were over when John Foxx left!'

Despite Ure's lukewarm review, I couldn't stop myself laughing. I was doubled over with it, partly the narcotics and partly the stream-of-consciousness abuse being hurled at Ure, but mostly I was laughing at the chain of events that had somehow brought me to this place, right here, right now, having the prospect of playing out this rock star shtick for real. Who knew how long it would last for and where it would lead to?

* * *

From then on, it seemed that every other day I was in the back of a cab with a heavily coked-up Jonty, heading off to some record company pitch around the West End of London. And just to be clear, it was *they* who were pitching to *us*!

There was mounting interest in the band from several major labels but they were all reserving judgement, much less commitment, until they could catch the now-fabled live act for themselves. It seemed that anger – authentic, unmanufactured anger – was a rare, marketable and a much sought-after commodity, and we had it in spades. It came through on the records, it came across in the interviews, and all this only fuelled the rumours of the intensity of our Belfast gigs. Punters wanted to see the band perform. A&R men wanted to see the band perform. Christ, *I* wanted to see the band perform!

Hot to trot

Two showcase gigs were arranged. The second was to be in Dingwalls in Camden Town, but first, we were to travel to that mecca of Northern cool, Factory Records' Haçienda club in Manchester. Both gigs would be attended by interested parties from amongst the big beasts of the world's record labels. Let the bidding war commence – or so we hoped.

It was becoming apparent, however, that Jonty was badly out of his depth, and I even more so. In an uber-politicised Britain, almost everything about our politics was on the left. We were at street corners collecting for Miners' Aid in plastic buckets. We hated Thatcher with a passion (who didn't?) Yet here we were, a couple of blokes from North Belfast, looking to broker a licensing and distribution deal for Jonty's and Neil's small indie label, Kasper Records, with multi-national entertainments companies. To say we were conflicted and confused is an understatement.

Add to this Jonty's very messy and unresolved break-up with Valerie, an accountant who, with her new boyfriend, was now sharing the same house as him. It was a shit show that had all the makings of an epic fail. He was drinking and snorting to help him cope with his insecurities regarding his new management role, and it was affecting his judgement and focus. I simply believed this was how the music biz rolled and allowed myself to be swept up and along with it.

According to Jonty, alienating and insulting record company executives who were showing the band love was just 'playing hardball'. But soon, we began to get a (deservedly) terrible reputation on the grapevine as unprofessional and clearly in over our heads. Suitors were melting away like snow off a ditch, and when the game of musical chairs eventually ended, just two executives were left standing.

Rob Dickens, the Managing Director of WEA Records (Warner Music Group), was hugely enthusiastic about the band for reasons I was never quite clear on.[1] He outlined a detailed, phased, career-building process, with long-term goals, that would develop Ruefrex over a period of time. It seemed perfect to me, the kind of deal that Paul McGuinness and U2 probably got.

We were sitting in his office one Thursday morning as he laid it all out for us when Jonty, without any warning, told him to 'fucking stuff it!'. Then, standing up, he announced that we were leaving. I was shell-shocked.

In the cab afterwards, he explained to me – coked-up words machine-gunning from his lips – that Dickens's proposed phased development failed to capitalise on the buzz and momentum currently surrounding the band. Furthermore, he claimed, it was an attempt to take us out of the running and ensure that WEA's competitors couldn't sign us.

He looked distractedly out of the cab window. 'They'll put you on a shelf and forget about you', he said. Then he went on a rant about 'not being taken for mugs' and enthused about The Three Johns as the greatest band to emerge in the last five years.

As I looked at him – his bug eyes, his dilated pupils – and heard his paranoid ramblings become ever more bizarre, I felt sick to the pit of my stomach. We had just fucked up big time and I'd just sat there and let it all happen.

That left only the infamous Dave Robinson and Stiff Records still standing. Dave Robinson had clearly impressed Jonty. Leering madly, he assured me that Dave was 'hot to trot!'

NOTE

1   WEA was a major international force in the industry, with a US parent company to boot.

22

If it ain't stiff, it ain't worth a fuck

Dave Robinson was one of those quintessential Irishmen, perhaps best defined by the term 'chancer'. Invariably a man rather than a woman, a chancer in Irish lore enjoys something resembling begrudging respect – sometimes awe – from the wider community. He is the quintessential lovable rogue, particularly if he is using his charm and guile to part a fool from their money, or undermining and humiliating a faceless, uncaring bureaucracy, especially if the target in question is English. The bigger and more outrageous his success, the more audacious and brazen his cheek, the higher esteem in which he's held.

Down the years, notable Irish chancers who have blagged and bluffed their way to success and riches could be said to include famed punter Barney Curley, former FAI Chief Executive John Delaney, rock star and (eventual) philanthropist millionaire Bob Geldof, a plethora of Irish taoisigh and perhaps even Oscar Wilde, who led English high society a merry dance before coming to grief. Terri Hooley's activities emphatically affirm that 'chancership' is not confined to south of the Irish border.

There is something of the rebel in the DNA of the Irish chancer that people often fall for, despite their better judgement. Ironically, it's the English themselves who invariably and wholeheartedly embrace the amiable, charismatic Irish chancer, oblivious to the fact that they themselves are his mark. Indeed, it is this mischievous quality that English people are often attracted to, believing it to be characteristically 'Irish'.

It was with the chancer's charisma, the glint in the eye and the winning smile, that Dave 'Robbo' Robinson was able to get other people to do what he wanted them to, often things that weren't always in their own best interests.

Following an erstwhile career on the fringes of the scene (he reportedly managed Jimi Hendrix when in London), Dave moved into the music business proper, establishing Stiff Records with Jake Riviera in 1976. Over the years, Stiff signed various punk and new wave acts such as The Damned, Lene Lovich, Elvis Costello, Ian Dury and the Blockheads, and Devo. In the 1980s, with most of their early signings having moved on, the label found commercial success with Madness, The Pogues, Tracey Ullman, Dr. Feelgood, Kirsty MacColl and others. In 1984, Island Records bought fifty per cent of Stiff, and Dave ran both labels as part of the deal.[1] So he had already acquired mythical status in the industry, famous for his cut-throat deals and practices. He used to joke that he put a list of his creditors into a large sombrero hat that hung on the wall and whoever he drew out would get paid that week.

Stiff/Island's offices were based at 22 St Peter's Square, in Hammersmith, London, a grade II listed building that had been converted to an open-plan, glass-walled, humming hub of music business activity. Cool artefacts from radio stations and world tours littered the floors and adorned the walls, and framed gold discs by legends, many of them my heroes, were everywhere.

If it ain't stiff, it ain't worth a fuck

I was shown into the great man's office by a very sexy PA who wore the world-weary look of having seen it all before, instantly quashing any amorous intentions I might have had. Dave sat, feet clad in cowboy boots up on the desk, talking on the phone. Mounted on the wall behind his head was a baseball bat rumoured to be the brokering tool in many a deal. His complexion was dark; his receding wavy hair, arched heavy brows and intense stare suggested something of the gypsy vagabond.

'Yes, I have Paul Burgess from the band with me now. Yeah ... well, we're hot to trot at this end. [*There was that phrase again*] Okay, leave it with me.'

He hung up and gave me a killer smile, flashing gold teeth and transforming his entire face in an instant. 'That was the States,' he explained. 'They're hot to trot.'

Whether there actually was an American promoter on the other end of the line or whether it was staged for my arrival mattered not. I was already so far in over my head that it was all I could do to not to blush even more than I already was and clam up completely.

'There's love for you on the US college circuit. Could go a long way to breaking you in the States. We have The Pogues going out there later in the year. You know The Pogues?'[2]

'Sure,' I blurted out.

'We have to jump on this right now, while you're flavour of the month.'[3]

Phones were buzzing, people walked around the office clutching sheaths of papers. His PA, Alison, came to the glass door, but he signalled 'not now' with the palm of his hand. His own phone buzzed but he pushed a button, holding the call. For the moment it was all about me. Me and my band.

We were joined briefly by Stiff's Head of A&R, former Queen's Guardsman Nick Stewart. He was a tall, patrician gent who, speaking in a plummy accent, told me how much he liked the band and that he had served a tour in Belfast before quickly leaving again. He seemed an odd confederate for Dave Robinson – and indeed for someone in this counter-culture – but all of my preconceived notions had already been shaken. What was one more?

Dave picked up where he had left off. 'You're from Belfast. I remember when Van the Man first came off the boat – didn't have a clue. Green, like yourselves.'

I tried to be cool and in awe at the same time. Christ knows what that looked like. I wasn't taking in half the things he was saying to me.

'I'm told you boys need some money for equipment? What kind of drum kit do you want?'

I was thrown. Off the top of my head, the best make of kit I could think of was a Gretsch. So I said so.

He looked at me, frowned a little and smiled knowingly. 'You'll grow into a Gretsch,' he said. 'We'll get you a Yamaha.'

I grinned and nodded compliance.

From there on in, I pretty much submitted to him on everything he suggested. It might have been the Prince of fucking Darkness sitting right there in front of me, but like everyone else who had gone before me, I just wanted to be his friend, to bask in his charisma, in the life he'd led and the people he'd associated with. I just wanted to let him make me a star.

Of course, he knew all that.

'Now, about booking you in for some studio time to record the album …'

There it was, the words I'd been longing to hear since the days when TC and I had sat cross-legged in his basement trying to solder a broken microphone back into operation.

If it ain't stiff, it ain't worth a fuck

Dave paused for maximum effect, his eyes narrowing inquisitively. 'You're not still thinking about going with someone else, are you?' He seemed incredulous, as if the very thought of it was lunacy.

A small voice somewhere in the back of my mind counselled a mannered withdrawal, time to think and reflect. But he held my gaze unremittingly.

'Any thoughts on who you want to produce it?' he asked.

'Sorry?'

'Your album ... who do you want to produce?'

Again, the door seemed to be held wide open. I just needed to walk through.

'Brian Eno,' I burbled. 'Or Bob Ezrin.'[4]

'Leave it with me. I've some ideas of my own.'

Alison pushed the door open a crack. 'Paul McGuinness on line two.'

I of course recognised the name of U2's manager.

'I have to take this. Alison, will you take Paul here down to the warehouse?' Then to me: 'Take whatever you want from the back catalogue and come back and see me.'

She ushered me out and down into a large basement area. I was now floating a few inches off the ground, operating on autopilot, still trying to take everything in and petrified of doing or saying the wrong thing. When I returned to Dave's office clasping an armload of LPs, from Costello through Madness to The Pogues, I found him pulling on a leather jacket.

'Where are you living in town? I'll give you a lift,' he said.

I thought it remarkably generous that he should take time out of his busy schedule to accommodate a newbie like me.

As we walked to his top-end Mercedes Benz, he told me that he and some of 'the posse' would be making the journey up to the Haçienda in Manchester the following week. They were all very excited about seeing us live at last.

The Stiff lawyer had furnished Jonty and Neil with the requisite forms, outlining the licensing deal for Kasper Records (about which nothing had been said to me) and the terms of our recording advance, etc. Publishing would be dealt with separately, but he assured me that this was in hand, likely with Zomba Music Publishing. All that remained was for me to sign on behalf of the band (subject to a tour de force at the Haçienda, of course).

It had begun raining – more like early December sleet – and the bustling streets were dark and inhospitable in the evening rush hour. Dave's wipers swept back and forth as he talked on, incessantly name-dropping, seemingly without really realising it. I pushed back deep into the leather, enveloped by the heated seats, and enjoyed feeling cocooned from the little people outside, lulled by the low hum of the engine and the orange glow of the instrument panel. Olive Road was some distance away and for now I could relax. I could get used to this.

So I was surprised when, after what seemed like only two or three minutes, Dave pulled the big Merc over to the kerb.

'There you go. You can get your Tube from here.'

As I stood outside Hammersmith Tube station at rush hour, watching his red taillights disappear into the winter gloom, I couldn't help but think that this must be how girls feel when, having had undying love pressed upon them all night long, are left on the side of the road with a hastily scribbled number on a scrap of paper.

NOTES

1   Island Records was founded in Jamaica in 1959 by industry legend Chris Blackwell and associates. Before Blackwell sold the label to PolyGram in 1989, it signed artists such as Bob Marley, Roxy

If it ain't stiff, it ain't worth a fuck

    Music, King Crimson, and U2. It is now a multinational label owned by Universal Music Group.

2 Pogues manager, fellow Dubliner the late Frank Murray, was also a renowned chancer on the music circuit.

3 Later inquiries revealed that there *was* in fact considerable interest in Ruefrex stateside according to Cactus World News, a Dublin band beloved of Bono and U2 (who produced their first album). In an interview given in 1986 in San Francisco, Eoin McEvoy, the band's singer, said: 'Certainly, Americans just seem to be eternally enthusiastic about music ... and you would think, you know, they've seen it all before, but their knowledge about new British bands just embarrasses me. I was doing one radio interview in Boston and the deejay asked me what I thought of the new Ruefrex album and it was like ... well, I can't say because I haven't got around to hearing it yet. Embarrassing.' (Barry McIlheney, 'A Beach Too Far', *Melody Maker*, 20 September 1986; http://cactusworldnewsband.com/archive5.html).

4 Bob Ezrin was producer of Lou Reed and Alice Cooper.

23
The fourth estate

Can there be any more life affirming experience than to emerge from the London underground in Oxford Street and be immediately met by the sight of a newspaper vendor's billboard with your face on it? Or to have the name of your project, something that you've conceived and worked on, emblazoned on the front cover of glossy magazines, piled high on busy West End street corners while tens of thousands of commuters, largely oblivious, play out their daily lives in the capital?

Despite all the usual caveats – 'It'll be lining the bottom of a budgie cage tomorrow' etc. – as a twenty-five-year-old on a mission, I was happy to bask in the warm glow of affirmation that this all seemed to be offering.

This love affair with the press in 1986 had begun with some lower-profile *NME* coverage: a review by Muir MacKean of a Ruefrex gig at Jules, a secret nightclub in Belfast. He wrote: 'Ruefrex are powerful, mature and on the ball and only need a decent sound system to be heard as one of the most important bands in Britain.'[1] Unbeknownst to us at that time, his short article was to go on to punch way above its weight.

In the way these things go, the phrase 'the most important band in Britain' was later to be leapt upon by promoters,

The fourth estate

record companies and other publications. It re-appeared (often out of context) on promotional posters, record sleeves and magazine reviews. DJs and radio commentators cited it as gospel. Like a snowball rolling downhill, it gathered weight and momentum. It proved to be a salutary lesson in how PR works, and useful experience in holding on for dear life (if you're lucky, you'll enjoy the ride).

The front cover profiles were down to the backing of the good people at *Melody Maker* (the magazine was enjoying something of a golden period in sales and popularity at this time). A cabal of their hottest writers held court at the Oporto Pub in High Holborn. (This and the Coach and Horses in the heart of Soho remained our go-to hostelries in the West End for the duration of our odyssey.) The *Melody Maker* gang largely consisted of Barry McIlheney, Colin Irwin, then editor Allan 'Jonsey' Jones, staff photographer Tommy Sheehan ('Just a gnat's dick to the left') and Steve 'Stickboy' Sutherland. An environment dripping mostly in testosterone did not deter sporadic appearances from Carol Clerk, who could party with the best of them. While ostensibly surfing what seemed like a dream job of endless free perks, while rubbing shoulders with celebrities, most of this happy band had half an eye to a more sedate, stable career within the publishing establishment (and many went on to achieve just that).

To most of the English contingent, Barry and I were simply 'Irish', with few qualifying factors placed upon that designation. It was no bad thing at the time, for Irishness or Celtic identity was held to be desirable, alternative and authentic. Sure, some of the usual stereotypical attributes might have been expected – hard-drinking, hard-partying, troubled, prone to soulful reflection – but most of our fellow exiles (including Barry and I) were more than happy to comply.[2]

Wild colonial boys

It is to their credit, then, that *Melody Maker* were prepared to dedicate a healthy amount of coverage to reflect on the more nuanced political and cultural interpretations of (Northern) Irishness as represented by Ruefrex and others. They offered an important platform to air the often-complex political ramblings of someone like me, and I remain grateful for that.

These most notably took the form of an initial semi-biographical piece and two front cover slots. One featured a centre page spread, with a large portrait of a tattooed Clarkey on the front cover. The other, as part of a 'music meets football' article, was presented in the run up to the Mexico 1986 World Cup finals.

The idea with the football-themed edition was to showcase short articles from Robert Smith (The Cure, from England), the late, lamented Stuart Adamson (The Skids/Big Country, from Scotland), and me, from Northern Ireland. Befitting our respective chances in the football competition, Fat Bob and Stuart were given the lion's share of the cover page, while perennial plucky outsiders Northern Ireland (and Ruefrex) occupied a small box further down. Nevertheless, I was thrilled to be included.

We were all photographed wearing our country's football jersey and I was happy to kid myself that I was representing my beloved province in the game itself. (Jake Burns would have killed for the opportunity!) The photo shoot also afforded me the chance to meet one of my heroes.

Robert Smith and The Cure had been firm favourites of mine from the outset, with *Three Imaginary Boys* in 1979 and *Seventeen Seconds* the following year. Smith was a regular customer at the Video Palace and friendly with the *Melody Maker* crew, so there were some things we had in common in order to strike up a conversation. In the spirit of

Illustration S2.3 'Green and White Army.' Portrait for *Melody Maker* World Cup feature.
Photo by Tom Sheehan

the footballing theme of the photo shoot, he recounted one of my favourite rock n' roll stories.

Smith was a lifelong Queen's Park Rangers and England fan and, while on a European tour with the band in France, he and fellow Cure founder member Lol Tolhurst were desperate to see England's vital (if ultimately futile) qualifying game for the 1984 UEFA European championships. Unable to attend the live match, the boys opted for the next best thing. They privately hired a cinema, had the game beamed in live and, dressed in full England kits, kicked a ball up and down the aisles while the real drama played out on the big screen as a backdrop. I was impressed!

Football and the arts overlapped for me on other occasions as well. We used rehearsal rooms in North London that were shared with popular duo Everything but the Girl. Tracey Thorn didn't engage much with us, but during breaks in the day's work, Ben Watt insisted that we retire to a nearby green area where we saw how many penalty kicks we could get by him. We won!

Around this time, perhaps inspired by my new-found role as international music emissary for the national team (in my head anyway), I was endeavouring to keep my hand in on the football field myself. Old teammates from Belfast contacted me about an amateur tournament that took place annually in Holland. Apart from the opportunity to catch up with friends, the craic at the event itself would be mighty. So in the week that the football article appeared in the *Melody Maker*, I was in transit to Delft to take part in a game of my own.

As I waited for my flight to be called, I looked across the sparsely occupied lounge and did a double take. Was that … could that be … Seamus Heaney? It was some ten years before he was to be awarded the Nobel Prize in Literature,

The fourth estate

but I was already an enthusiast. The great man was unaccompanied and apparently also awaiting a flight call. Flushed with my recent press profile, I summoned up my courage and decided to approach him. Nowadays, I might simply have asked for a selfie and left. Back then, I asked if I could buy him a drink.

He indicated that I could and, if memory serves, he had a half of Guinness. I sat down with him and he confirmed that he was indeed awaiting a flight to the US (where he was Boylston Professor of Rhetoric and Oratory at Harvard). And that's when it all went pear-shaped.

Instead of allowing the great man to wax lyrical about anything – the weather, the price of a pint, the iambic pentameter – I just wouldn't shut up! I told him I'd studied his work at the University of Ulster for my literature degree, that I'd been supervised by his contemporary, poet and songwriter, the late James Simmons, who had written 'The Ballad of Claudy'. I told him about the football article in *Melody Maker*. I told him my life story and about the peacebuilding mission of my band. I gave him my tuppence-worth of working-class Loyalist perspectives and what I thought was needed for a road out of sectarianism. And rather than ask him what he was working on, I recited my own lyrics and poems at him as he sat there, patient and glassy-eyed. In short, full of myself, I behaved like a massive asshole. And I regret it to this day.

It must have been a huge relief to him when his flight was called, and he made his apologies and left. (Reader, he did not buy his round!)

* * *

Relations with the press and the media in general were not always as supportive and affirming as those we enjoyed with *Melody Maker*. In fact, in some respects, some journos were downright hostile.

Take the case of journalist and second-generation Irishman Danny Kelly, later to be editor of *New Musical Express*.[3] Kelly was a staffer at *NME* when I received an invitation from him to come for a photo shoot at their Carnaby Street offices. The photo was to accompany an interview that I'd given Gavin Martin earlier, a balanced piece which reflected the difficulties of trying to walk the political middle ground when writing songs about the Troubles. In the piece, Martin had observed that 'In the liberal press these [Ruefrex lyrics] are not fashionable sentiments,' and I had conceded: 'I know we stick out like a sore thumb in that respect. It's not trendy if you're not for "the struggle." '[4]

The photo session was to be carried out by Australian photographer Bleddyn Butcher. He was on the staff of *NME* throughout the eighties, and his interests in the music industry and his friendships with fellow expat musicians (Nick Cave in particular) provided the impetus for much of his work. He was already well on his way to career success, having worked for several leading publications.

When I arrived for the shoot, I immediately sensed that Kelly and Butcher had some private joke running between them. They were all sly innuendo and smart double entendre. When Kelly suggested that we might go up to the roof of the building to try out an idea they had for the session, I reluctantly went along with it.

Several floors above a busy Carnaby Street, the flat roof area of the building had its fair share of pigeon shit and building materials strewn around. Spotting a section of chain link fencing lying on the ground, Kelly lifted it and, smiling, said, 'Oh look, the men behind the wire!' It was, of course, a reference to a popular Belfast IRA/republican song.

The fourth estate

In that moment, I realised that he was fully aware of what I'd said in the article, my politics and my background, and that he did not approve. His own allegiances were becoming obvious.

Butcher then suggested that it would be a good idea if I were to be dangled out from the edge of the building as he stood above me, firing off shots on his camera. I wasn't to worry, he said, as Kelly would be sure to hold my legs. They both sported broad grins.

To say I was uncomfortable with this proposal would be putting it mildly, but eager to please, I tentatively agreed to give it a try. Then Butcher wanted my expression to show more abject terror and they briefly joked about how they might conjure up a more authentic reaction. At that point, I let them know it had gone far enough.

In the end, Butcher decided to shoot me resting my head on an illuminated medical light box, the kind used for reading hospital x-rays, with a large plastic trout next to me. (Again, I imagine there was some in-joke between the two here.) And that's the image they ran with in that edition of the magazine.

Other interactions with mainstream publications were not as hostile but proved every bit as dangerous to life and limb.

Bill Graham was a stalwart of old-school music journalism and played a seminal role in the breaking of U2. In addition to authoring several books, he wrote for *Hot Press* magazine from its founding.[5] Bill arranged to meet me under a tree in Battersea Park and immediately tapped me for a tenner. I was a little put out as I had become fond of the trend for staffers to buy me liquid lunches during interviews.

He was an amiable sort with a penetrating insight that, from his somewhat dishevelled manner and tendency to eccentricity, may not have been apparent straight away. Above all, he had an interest in and understanding of the Northern Irish conflict. That was rare enough amongst his peers.

Despite my growing weariness of having every interview turn into a political polemic from me (only a third of the tracks on our album *Flowers for All Occasions* were overtly about the conflict), when I found us drifting again into the machinations of the Irish question, I felt confident that Bill Graham would faithfully represent the complexities I was trying to convey.

And this, in the main, he did. However, my blood froze when I saw the published full-page article. In what might be called 'click-bait' in today's parlance, above a picture of the band screamed the headline: 'We Are Supposed to Be a Voice of Loyalist Extremism'.[6] If readers took the time to read the article, they would soon realise that that was not what I said, but for those simply flicking through or, worse still, deliberately seeking to reinforce already existing prejudices about the band, it was a nightmare. Furthermore, given the tensions at home at that time, and aware that *Hot Press* was purchased by a largely Republic of Ireland readership, I felt that a large bullseye had just been drawn on my back.

I prefer to believe that Bill Graham would have been sensitive to this and that perhaps it was a sub-editor who sanctioned the headline. Nevertheless, it was another sobering example of how the fourth estate could hinder, rather than help, one's best intentions.

In a similar way I had high hopes for an article written for the *New Socialist* in 1986.[7] When I agreed to do this, I was flattered that the band and songs seemed to have transcended the music press to find a platform in a dedicated political magazine, and delighted that my own left-wing, democratic socialist views were now being given credence over the easier Loyalist identifications that lazy journalism often favoured. How wrong I was.

I was (and remain) someone who fervently believes that the British Labour party should field candidates in Northern Ireland elections to offer a disenfranchised Protestant socialist electorate an alternative to the traditional unionist parties who tend to focus solely on constitutional/sectarian concerns.[8] But the *New Socialist* article could not resist the temptation of contrasting my songs with those of That Petrol Emotion, a Derry band formed from the remnants of The Undertones, which espoused unambiguous support for Sinn Féin and the 'armed struggle'. As the British Left has always entertained a tacit support for Irish unification, it should have come as no surprise that Ruefrex's lyrics were found wanting when compared to That Petrol Emotion's, the *New Socialist* article describing my songs, motivations and bona fides as 'overburdened by the weight of [his] own Loyalist imagery.' The political left's unease in dealing with the socialist views emerging from the Ulster Protestant working classes was also revealed when Ruefrex threw their weight behind the Red Wedge initiative in 1985.[9]

* * *

In the final analysis, the media know that a symbiotic relationship, whereby both parties need each other for mutual benefit, will always drive you back into their dubious embrace. Guitarist Forgie was now regularly complaining that his artistic integrity was being increasingly prostituted and his commitment to the creative process stymied by the need to promote the record. So when a little-known US news outfit called Cable News Network scheduled a camera crew to call with us during a rehearsal session, we reluctantly agreed.

The crew arrived, set up and shot in a perfunctory manner, carrying out a general Q&A with me. I imagined the spin stateside: 'War Kids Make Music for Peace' or some such. But I was aware that our records were getting airtime on the all-important college radio circuit, a major prerequisite for breaking the States, should it ever come to it, so I was happy to comply.

As they said their goodbyes, I asked the departing cameraman who might be watching our segment and where we could see it ourselves.

'CNN broadcast twenty-four hours a day, seven days a week,' he said over his shoulder on the way out the door. 'We go out to more than one hundred million households and are in more than five million hotel rooms. Have a nice day.'

I was stupefied. We finished rehearsals early and sat on the floor, passing a joint around. I simply couldn't get my head around it.

'I mean a hundred fucking million homes. There could be someone being murdered in a New York tenement building, a baby being born in a New Orleans shotgun shack, a sea of screens stretched out across a Vegas casino floor, all with us playing in the background. All human life is there … and so will we be.'

There was a long, stoned silence as we let that sink in.

Eventually The Dean, who rarely offered an opinion on anything at all, spoke up: 'See the mice in their million hoards. All we did was play some minor chords.'

We looked at him, puzzled and surprised.

The fourth estate

'I'm a poet and I don't know it!' he said with a broad, wasted smile.

Stoned as I was, it seemed in that moment the most profound thing I had ever heard him say.

NOTES

1 Muir MacKean, *New Musical Express*, 25 February 1984, p. 41.
2 The notable Northern Irish journos working on major music publications at that time were Barry McIlheney (*Melody Maker*), Gavin Martin (*NME*) and Stuart Bailie (*Record Mirror*). We had known Gavin from his days editing the fanzine *Alternative Ulster*. Stuart Bailie was younger and perhaps more ambitious, even then. His prominent role in the subsequent development of Ulster punk as popular culture came as no surprise.
3 Kelly relocated to the Republic of Ireland some years later, where he lives today. He has since moved into mainstream football journalism.
4 Paul Burgess interviewed by Gavin Martin, 'Plight of the Middlemen', *New Musical Express*, 7 September 1985, p.8.
5 Sadly, Bill died of a heart attack, aged only forty-four, in 1996.
6 Bill Graham, 'We Are Supposed to Be a Voice of Loyalist Extremism', *Hot Press*, p. 14.
7 The *New Socialist* of the 1980s stated that it aimed 'to renew democratic socialism' by engineering a broad political coalition. It should not be confused with the current manifestation of the publication, founded in 2017.
8 The British Labour party has always maintained that its sister party, the SDLP (Social and Democratic Labour Party), fulfils this role. However, the SDLP manifesto states the party's aspiration for a united Ireland, thus nullifying support from the Loyalist working classes. The Progressive Unionist Party, a potential alternative, has associations with paramilitary groups, which limits its appeal for many.
9 Red Wedge was a socialist musical collective formed in 1985 to encourage young people to vote Labour in the general election in 1987.

24
It's too late to stop now

For most of the period leading up to the recording of our first album, *Flowers for All Occasions*, and its subsequent promotion through tours and television appearances, only Forgie and I lived in London. TC had made his intentions (if not his antipathies) clear and Clarkey travelled from Belfast only when absolutely necessary and on a schedule that suited his availability. (I had not yet asked Gordy Blair to step in as I felt that TC had to be allowed his swan song at the two remaining showcase gigs.)

Throughout this time, largely out of a sense of loyalty to TC, my old buddy and co-founder, I reported back to Belfast by phone on an almost daily basis. As well as wanting to keep band absentees as informed as possible about developments, I also still leaned heavily on TC for guidance when it came to artistic decisions relating to set lists, arrangements and matters relating to the integrity and vision for the band. We remained, after all, proud parents of the venture, despite the fact that one of us was seeking a divorce.

In TC's absence, Forgie sought a greater role in the decision-making process, and although this led to some fruitful and rewarding co-writing collaborations between us, it came at a high price. While we had many interests

It's too late to stop now

in common, shared a similar sense of humour and enjoyed, I liked to think, a genuine filial comradeship, he had a tendency to down tools and adopt a 'work-to-rule' policy if he didn't get his own way.

He seemed to be perpetually staring into a chasm of unresolved self-doubt, and this meant that he constantly needed to assert himself to feel 'important', to know that he was being taken seriously. It proved emotionally draining to be around and also professionally challenging.

His politics at the time were like Rick's in *The Young Ones*.[1] There was barely a popular cause that he did not align himself with. It was clear that the burdens of being publicly associated with and allied to the most 'uncool' and politically unappealing community in Europe gave him considerable cause for concern. The band's raison d'être simply did not fit comfortably into the many left-field causes that he rushed to champion. His adopted self-image as the only 'true' musician and artist in the band led to a preciousness and pomposity that only got worse when it was indulged. And as our continued success attracted sycophants who bolstered his delusions, the writing was perhaps on the wall.

Nevertheless, we were back at full strength for the Haçienda gig, which was just as well, as it was to determine whether we'd be signed by Stiff Records or not. TC and Clarkey travelled over and stayed in London the night before. Right away I felt uneasy. Something wasn't right. Despite attempts by all and sundry to welcome them and make them feel at home, they remained aloof and almost exclusively in each other's company. This continued on the journey north to Manchester.

We piled most of our gear into a hired van and the band travelled in Frank Toner's estate car. Frank was taking care of our onstage sound mix, while some of our other housemates were acting as roadies. (This would essentially remain the set-up for the duration of our live performances in England.)

In response to my pre-gig team talk, outlining the importance of the event, there were smirks and whispered jests between Clarkey and TC. Something was definitely up. I thought that the prospect of members of Joy Division/New Order being present at the performance might spur them on to great things. It did not.

As we sound checked, then prepared backstage, I was alarmed at the amount of beer and vodka they were putting away. There was an unspoken rule that the performance should not be compromised by pre-gig indulgence – there would be plenty of time for that afterwards – but I knew that any attempt to point that out would only be counterproductive.

The club was filling up. I recognised the faces of some of the Stiff staff from my visit to their offices. Again, I appealed to TC. All roads had been leading here, to this night. 'Please don't fuck it up now!'

But even as I spoke the words, I realised the truth: TC was intent on bringing down the curtain once and for all, not only on his own involvement in the band, but on the band's very existence, and predictably he had enlisted Clarkey to his cause. Watching them in the dressing room, well-oiled and acting the fools, I felt absolutely crestfallen as we took to the stage.

In what seemed like the longest show we'd ever performed, Clarkey forgot or repeated verses of songs while drunkenly haranguing the audience (who couldn't understand a word he said). Meanwhile TC 'played jazz', as he always jokingly claimed to when too sozzled to keep it together. Then there were the false starts, fluffed endings, ear-splitting feedback.

It's too late to stop now

Forgie, The Dean and I looked around, bewildered. Only I fully realised what was going on.

Only one other performance matched the Haçienda for awfulness born of alcohol, petulance and bad temper. It was later, at the Rock Garden in Covent Garden. Our producer, Mick Glossop, had asked along Tom Verlaine from the band Television as a special guest. Both Forgie and Clarkey drank way too much and I sulked and stormed off stage, kicking my drum kit over into the audience in the process. Divas all!

I felt simultaneously humiliated and betrayed. All of our unshakeable self-belief, our iron will to succeed, had seemingly evaporated, sacrificed at the final hurdle. And for what? It looked like sabotage, pure and simple.

Distraught, I couldn't speak to anyone on the journey back to London. Housemates at Olive Road tried to make encouraging noises. Even Stiff personnel gamely lied about how much they'd enjoyed it. But we'd fallen far short of our self-imposed high standards and our hard-won reputation as a live act.

The next day, TC and Clarkey flew back to their lives in Belfast, still wisecracking and showing no remorse whatsoever for the previous night's debacle. It didn't seem to occur to them that Forgie, The Dean and I could not blithely up sticks and go home. We had bet all our collateral on that one roll of the dice.

Then incredibly, it seemed all was not yet lost. Whether the chaos that ensued on the Haçienda stage was in some way accepted as 'punk', or whether the A&R execs at the gig were so bolloxed themselves from the free bar that they couldn't tell the difference, we were told that the signing was to go ahead with Stiff and the album recording was duly scheduled.

I phoned TC to tell him the good news, and while I spoke of my disappointment at the Manchester show, neither of us broached the subject of any deliberate disruption on his part. It remained unsaid, and has done to this day.

Also unspoken was my now unswerving determination that the show would go on, with or without his blessing. Yes, I would ensure that his writing credits and his invaluable contributions were recorded in sleeve notes and credits, but any further input from him was now at an end, just as he wanted. It must have presented him with a welter of conflicting emotions when, through gritted teeth, he wished us well. I prefer to believe that deep down, some part of him genuinely meant it.

Despite everything, it still seemed bizarre and unnatural to me that the circus should move on without him. Somewhere, regardless of the heady mix of avowals and boyhood dreams made real, I knew that the band would not, *could* not, ever be the same again. A small whisper of misgiving tried to insist that it was all over before it had really begun.

But all such thoughts had to be pushed down for now. There were enough hangers-on around to convince me that there was all still to play for. Suddenly, people were depending on me: my fellow band members, the people at Kasper and Stiff, those in my immediate circle who were picking up roadie work, others like Sean O'Hagan who were selling us second-hand equipment for a few needed shekels, the lads at *Melody Maker* ... Christ, even TC himself, whose songs and legacy were now solely in my hands.

I was confident that Clarkey's ego and desire to make the album would trump any further malign influence or intent on his part. And so it proved. He happily agreed to return for the Dingwalls gig, where once again, record executives and press would be present. We rehearsed feverishly with new bassist Gordy. As an accomplished musician who was already familiar with much of our set, he hit the ground running.

As luck would have it, and as is sometimes the way with these things, the Dingwalls gig turned out to be one of the finest performances Ruefrex delivered in London, or anywhere else for that matter.

Dingwalls, next to Camden Lock, had become a popular punk venue over the years. The performance area was notable for having a long hall and a low ceiling, thus ensuring that the sound feeding through the speakers onstage punched right out to the audience at head and shoulders level. Get it right, and you could decapitate them sonically!

As the house lights dimmed, we went onstage to a pre-recorded excerpt from 'Grand Finale' (taken from Alice Cooper's *School's Out* album). And we destroyed! Clarkey, at his menacing best, left the stage and roamed through the crowd, offering the mic to at first sheepish, then ultimately bellicose punters to bellow 'One by One' or 'Make your peace with God, forgive your debtors ...'. Three encores included 'Ex Lion Tamer' by Wire and a left-field version of 'Last Train to Clarkesville' by the Monkees. At last, people could see what all the fuss was about.

Stiff provided a booking agent, The Agency, and a steady stream of gigs followed at some of London's most iconic club venues (now mostly gone): The Roxy, the Bull and Gate in Kentish Town, the 100 Club, The Marquee Club, The Cricketers at Kennington Oval, the Rock Garden.

Dates were also arranged for up north, sometimes disparagingly referred to as 'the toilet circuit' by touring bands, with JB's Dudley in the West Midlands presenting a particular challenge. Incomprehension between the Belfast and Brummie accents ultimately proved to be no barrier to common cause. Loud, aggressive and dripping with attitude, Ruefrex won over a primarily heavy rock audience to our banner.

The buzz regarding our live performances was spreading thanks to a phalanx of stellar live reviews in the music and mainstream press. Colin Irwin of *Melody Maker* caught the tone: 'Next time they play ... be it snow, hail, earthquake or hurricane ... no excuses, be there.'[2]

The physical cost of consecutive gigs, night after night, was one we were not used to, and it began to take its toll. Playing drums while singing is perhaps the most physically demanding task in a (punk) rock band. Many of the songs were driven along at a furious pace and it was a struggle not to allow these exertions to swamp the quality of your vocal performance. Additionally, blistered fingers and knuckles that have bashed off cymbals, drum rims and stands get no time to heal. You come off stage, soaked in sweat, into the cold night air, when you immediately partake in copious amounts of alcohol, illegal substances and fast food.

Don't believe the hype. Life on the road remains to this day some of the most physically demanding work I've ever done. But even at twenty-five years of age, something had got to give, sooner or later. It would have to be later. Contracts had been signed with The Agency, tickets had been sold, venues booked, and press engaged. The cardinal rule was 'never cancel', for the professional backlash could terminally damage a band's reputation.

Irrespective of the health and well-being of band personnel, we had another underlying malady that might prove fatal to our prospects: Clarkey was presenting us with some outrageous, if predictable, challenges.

Illustration S2.4 'He'd fly through the air with the greatest of ease ...'. Dingwalls gig, 1985.
Photo by Andrew Catlin

He was undeniably synonymous with the band's image, and for the many promoters, record label owners and publishers now rallying to our cause, he was indispensable to the band as a 'product'. But as Clarkey himself came to understand this, it created all the well-worn tensions concomitant with a frontman's ego and the band collective.

He was still living in Belfast, and it certainly didn't help that he had many voices there, whispering in his ear, telling him how he might claim more money for his services and insist on more flexibility regarding his availability for tour work.[3]

Over these years, those influencing him were often wives and girlfriends, working-class Belfast women with their own dreams and aspirations that they felt Clarkey might be able deliver for them. Then there was the fear of his role as a fifth columnist in the ranks. When at after-show house parties in London, usually thrown by well-wishers and attended by the 'too cool for school' brigade, he would invariably incite a confrontation and act up accordingly, smashing something against a wall or haranguing an unfortunate punter who had irked him. Inevitably it required an intervention and an early exit, with Clarkey seeking to justify his actions: 'He was looking at me funny ...'.

With hindsight, I expect this was all a reaction to him feeling out of his depth and unable to adapt to the repartee and smart-arse, 'in the know' posing that passed for social currency at these gatherings. It all seems more understandable now. He simply didn't see any difference between performing for these people a few hours earlier onstage and socialising with them afterward. They were looking for something larger than life and he wasn't going to disappoint

It's too late to stop now

them. But when he suggested that the band/label pay for his then girlfriend, Sharon, to accompany him on trips to London, it upped the ante.

Then came the phone call from Belfast: Clarkey would be indefinitely indisposed due to a pending court appearance concerning the assault of a punter in a public telephone kiosk. Apparently, our singer had bashed him around the head with the receiver!

Those of us in London were furious; we were left holding the baby (literally, in Forgie's case) and, suspecting a ruse, insisted that official documentation be provided to the parties affected by the gig cancellations. This duly arrived from his solicitor and so, just like his victim in the telephone kiosk, we simply had to take it on the chin.

But real disquiet was growing within the Kasper ranks, the Stiff people, the live venue folk and the band ourselves. Everyone loves a bad boy, but not, apparently, when it's bad for business. All these people had been humouring and feting Clarkey with praise and attention. Only Forgie and I realised that this was adding fuel to the fire. Tumult was not an act with him; it was his default position.

If ever there was a time to call his bluff, it was now. Whispers were rife. Should we place a 'Singer Wanted' ad in the music mags? Might I summon up the courage to front the band and sing my own songs?

I considered phoning TC. He more than anyone could keep Clarkey in line. But I was still unsure of his feelings toward 'Ruefrex Mk II', which had taken the next step without him.

No, clearly Clarkey had us by the short and curlies, and he knew it. We had an album to record within weeks and we needed him to deliver on it.

Wild colonial boys

NOTES

1. The character Rick was played by Rik Mayall. *The Young Ones* was a sitcom on BBC TV that ran from November 1982 to June 1984.
2. Colin Irwin, 'Wild Boys', 'Ruefrex. The Marquee, London'. *Melody Maker*, 7 December 1985.
3. Clarkey insisted on remaining in Belfast while the band lived in London, resulting in exorbitant travel costs and telling absences from the rehearsal and song-writing process.

25
Sarm East is east, Sarm West is west

Sarm West, established by Chris Blackwell of Island Records, and Sarm East recording studios were owned and run by husband-and-wife pair Jill Sinclair and Trevor Horn (of Buggles, Yes, and Art of Noise fame). Sarm West was in Notting Hill, and Sarm East, in Osborn Street at the southern end of Brick Lane. Over the years, almost all the Island Records roster recorded there, and that's some list!

Many of my favourite artists from my youth, including Mott the Hoople, Roxy Music, Brian Eno, Sparks and King Crimson, had worked there. Non-Island performers also recorded there – Madonna, The Clash, Depeche Mode, Queen, The Eagles, Led Zeppelin, Bob Marley & the Wailers, Genesis and The Rolling Stones, to name but a few. Band Aid recorded 'Do They Know It's Christmas' there.

Dave Robinson's Stiff/Island connections meant that we had been lined up to record in Sarm West from 16 to 29 October 1985. Music history seeped through the pores of the place and my head was spinning to be in such exalted company. It was enough to make us tentatively start to believe that we'd actually *arrived*. But talk was cheap in the music business, as I was beginning to realise.

Wild colonial boys

Short-lived super group The Firm, featuring Jimmy Page (ex Led Zeppelin) and Paul Rodgers (ex Free), pitched up looking for those dates as well, and as they were considerably further up the food chain than us, we were bumped. The Music Works Studio was scheduled as a replacement, with an undertaking that we would return to Sarm West for the album mix from 4 to 8 November.

Legendary producer Mick Glossop was booked in for the sessions. Hailing from The Wirral, on Merseyside, this lanky 'long-hair' resembled Frank Zappa on first take. His laid-back, easy affability and Scouse good humour belied an unerring attention to detail and a CV to die for. Having engineered most of Van Morrison's work (the Belfast connection a qualification that informed Robinson's decision to affiliate us), Mick went on to produce a catalogue of punk and post-punk classics from Magazine, Public Image Ltd, The Ruts, Skids, The Waterboys and Penetration.

The relationship between artist and producer is seminal in delivering on the musical vision a band has for its album, and trust is paramount. Mick immediately endeared himself to us with his openness and enthusiasm. Realising I was something of an orphan émigré caught in the eye of the storm, he immediately invited me to his home for dinner with his partner, Elva.

We felt confident that he understood what our mission was. His guidance on song arrangements, guitar parts and mixing undoubtedly helped us develop as musicians and song writers. But Dave Robinson also had an agenda as to how the album should sound, and later, I came to realise that he had Mick's ear in these matters as well. Nonetheless, it seemed churlish to question decisions made by such old hands, who were spending money and time on our behalf to help us deliver our dream. It rarely occurred to me that it was 'just business', that Stiff's prime motivation was to 'shift product', that no one, other perhaps than the band itself, was in it for purely artistic or political reasons.

The Music Works Studio was a state-of-the-art facility and made all the studios we had worked in up to that point appear obsolete and archaic. It was like comparing the deck of JJ Abrams' USS Enterprise with the 1960s TV original!

A well-equipped recording studio is one of the most exciting environments for a creative to find themselves in. (I imagine the film editing suite for a movie to be the same). It is womb-like, a cocoon in which to generate ideas and new musical forms from sometimes tired and long-established arrangements, or to try new instrumentation overdubs and vocal multi-tracking. The ambience and intimacy make it easy to lose all track of time and place, and you become so focused on the task at hand that you forget to eat or even sleep. You feel like a kid in a sweet shop, wanting to stay until musical permutation after permutation is exhausted in the search for that holy grail of mixes, the definitive version.

The process itself is essentially divided into two tasks: recording and mixing. Recording is arguably more important because the foundations upon which the song will be built must be rhythmically solid and without deviation. Much can be done later in the mix, but if the rhythm of the track speeds up or slows down during the original recording of the song, other instruments recorded over it will drift in and out of sync and no amount of high-tech tweaking will save you in the end. (The more reliance on technical fixes, the further you move away from that authentic organic sound.) Logically, then, it falls to the rhythm section – and the drummer in particular – to nail down the backing tracks before anyone else can record their contribution. This task brings with it no small degree of responsibility and, therefore, pressure.

Mick exhorted me to 'hit the drums harder', despite the kit being festooned with microphones, and I learned that this was more about the acoustic sound the drums made when struck than anything to do with volume. Thanks to his good-humoured cajoling and years of experience, my technique (and knowledge) improved exponentially. It was the same for the others too.

Meanwhile, the prima-donna-esque posturing of our frontman had taken on new levels of perversity. Clarkey insisted that he be flown back and forth to London on the same day that he was required to contribute. All expenses for this (as well as the recording sessions themselves, of course) were to come out of the band's advance from Stiff. It was eating into what little cash we had and causing a considerable amount of bad feeling. But at least it meant that the rest of us could continue unencumbered, getting on with the job of recording the music.

Periodically, friends and housemates dropped by with a carry-out or two, and while this was welcomed by the band, Mick pointed out that we were both on the clock and pissing away our own money. It would be better if we adopted a workmanlike attitude to proceedings.

The guitar sound soon became a matter of contention. The preference at that time was for 'jangly' guitars, in the style of The Smiths, REM and early U2. This was often accompanied by a huge, cacophonous tom-tom sound for the drums, but this combination was an obvious indication of how far we had strayed from, and betrayed, our Belfast punk roots.

We pushed Mick hard for an overdriven, sustained, power-chord guitar sound, but it was becoming apparent that Dave

Sarm East is east, Sarm West is west

Robinson was pushing for a more radio-friendly sound. We didn't realise it then, but it was this compromise in our sound that gave rise to the accusation of 'sell out' from our fan base back in Belfast. In essence, what had made us popular with the patrons of the Harp Bar was being chipped away at. Yes, this was a much better sound, with high-end production values – cleaner and more professional – but it did not represent who we believed we were musically.

Nonetheless, we couldn't help but be seduced by aspects of the performances and recordings that Mick was coaxing from us. The professional sound that was alienating the old guard was also a gratifying indication of our application to the task. I was reminded of the adage that gaining of experience necessitates a loss of innocence, and that was how it seemed to me then.

By the end of our time in Music Works, we had finished ten songs. Only around a third of them could be said to be overtly political and concerning the conflict in Northern Ireland. We had no agreed track order, as mixing was still to take place; only in the final pre-release playback would this be decided.

The tracks that made the cut were:

'One by One', the song that had been our first release on Good Vibrations, but now sounding like it was on steroids and very different from the original.
'The Ruah', intended as a slow-tempo, tango rhythm similar to Bowie's *'The man who sold the world'*. It was an ode to the Holy Ghost of my childhood Sunday school classes but it somehow morphed into a lively, jangly-guitar oddity, a million miles removed from my vision for it.
'The Wild Colonial Boy', the breakthrough song that we had now become known for.

'In the Traps', which unashamedly played to our power-pop sensibilities. The lyric was a scathing indictment of the limitations of a meritocratic educational system.

'Even in the Dark Hours', an unapologetic rock ballad and one of the two longest tracks on the album. It featured Forgie and Clarkey's finest recorded performances and was augmented by a one-finger contribution on keyboard by Microdisney's Cathal Coughlan.

'Mr Renfield Reflects' was a homage to both Bram Stoker and Alice Cooper. Later, at my request, Barry McIlheney presented our album to Alice during an interview he carried out with him when in the US. On hearing 'Renfield' Alice remarked, 'Hey, I know this guy', referring to his own song 'The Ballad of Dwight Fry'. To say I was pleased with this – and the glossy pic he signed 'To Paul … your pal in blood, Alice Cooper' – is something of an understatement.

'Correct Your Fireside Manner' is the second of the 'biggies' on the album (it clocks in at over six minutes long) and is augmented with an instrumental section, 'The Forces and the Energies'.

'Flowers for All Occasions', the album's title track. It's an acoustic ballad lamenting the tragedy of sectarian murder and the ordinary families that it decimates.

'Paid in Kind', first released in 1984 and seeking to draw on Tom Waitesian imagery in creating an aural tableaux.

'By the Shadowline', was inspired by a novella by Joseph Conrad. The song belted along at a furious punk pace and was favoured for plays by Radio One. To my delight, I was once assailed, via a detailed critique of the lyrics, by an English journalist who claimed that the song was about a British Army jeep, patrolling the peace line in

Belfast. What would I know? I only wrote it! On reflection though, this seemed like a very good call.

So now it was all in the can, so to speak. Perhaps it was not entirely true to the vison we shared for it, but we were all agreed: we certainly had something. During the cab journey home, it somehow felt post-coital. After a brief hiatus to reflect, it was now on to the all-important mix.

26
Brixton nights

After hours, I had taken to spending more and more time at the Brixton high-rise flat of Grimmo and Karen. It was a small municipal flat on the 22nd floor that someone had somehow managed to get a grand piano up to.

It overlooked the main Brixton railway junction, a jumble of intersecting tracks and signals. Trains clunked and brakes squealed; the rat-a-tat-tat of the metropolis's metal arteries rarely stopped. The furnishings were basic and the small kitchen less than sanitary. But the assembled bric-a-brac, reclaimed furniture, piano and the neon cityscape that stretched out below us gave the whole place something of a *Blade Runner* vibe. One wall of the small living area was designated a 'media centre' where ramshackle shelving and industrial racking housed all the audio-video equipment that had been salvaged from many house moves.

Grimmo, a tall, thin, handsome, sallow-skinned guy of German-Irish descent, was a bohemian right up to his high cheek bones. He had a passion for Werner Herzog, Beethoven sonatas, Miles Davis and Keith Richards. An accomplished guitarist, he had become disillusioned with the corporate packaging of his first band, Zerra One, and formed The Velvet Underground-esque My Baby's Arm before going on

Brixton nights

to play with Cathal Coughlan for art-rock outfit Fatima Mansions.

As a host, he was a whirlwind of seamless, apparently effortless, activity. Spliff in hand and in constant motion, he flipped playback sources from his turntable to cassette deck to BBC Radio 4, sometimes changing the visuals from TV stations or videos, played on a small black-and-white set with the sound turned down, all the while brewing up Arabian coffee on his gas stove-top coffee maker and pouring Irish whiskeys. Occasionally he would pause mid-action, eyes closed, as if held in some sublime moment of a minor chord, or drift to the piano and, seemingly lost in thought, attempt an impromptu arpeggio. However, any impression you might have that he was some kind of effete intellectual were quickly dispelled by his infectious hoot at something or other, followed by an exclamation of 'Me fookin' arse!' in a broad Dublin accent.

Karen was the polar opposite of an ingénue. Originally from Dundee, with chalk-white skin and red hair and sporting blood red lipstick – like some Caledonian Dorothy Parker – she was both desired and feared by the men who strayed into her gravitational pull. Not that they had any say in the matter. Known for her intuitive reading of the zeitgeist, her whip-smart intellect, and her withering put downs, she invariably got what she wanted. These qualities ensured her corporate success in both the music, and latterly, film industries. The flat share with Grimmo was a purely pragmatic, platonic arrangement that suited both parties.

The location of the flat in Brixton – with junkies shooting up in the stairwells and an overwhelming smell of piss in the dangerously erratic lifts – soon filtered out the wheat from the chaff. Only serious party animals, sub-culture devotees and perhaps those who themselves originated from urban zones of high tension ventured here after dark. I loved it, just as I increasingly loved pot, weed, grass, hash, reefer – call it what you will. It became my drug of choice.

'Dope is for dopes,' counselled the stick-thin Cormac back in Olive Road (he preferred lakes of white wine and amphetamine). But for me, Grimmo and the many Rastafarians who frequented the pubs of Coldharbour Lane and Electric Avenue, we were definitely in the right place.

This was how I found myself standing, somewhat the worse for wear, outside the Atlantic Bar late one Friday night. The pub had a fearsome reputation as an exclusively Black bar, and six-foot-high PA speakers thundered out bass lines from Robbie Shakespeare and Aston Barrett. Stories had been circulating that, just the previous week, some West End media type had been robbed in the toilets. Despite offering up his wallet willingly, the young Rude Boy had slashed him across the face with a Stanley knife.

So if a sozzled white boy like me was loitering outside, it was for one reason only and everyone knew it – to score dope. Grimmo had warned me against this. He had been adopted by the local Jamaican émigrés at the Coach and Horses, further down the road where a couple of games of pool and a few pints of Guinness with the regulars meant he never went short of ganja. Miss Ruby, the elderly patron, turned a blind eye and the whole scene was a model of race relations.

Not so at the Atlantic. It was dark and I was short of cash. So a £10 deal was all I was after. It didn't take long before two likely lads wearing baseball caps, sneakers, leather jackets and gold chains furtively approached me.

'What you need, mon?'

Brixton nights

'Just a ten spot if you can do that.' I thought I caught a snort of derision.

'You wait here, right?'

Then they disappeared into the Atlantic.

Not much time passed, but I was sobering up fast and starting to think better of the whole enterprise as I looked this way and that for police patrols.

Suddenly a guy was there, up close, same clothes and demeanour as the other one. 'What you need?' he asked.

I hadn't been paying attention. Was this a different guy? I wasn't sure. 'I was just telling your friend ... ten.'

He stretched out his arm. The familiar black nubbin of a hash deal, swathed tight in clear cling film wrap, sat in the palm of his hand.

I handed him the cash and took it.

'Sweet,' he said.

Just at that moment, the two guys who had gone into the bar emerged. Cursing loudly, one ran at my salesguy, who took off immediately and they both disappeared, one chasing the other into the shadows. The other guy just stood there, staring at me with a look of utter contempt.

I realised then what had happened, of course. This was their patch and my guy was an interloper.

'I thought he was with you', I muttered, rising imperceptibly onto the balls of my feet, ready to bolt.

'You want this or not?' He held out a small ziplock bag of weed.

'I gave him all the money I had', I whined. I felt pathetic.

He sucked his teeth loudly and spat on the ground while I anxiously wondered what wasting his time might ultimately cost me. To my utter relief he simply turned and walked away. I did the same, moving quickly in the opposite

Wild colonial boys

direction. At least I scored the deal, I thought. Grimmo and I can laugh about it over a joint and a whiskey when I get to the flat. The bounce in my step returned and I started to feel a little bit like a gangsta.

When the Rizlas were laid out, I told my story as I unwrapped the cling-filmed package. But instead of finding a lump of hashish inside, what sat before me was ... a black treacle toffee. Grimmo and I stared at it, sniffed it a few times, then stared at it again. 'Sweet,' the guy had said, and it seemed he'd meant it literally.

But within the week, my ham-fisted misadventures in the drug trade took an unforgettable turn for the better.

We had decamped to Sarm West Studios to multi-track mix the fruits of our labours from the Music Works Studio. The décor and general vibe of the place oozed success – all soft furnishings, Scandinavian blond wood and smoked glass.

'Be sure to try the food while you're here,' Mick Glossop advised. 'It's the finest Caribbean cuisine you're ever likely to enjoy – jerk chicken, rice and peas, sweet potato and black bean curry, saltfish and ackee.'

None of us had the slightest idea of what he was talking about but when he revealed that the resident cook on the premises was Lucky, Bob Marley's personal chef ... well, we were hooked.[1]

We met him in the studio kitchen at lunch time on our first day there. He wore a 'tam', the red, green and gold Rasta hat; Around his neck he sported a wool pouch in the same design. He was handsome man, getting on in years. I had no knowledge of his colourful past or, indeed, his place in British social history beyond his relationship with Marley and the Wailers.[2]

Following a delicious lunch, and before returning to the studio, I wondered aloud to Mick if the chef might know

Brixton nights

locally where I could score some grass. Lucky overheard me and, laughing, enquired how much I was looking for.

'Is £20 okay?' I said.

Without answering he looked around the room. Spying a copy of that week's *Radio Times*, he rolled it into a cone, reached into the pouch around his neck, fished out two fistfuls of weed, stuffed it down into the funnel, and handed it to me. I nodded my gratitude and gave him two tenners. I was speechless with delight and grinning from ear to ear. I had just scored ganja from Bob Marley's cook!

We must have been becoming complacent, because when the engineer told us that Queen were using the same studio during the evenings to work on tracks that later featured on the *Kind of Magic* album, we weren't that surprised. Perhaps we were beginning to believe our own press. But it didn't stop us from pressing him for sordid details of what went on in those sessions. None were forthcoming. However, he did tell us that, such was the animosity between band members, they rarely met each other in the sessions. Each member came in separately and laid down a succession of takes to be decided upon later. Brian May might be in alone one evening, Freddie the next. It seemed like a bizarre way to work, and it disconcertingly reminded me of our own deteriorating collegiality within Ruefrex.

On more than one occasion, I had entered a room where the others had gathered ahead of my arrival and immediately, voices dropped, conspiratorial glances were shot my way. I felt for all the world like a manager venturing on to the shop floor. I was deeply hurt by this development and felt lonelier than I had ever been since leaving home. Was this how they now looked upon me? As an employer? As management? I wanted desperately to plead my case, to explain that I was a writer, a musician, a creative like

Wild colonial boys

them, that circumstances had dictated this situation, that *they* hadn't wanted to liaise with a phalanx of music and publishing executives, studio and pressing plant workers, agency bookers and road and travel managers for gigs.

I wanted the rock star idyll we had all hoped for too – to stay high and drunk as much as possible and only worry about the songs, to stay up late, oversleep and have someone else pour me into a waiting taxi next day.

There was no one else to do all this except me. I had been feeling cheated. Now I felt wounded as well.

In one key respect, it wasn't surprising. I had been managing the band finances with Kasper/Stiff and had opened a bank account with our dwindling advance. This meant that I had to write cheques to the other band members, often for rental deposits, musical equipment purchases or (in Clarkey's case) fines for criminal damages.

'How sharper than a serpent's tooth it is to have a thankless child', lamented both TC and King Lear. TC's prophecy had come to pass. Democracy had perished; benign dictatorship was in full effect. And I profoundly felt the sting of the others' resentment.

NOTES

1. Aloysius 'Lucky' Gordon was born in Kingston, Jamaica. A jazz singer and hustler, he stowed away to Britain in 1947.
2. Lucky Gordon became involved with nightclub hostess Christine Keeler. This ended acrimoniously and Keeler sought protection of another lover, Johnny Edgecombe, culminating in a public fight at the Flamingo Club in Wardour Street in October 1962. This in turn set in motion a chain of events that would eventually result in the public revelations of the Profumo affair.

27
On *The Tube* with Sonnie Rae

The late Frank Murray was some pup. His early career in the UK music business was not dissimilar to that of fellow Dubliner Dave Robinson. Both of them were opportunistic Irishmen who earned their spurs as managers, confidantes and sometimes muses for some of the most successful emerging talent of the period.

When I first met Frank, he was enjoying the breakneck ride as manager of the wildly popular Pogues. Ruefrex could certainly have done with such a champion and powerful advocate in their corner, although the thought of him (or Robinson) acting as the sole custodian of our band's financial affairs might have been somewhat scrotum-tightening.

The Pogues, our stablemates at Stiff Records, were trading off a particular brand of 'Oirishness' that fused punk rock attitude with Irish traditional mores to produce a live sound that was perfect for mid-eighties London and further afield. (Someone once described them as 'The Dubliners on speed'.)

Frontman Shane MacGowan's reputation for hard drinking was legendary from the outset, and the band's live concerts were often raucous, stage-diving celebrations of excess. Their musical hard edges were smoothed by the talented songwriter and guitarist the late Phil Chevron, previously of

Wild colonial boys

Dublin band Radiators from Space. A thoughtful and astute individual, it was Phil who turned up as representative from The Pogues to share an interview with me for one of the big London independent radio stations.

The focus inevitably turned to Irish politics, and while this was a topic I had become adept at fielding, I was wary of a pro Provos stance from a band whose membership and followers made no secret of their uber republican credentials and politics. So I was both relieved and surprised when Phil offered a balanced, nuanced and considered take on the current situation in Ireland. This was a rare enough perspective within the music business, where anti-Thatcher sentiment equated with Irish nationalism and 'the struggle for liberation'. But for a member of The Pogues to resist these lazy oversimplifications ... well, I was impressed. The same could not be said, however, of some of the other band members or the entourage that travelled with them, and this became all too evident as time went on.

Dave and Frank decided to award Ruefrex the support slot to The Pogues on a short UK tour. It seemed like an obvious mismatch, but that may have been precisely why they thought it was a good idea – that and a variety of practical and fiscal synergies that kept everything in-house.

Robinson, who had continued to hold out the prospect of an American adventure for Ruefrex, citing our enduring popularity on the US college radio circuit, believed that the forthcoming Pogues tour there was an ideal vehicle for this. So it's fair to say that expectation and trepidation washed over the band in equal measure.

Everything now seemed to be coming at us apace. The late Janice Long, new to BBC Radio 1 and *Top of the Pops*, took a liking to Ruefrex. She phoned me, unannounced, while she was live on air one evening. I was alone at home.

On *The Tube* with Sonnie Rae

The others were at the local Indian restaurant or at the pub. I was seriously hung over from the previous night's excesses and fancied a quiet night in.

Taking the call, I worried aloud that I would seem like a Billy No-mates to listeners. The conversation went back and forth in a casual way until she had to play the next record, one of ours, 'By the Shadowline'. As an aside, she announced that we would be coming into the BBC to record a session for her show. It was the first I'd heard of it! All in all, it was invaluable coverage for us.

The next day, summoned by Robinson, I travelled to Stiff offices. The big news they had to impart was that Ruefrex were to perform live on *The Tube*, a popular TV music show that served as a showcase for many emerging 1980s bands, as part of a politics-themed edition around the Red Wedge initiative.[1] This was marvellous news, of course, for all the obvious reasons, but for me, it felt like a personal validation. For Ruefrex to be so strongly associated with this socialist initiative seemed like a vindication of all I had been saying through my songs and in my interviews.

The train journey north to Newcastle, where the programme was filmed live for Tyne Tees, was a tense affair. We had been allocated a PR minder by Robinson, an indefatigable woman with the improbable name of Sonnie Rae. She was ostensibly there to keep the band in general, and Clarkey in particular, out of trouble.

There had been much talk of what to wear and what *not* to say on live TV. Clarkey plus mic plus live TV … what could possibly go wrong! We virtually begged him not to use the opportunity to namecheck his various family members watching back in Belfast. Instead, we implored him, he should realise the importance of the opportunity

Wild colonial boys

and respond accordingly. So when he engaged in a protracted disagreement with Sonnie Rae about whether he should wear a hat onstage or not, we knew that nerves were already fraying.

The show always started with a sequence captured in a mocked-up pub area where the acts for the evening were filmed, supposedly relaxing with a drink. We spotted Elvis Costello across the bar (he later performed a mimed version of 'Please Don't Let Me Be Misunderstood'). He had been hanging around with The Pogues, ostensibly producing their latest album and revisiting his Irish roots as Declan Patrick McManus, but with the intention of wooing their bass player, Cait O'Riordan. So our paths had occasionally crossed in different settings. Proffering a wave in his direction, he turned his back on us in a studied snub. It did little for our confidence or our increasing pre-performance anxiety.

Next up was the sound check. Again, Clarkey sought to impose his will on matters, in the manner of someone who knew they held all the cards. The sound mix on *The Tube* was often notoriously poor, giving everything a curious quality – particularly guitars – of having been 'phased' (electronically washed to produce a bland consistency). So it was evident that the film and sound crews had to be finessed. After all, they were responsible for making you look and sound good in front of millions of viewers. We were to perform two songs: 'The Wild Colonial Boy' and 'The Ruah', the latter chosen because it featured acoustic guitar, and we wanted to let everyone know we had a greater range than your average Punk rock outfit.

The floor manager was especially insistent that, during the live broadcast, we should keep to the areas we had occupied in rehearsal. This, he explained, was to ensure the best camera angles.

On *The Tube* with Sonnie Rae

A fraught, seemingly endless period of waiting followed during which we sat in our dressing room, we bickered, smoked, bit our nails to the quick, peed with abnormal frequency. Eventually we were called.

Tom Robinson, a supporter of Red Wedge and known for his activism around gay rights, introduced us, name checking our first single 'One by One', which he had previously reviewed.

And we were on.

Immediately, Clarkey deviated from his agreed stage routine, climbing on the drum riser and launching himself into the air. Coursing adrenaline drove us to speed through the performance at a faster pace than intended. All the while, our singer prowled the stage's edge, fashioning his mic stand into a gunsight and generally terrifying individuals in the crowd, and careering across the stage, causing the handheld cameramen to bump off scenery and catch each other in shot (something they deplored as it made them appear amateurish). And adding a final insult to injury, he blurted out 'Hiya Sharon' on the closing crescendo of 'The Ruah' before they cut to commercial break. Suffice to say, it was not all I had hoped it would be.

On the train journey back to London, instead of being on a high, I felt far away from home and lonelier than I ever remembered. I kept thinking of the old maxim, 'Be careful what you wish for. You just might get it'.

We shared a carriage with Heaven 17, who had performed their massive hit 'Temptation' on the show. Collapsed deep into my seat, I watched the dapper Glenn Gregory joke around with their two incredibly attractive backing vocalists and remembered Ziggy's belief from what now seemed a lifetime ago, 'I can make it all worthwhile as a rock and roll star'.

Wild colonial boys

NOTE

1 *The Tube* broke the careers of presenters Jools Holland, Paula Yates and Muriel Gray and started with a magazine section consisting of interviews, fashion items and comedy appearances and featured live performances from three or four acts each week.

28

Shane MacGowan's smile

When I first met Shane MacGowan, there was little evidence of the individual who would become the beloved icon of Irish culture we know today, lauded for his songwriting abilities and artistic contributions to the canon.[1] I always found him personable and self-effacing. While the other band members might gather in rowdy communion, when in his cups Shane liked nothing better than to find a quieter corner to settle in alone with his drink. And his intake was indeed prodigious.

His reputation preceded him. No one could imbibe *that* much and still get up onstage to front a band, could they? But this he did – albeit sounding incomprehensible for most of the set, the raucous, pogoing crowd not minding one jot.

So when friends – activist Ken McCue and journalist Henry McDonald – invited me to appear with Shane on an RTÉ Saturday morning show, I was pleased to do so. It was identified as an opportunity to promote the peace-building work of New Consensus and talk about the anti-sectarian efforts of Ruefrex.

We arrived in RTÉ studios around 8.30 a.m. for a 10.30 a.m. slot and were told that Shane was flying in on a chartered flight from Portugal, where the band had been playing the

Wild colonial boys

night before. He arrived about 10.15 a.m., clearly the worse for wear. Carrying opened bottles of port and rum, one in each hand, he routinely swigged from both. When introduced, he seemed to remember me and offered a hug. His broad smile revealed a mouthful of blackened tombstones and dripping gums. Then he presented the two bottles and, with a gesture, invited me to join him. I had to ignore saliva and slobbers to partake in a kind of liquid breakfast camaraderie, and did so happily.[2]

It was another few months before we met again, this time backstage before our support slot to The Pogues in Portsmouth. We had witnessed hijinks aplenty on this short tour, both behind the scenes and during the gigs, but Portsmouth was a new low. Students, shore-leave sailors, and locals beat the shite out of each other in spectacular fashion, while the band(s) played on.

By this time, we seemed to have added a whole assembly of peripheral personnel to our payroll. Valerie, Jonty's former accountant girlfriend, was now in a relationship with Ray, a work colleague from Dublin. This meant that a succession of their friends from Dublin, looking to gain a foothold in London, were now kipping around our house in Olive Road. Some of them turned up on the guest list at our gigs. Others seemed to have acquired random roadie jobs, carrying equipment willy-nilly from one side of the stage to the other. With increasing frequency, I found myself sitting at the bottom of my bed, cheque book in hand, while Jonty ushered in individuals to be paid: 'This is Enda. He helped set up the amps at the Brighton gig. He'll need fifty quid.' The uneasy feeling that I was now a fully-fledged dupe for strays and waifs was hard to shake. There was also something crazy feeding into all of this, something to do with Jonty's unresolved relationship issues with Valerie. But sign

Shane MacGowan's smile

cheques I did. Giving away the band's money was one thing. But being put in the invidious position of paymaster was quite another. I hated it with a passion. With strangers, it was unpleasant enough, but with my fellow band members – who regularly came to my room on a Wednesday afternoon for the same purpose – it was beyond the pale. This was definitely *not* what I signed up for.

Meanwhile, back at the dressing room in Portsmouth, Phil Chevron pushed his way through the band members, entourage and bouncers to make sure his support act was doing okay. As we chatted, I could see the unmistakable figure of Elvis Costello join the post-gig melee. He looked over in our direction.

Like many people, I always imagined Elvis to be the skinny nerd that he appeared to be in his early appearances with The Attractions on TV, the suit, tie and gawky glasses suggestive of the perpetual loser. But the character who showed up that evening in Portsmouth was tall and bulked out. He was also loud and aggressive.[3]

As I talked with Phil, I heard Elvis say loudly to a few Pogues and sycophants, 'Why is he talking to those Orange bastards?'

I immediately darted a look in Clarkey's direction. Mercifully, Clarkey didn't seem to have heard the comment. Then Elvis exaggeratedly adjusted his glasses, squinted towards us and held his stare in our direction, seemingly inviting, even daring, a reproach from our side of the room. When he got none, he turned and melted into The Pogues' entourage and the mocking laughter that had greeted his remark. I thought Phil Chevron, who had clearly heard him, might challenge him there and then, but he simply squeezed my shoulder reassuringly and pushed on through the crowd.

Wild colonial boys

I know that recalling this incident is not something his many fans will find palatable. Nevertheless, now, as then, I thought it a cheap and lazy way for someone in his position to curry easy favour and bolster his Irish 'rebel' credentials. More damagingly, it showed a lack of understanding for what Ruefrex were trying to achieve through our music and undermined our efforts to challenge the sectarian dichotomy of Orange and Green. Later I learned that Costello had previous form in these matters, this time regarding racist remarks:

> Costello was already drunk when Stills and friends walked in. As he got drunker, his words got nastier in a desperate attempt to inflame the sensibilities of his elders. Stills soon left to go to his room. Backing singer Bonnie Bramlett (of Delaney and Bonnie fame) continued to engage Costello, who kept disparaging America and its most hallowed rock stars. After 2 a.m. he described James Brown as a 'jive-arsed n—' and Ray Charles as a 'blind, ignorant n—.' In response, Bramlett backhanded the twenty-four-year-old up-and-comer. It all ended in a brawl, quickly broken up by the bartender.
> Elvis was branded a racist and his steadily rising American popularity was truncated. Death threats came in by the hundreds. A New York press conference was slapped together to hasten the bleeding and allow Costello to explain himself. Excuses were offered. An apology was not.[4]

Elvis himself later refers to this US incident in his memoir,[5] but that night in Portsmouth, he must surely have felt he was on a surer footing when surrounded by fellow travellers. Nonetheless, it remains my belief that he indirectly disparaged two thirds of the national flag of the country that he purported to love so much.

The following week, perhaps still stung by the incident, and increasingly disillusioned by the realities of life on the road, I gave an ill-considered interview to *Melody Maker*.

Shane MacGowan's smile

The opportunity presented a significant development for the band in that we were guaranteed a double-page spread and the cover shot (a full head and torso shot of Clarkey flexing his heavily tattooed biceps). It was substantial by any measure and a high point in terms of band profile. In short, it was too good to turn down. The strapline for the article was 'Look Back in Anger'.

While Colin Irwin wrote a very positive piece, Clarkey revelled in his hardman persona, essentially insisting that he had been misunderstood while recounting lurid stories that suggested quite the opposite. I rambled on about the many slings and arrows that beset the band's mission in London. I had a good rant about the short-sightedness of political unionism and their stance regarding the Anglo-Irish Agreement. (This was playing out in the background to this period and was the inspiration for a new song I wrote at the time, 'Playing Cards with Dead Men'.)

I also put down Stiff Little Fingers at length and whinged that the music biz was far removed from all it was cracked up to be. If things didn't change, then I'd be back on the boat to Belfast tout suite to resume my teaching career. No one reading this much cared, of course, except perhaps the thousands of other young men in struggling bands up and down the country who would have sold their souls for the chances I was now disparaging. I was abrasive and dismissive of the industry I had ached to be part of for so long. Above all, I made it abundantly clear that we, as a group, were trouble. We stuck out like a sore thumb and were proud of it. Anyone who had a problem with that could fuck right off. (Any record labels, A&R men, booking agents, radio DJs and music management personnel who hadn't already been alienated by us most certainly were now.) As a parting rejoinder, I sneered that The Pogues were 'professional Irishmen.'

Within a day of the magazine going on sale, I received word that Frank Murray had removed us from the support slot on the American tour.

We were gutted, of course, but I allowed myself a wry smile. It had come to something when a band from the Loyalist Shankill Road could so offend the musical wing of Irish nationalism by pointing out that *we* were more Irish than *they* were.

NOTES

1. It seems there is no limit to the status and high regard in which Shane is held in Ireland. Most recently we've been told that he was reading Dostoyevsky by age eleven. It's a far cry from the self-destructive oblivion of early Pogues' gigs.
2. I commemorated the moment in my song 'Shane MacGowan's Smile'.
3. Shane has talked about this period in the documentary *Crock of Gold: A Few Rounds with Shane MacGowan* (2020). He suggests that Costello was struggling with drug withdrawal and a difficult separation from his then wife.
4. Bryan Wawzenek, '36 Years Ago: Elvis Costello Incites Brawl with Racist Remarks', 96.5 The Rock, 15 March 2015. https://965therock.com/elvis-costello-racist-remarks/.
5. Elvis Costello, *Unfaithful Music & Disappearing Ink* (London: Viking, 2015).

29
Jumping the shark

It was becoming clear that Stiff Records were fatally holed below the waterline and taking on water at an alarming rate. Debtors could be held at arm's length no longer, rumours of bankruptcy abounded and some said Dave Robinson had his bags already packed. Where before there had been a crazy energy buzz and a can-do panache, now an air of pessimism hung over the offices and the depleted staff. 'If I were you, I'd get in there and take anything that's yours before the bailiffs come' was the advice from Simon Ryan, record sleeve designer and himself a former recording artist for the label.[1]

I had been working with him on the follow-up single to 'The Wild Colonial Boy'. Dave, reasoning that we might command daytime radio airplay again, opted for the most overtly commercial track on the album, 'In the Traps'.[2] Mick Glossop and I produced and mixed the hell out of it, a catchy power-pop ditty that used a dog race as an analogy for an unfair, meritocratic education system.

This attempt at a subversive, under-the-radar counter-narrative perhaps unsurprisingly went over most people's heads. For those fans who had been with us from the Belfast beginnings, it seemed far removed from the likes of 'One by One' and 'Capital Letters'. Worst of all, it appeared to convey to them the very thing I had feared most all – that we had irrefutably 'sold out'.

Simon had designed a sort of school badge, a Ruefrex crest featuring figures and emblems, including the Red Hand of Ulster (without the crown) for the 7-inch and 12-inch sleeves. It also contained a Latin motto at the base: 'Numquam Sapientes Ruefrex Femus'. I don't know how intentional it was on his part: a rough translation is something like 'Ruefrex will never know wisdom' (or in Belfast parlance, 'Ruefrex will never wise up'). Prescient in most regards.

Despite the portents of imminent financial demise, Stiff released the record. It met with lukewarm approval from most quarters. Soon after, the label went belly up.

The silence in the subsequent vacuum was deafening. No one in the band seemed to have anything to suggest about what we might do next or where we would go from here. It seemed like we were being called ashore, that our fifteen minutes of fame were well and truly up.

Clarkey was back in Belfast. Forgie was moving to his own place in Highgate, North London, and had embraced the role of house husband and parent while moonlighting with other bands. Gordy pretty much always saw himself as a gun for hire, so opted out of policy-making decisions. The Dean was as anonymous and inoffensive as ever.

Things in Olive Road were just as uncertain. There was still a steady stream of musicians, drunks and waifs passing through, and there was always the likelihood of the bizarre and the improbable happening. That at least kept things interesting.

That Halloween, for example, we had been taking it in turns to deal with the local kids who were trick or treating. But when it came my turn to answer, instead of finding

Illustration S2.5 Ruefrex crest for 'In the Traps' (Kasper Records). Design and art by Simon Ryan.

children lathered in their mother's mascara and fake blood on the doorstep, I was confronted by three shifty-looking guys. One was wearing what looked like a celebrity Sex Pistols rubber mask (they were all the rage at the time).

'We're here to pick up the loan of a bass guitar from someone called Sean,' he said.

I returned to the living room and flopped back down on the couch. 'Sean, there's a guy outside in a Paul Cook mask says you'd loan him a bass guitar.'

Of course, it turned out that it was in fact Paul Cook, the Sex Pistol's drummer himself. I was duly mortified.

Styling themselves 'proper' musicians, the Microdisney crowd, who often de-camped in our open house, were increasingly patronising and condescending toward our band. They were incredulous at our lack of professionalism ('You don't even know what gauge of strings you use?!') It was a long, long way from punk rock. And those now encamped in the house as long-term guests – Valerie and Ray's Dublin crew – became increasingly belligerent. All were from the Republic of Ireland, and they roundly condemned British and unionist positions during the Anglo-Irish treaty period at every given opportunity (fifteen Unionist MPs had resigned their seats in protest at proceedings.)

They boasted that then Irish Minister for Foreign Affairs Peter Barry was the man to take on the Brits and win, and it often seemed that their rancour was aimed indirectly at me. As I was myself a tenant in the house at Valerie's invitation, there was nothing to distinguish their status from my own. So my growing ire at their failure to contribute to household bills, rent or household chores had to be held in check.

Adding insult to injury, they crowed that the dole and rent allowance they received from the Brits was beer money. I was reminded of an old saying from back home about

Jumping the shark

opportunistic nationalists: 'Not too fond of the Crown but fond enough of the half-crown'. My opinions were far removed from any Tory/Thatcherite mantra about benefit scroungers, but listening to them – their politics, songs and reminiscences – it seemed that the only thing they wouldn't do for their country was live in it.

Things took a serious turn when the only other girl in the house – let's call her Eileen – spent more and more time alone in her room, so much so that I remember very little about her, except for her ruddy cheeks, nut-brown hair, rural Irish accent and wary half-smile. She occasionally ventured downstairs in the early hours when everyone else had gone to bed. It was subtly made clear to me by the Dubs that she was shy and didn't welcome attention or conversation – just another quirk of this lunatic domestic set-up, I figured, and thought little more of it.

However, as the weeks passed, Eileen could no longer conceal the fact that she was clearly pregnant. Bizarrely, no one talked about it, and my enquiries about her well-being were politely ignored. One of the Dubs spent more time with her than the others, but it was unclear whether he was the father or not.

Soon she was the size of a house, and while she was sometimes seen around the place, toiling up the stairs or shuffling into the bathroom, some unacknowledged omertà meant that not a word on her condition was mentioned. Clearly whatever small-town disgrace had driven her away, had managed to extend its tentacles of judgement and disapproval even to London.

Following the demise of Stiff, our star continued to wane; invitations and guest list privileges were becoming fewer and fewer. So when an offer to attend The Cult's Hammersmith Odeon gig for pre-concert drinks came in,

Wild colonial boys

I leapt at it. I liked the band well enough and would have gone along just to hear them perform 'She Sells Sanctuary'. But as the night's proceedings progressed, somehow I felt more and more like an imposter, like a B-lister, there on sufferance and for pity's sake.

Feeling low, I left early and climbed into one of the black cabs parked outside. Failing to see that the taxi was already taken, I offered my apologies and made to exit.

'Where ya headed?' asked my co-passenger in a thick Mancunian accent.

'North ... Neasden ... Cricklewood.'

'Raaaiit ... mint. That'll do. We can shaaaare.'

The voice sounded familiar. I looked up to see Mark E. Smith of The Fall ease back into the shadow of the cab.

Losing all pretence of cool, I immediately turned into a reverential fan and for the duration of the cab ride home, pledged my devotion to the band and their wonderful *Live at the Witch Trials* album.

I talked to him about Ruefrex and was pleased when he told me he had seen *The Tube* performance and had heard of us. Clearly having learned nothing from my earlier encounter with Seamus Heaney I bemoaned at length about how it had all gone wrong. Well known for being cantankerous and mercurial in equal measure, he listened patiently, nodded and smiled occasionally. I was relieved at his indulgence.

'It was all gonna go tits up the moment the bass player left. He formed the band with me, ya see ... we wrote all the—'

Mark E. let out a loud guffaw. 'Maaate, stop scrikin', fer fook sake! I've sacked sooooo many members of The Fall. I only just sacked me drummer again last night! Get ova yarself!'

Jumping the shark

I had to laugh. That cheered me right up.

When I got home and went into the upstairs bathroom in the early morning darkness, I was taken aback to find a heap of bedsheets, sodden with straw-coloured fluid, hurriedly dumped in the bathtub. It was obvious to me right away that Eileen's waters had broken at some point during the night. I felt for her – a young girl so far from home, so alone at such a defining moment in her life.

Later that day I saw Ray packing her clothes into black bin liners. On enquiring after Eileen and the baby, I was assured curtly that mother and child were doing well.

Neither she nor the baby ever returned to the house; her name never came up in conversation and I never saw Eileen again. Everything about the sorry episode felt wrong. I wondered about the fate of the child, and about the hundreds of other lone Irish girls forced to make life-changing decisions in the dead of night in London.

Things were coming to a head on all fronts now. Like Forgie, I had actively started to look for other accommodation. Clarkey was back in Belfast (and impossible to reason with most of the time). Gordy and The Dean were happy to stay as peripheral figures in their own worlds. Forgie had somehow morphed into the role of last musical collaborator standing and fellow keeper of the now dimming flame. But despite our shared interests in music, cinema, theatre and left-wing politics, things were rarely without rancour between us.

So when journalist Barry McIlheney, stalwart supporter of the band and sometime drinking buddy, contacted me to say that one of the two housemates he shared with was moving on, leaving a room vacant, I jumped at the chance. Something of a party animal at the time, Barry's professionalism, conviviality and easy bonhomie were reflected in his little black book of contacts and it was no surprise that he steadily made his way up the corporate ladder in publishing.

For me, it meant a move to South London for the first time, but the prospect of a residence in Battersea appealed. It was a fairly cosmopolitan area, with Chelsea just nearby, and it offered many green areas like Clapham Common as well as easy access to transport hubs like Clapham Junction.

In the mid-eighties, the Yuppie phenomenon was at its height. Well-paid, young middle-class fashionistas were looking to get on a rung of the property ladder, and the gentrification of previously undesirable addresses was in full swing with estate agents and auctioneers keen to rebrand. Streatham, SW2, became 'St. (Saint) Reatham', Battersea, SW11, became 'Ba-tterr-sia'. It was the era of Harry Enfield's 'Loadsamoney', with outsized mobile phones, champagne and cocaine everywhere. I was appalled, when on a trip to the old Highbury grounds to watch an Arsenal vs Liverpool match, to see Arsenal fans goad the Scousers by waving wads of cash at them while singing 'Sign on, sign on, cuz you'll never get a job' to the tune of the Liverpool anthem 'You'll Never Walk Alone'. It seemed that everywhere you looked, Thatcher's unequal Britain was to the fore.

Barry was rarely at home, and neither was my other housemate, Alison. An upper middle-class girl from somewhere in the Shires, she seemed constantly preoccupied with her boyfriend who worked in the City and owned a boat. On the occasions that Barry *was* there, we'd happily guzzle copious amounts of lager and whiskey while lounging on the couch, speculating about whether Pat Jennings's hair was really his

Jumping the shark

own. On TV, the prodigious mop never seemed to budge, despite his acrobatic heroics in goal.

This living arrangement suited me fine at first, giving me ample opportunity to lament the loss of what might have been and ponder my next move. London? Belfast? A return to study? A 'proper' job? But it seemed premature to jettison what had been so hard won simply because Stiff Records had gone down the pan. So I began to consider the possibility of one last hurrah. It had worked before.

Artistic collaboration was at an all-time low within the band, so I had taken to writing alone. There were some older songs that had never been recorded and could be re-energised and rearranged for one last album. But this was predicated on finding a new record label who would be prepared to front the money for recording, production, sleeve design, distribution and promotion.

Other more robust bands might have picked themselves up, dusted themselves off and sought to build on established successes. After all, it wasn't like we'd be starting from scratch again. But too many significant bridges had been burned. We'd proved ourselves too truculent and unreliable, and our allegiances, our message and our cultural reference points all came from the most uncool, reactionary and conservative tribe in western Europe – Ulster Protestants. So in both commercial and ideological terms, we were undeniably a busted flush.

Naturally, then, when independent label Flicknife Records expressed an interest, I grabbed it with both hands and held on.

Flicknife had started in 1980 and had The Velvet Underground's Nico and the legendary Hawkwind on their roster. Spanning hard rock, progressive rock and psychedelic rock, Hawkwind were retrospectively considered an influential proto-punk band. I fondly recalled blasting them out at ear-bursting volume from my bedroom window as a backdrop to Belfast rioting.

But first, Flicknife had to be convinced that they were signing a functioning outfit, one that would be ready to tour and promote any new release. As some band members were barely prepared to be in the same room as each other by this stage, this task proved daunting. But I told myself that another Ruefrex album was the end that justified the means … and lied through my teeth to Flicknife owner, Frenchy Gloder. I then set about pulling together enough original material to warrant a new release.

But given Forgie's sullen reticence to collaborate with me on the venture, it quickly became apparent that I would have to pull all the strokes and figure out all the angles by myself. It was then that I realised that I too had become a chancer.

At least I had learned from the best.

* * *

The songs were recorded live at the Chocolate Factory Studios, South London. No money was available for a big-name producer like Mick Glossop; in fact, there was no money available for *any* producer. So, enthused with the mug's confidence born of blithe ignorance, I willingly took on the role.

It was clear to me early on that this would be no second album. The dearth of creative input and the absence of genuinely fresh material meant that only five songs were recorded – more like an EP.

Originally to be entitled *Playing Cards with Dead Men*, the project centred around the extent of human suffering

Jumping the shark

that existed behind the statistics and news stories the public heard on TV and radio. I wanted to deride the insidious notion of 'acceptable levels of violence' and 'legitimate targets', and to challenge the malignancy of paramilitary control of working-class areas in Northern Ireland.

'Political Wings (Clipped 1969–????)', the track that the EP ultimately took its title from, was something of a dinosaur from the Harp Bar days. Written back then with TC, it sought to unswervingly challenge the terrorists in their role as political representatives for marginalised areas. Introducing a drum machine, overdriven guitar and funky bass, the song offered a hard-driving sound that incorporated elements of hip-hop and heavy metal. The overtly political lyrics were spat out by Clarkey, hip-hop style. Inadvertently, we had pre-empted the coming era of bands like Rage Against the Machine and Soundgarden. (If only we had taken it to the US!)

'Playing Cards with Dead Men' was a rousing call to arms for a unionist population feeling betrayed by the Anglo-Irish Agreement and it had perfidious Albion squarely in its sights:

> To keep us down in days gone by
> you played the Orange card,
> and European fields of war, like sheep,
> we'd rush to guard.
> Six county men have looked to you
> in past and present strife,
> six county men again have found
> you're betting with their life.

'Playing Adult Games' was another old song that had never been recorded before. It dealt specifically with how paramilitary gangs recruited from the young and vulnerable.

'Days of Heaven' was one of my more notable collaborations with Forgie, and it demonstrated what might have been possible had everyone been pulling in the same direction. It attempted to capture a sense of the nobility and honour inherent in working-class communities that, if nurtured and liberated from sectarianism, could endure.

Finally, 'On Kingsmill Road' was a self-penned ballad recounting a particularly detestable episode in the history of the Troubles when the Provisional IRA murdered ten workmen in a sectarian attack in South Armagh.

A couple of the tracks had already been committed to tape but required intensive revision. For the others, I convinced Clarkey to fly in for a day to lay down whatever vocal tracks remained. Gordy continued as taciturn and professional as always and The Dean took the lion's share of the guitar work. Forgie, staging some principled stand that only he was aware of, largely boycotted the recordings, staying away for the most part.

If I were going to do all the work and carry all the responsibility, then I'd be damned if the credits didn't reflect it. My sullenness played perfectly into the 'megalomaniac' spin that Forgie promoted about me to anyone who would listen. It all seemed such a depressing postscript to a once honourable undertaking.

For the cover, I again engaged Davy Pentland (who had been responsible for the *Flowers for All Occasions* and original 'Wild Colonial Boy' artwork.) In keeping with past provocative graphics and employing the 'playing card' motif in the EP's title, I suggested to him an in-your-face challenge, similar to his earlier 'Armalite wrapped in brown paper and string' sleeve.

I had him design a cover featuring a Death Head playing card, on the upper half of which is Gerry Adams punching

Jumping the shark

Illustration S2.6 'Losing hand'. *Playing Cards with Dead Men/Political Wings* EP (Flicknife Records).
Photo by the author

the air, the word 'VOTE' emblazoned behind him, and on the bottom half, a hooded gunman clutching a rifle. A fiery landscape blazes behind him. It was the perfect evocation of the Sinn Féin strategy of the ballot box in one hand and an Armalite in the other. On the back, and with a nod to the idealism of the track 'Days of Heaven', was a picture of me when I was about eleven years old standing outside our Shankill Road home clutching a guitar.

Wild colonial boys

Illustration S2.7 'Windswept and interesting'. The final line up, Primrose Hill. L–R Blair, Burgess, Clarke, Forgie, Ferris.
Photo by Tom Sheehan

In a half-hearted attempt at levity, for I realised this truly was our swansong, I included the famous Warner Brothers Looney Tunes goodbye, 'Th-th-th-that's all, folks'.

But really, no one was laughing. Least of all me.

NOTES

1. Lick the Tins recorded a Celtic version of 'Can't Help Falling in Love', replete with fiddle and penny whistle. It was exactly the kind of punt that had so often paid off for Robinson.
2. He gave us little choice, insisting it was this or that we cover a U2 song! That suggestion offers some insight into his lack of empathy or understanding for everything that defined Ruefrex.

30

Green and pleasant land

By this time it was 1988. Long days spent alone in Battersea dragged out and on. My housemates were rarely home, and my days were unproductive and depressing. I punctuated aimless walks around the area with occasional trips 'up West' to meet Cormac for drinks in Chinatown or to meet Grimmo in Brixton for a spliff and a game of pool. But I was floundering and I knew it. I had come to London for a reason and the death rattle of that purpose was now clearly audible.

Any remaining flirtations with 'the music biz' seemed limited to writing for the music mags – an occasional review of a gig or a critique of a band's new release. These were sometimes put my way by Barry McIlheney, Stuart Bailie or other kind gentlemen of the press.

All thoughts were now turning to Belfast.

I had of late began to somewhat romanticise my hometown, and Ireland as a whole. Perhaps it was all those maudlin memories of the Irish exiles I had spent so much time with. Or maybe it was the affirmation doled out by those English folk who only saw a one-dimensional ideal of what it was to be Irish (noble in the face of oppression; gifted in expression; vivacious; entertaining at parties). I had been listening to Paul Brady's anthemic 'Nothing but the Same Old Story' and it pulled at me.

And yet.

At times like these I had to consciously force myself to remember why I'd been compelled to leave Belfast in the first place: the awful fear of no-warning bombs; the car that slows to a crawl right behind you; the everyday tit-for-tat assassinations; the suffocating peer pressure to *belong* to one side or the other.

I was at a crossroads ... again.

So when an unexpected wedding invitation dropped through the letterbox, it provided both a welcome distraction and an opportunity to rub shoulders with the glitterati, probably for the last time.

Neil Cuthbertson, the irrepressible South African owner of Kasper Records, and Sophie Richardson, the sister of TV comedian and director Peter Richardson, were to be betrothed. Perhaps because his side of the church would be woefully under-represented compared to the bride's, Neil had been generous when issuing his invitations. Several of the old guard from the Video Palace were included, as was I.

The Richardsons hailed from the south-west of England and so, with that quintessentially English bravura beloved of the show business fraternity and bourgeoise, the service and reception were to take place in rural Dorset. The family's parish church was in a small, picturesque village, and the reception was to be held at the Richardson family home. It was picture perfect.

I contacted Jayne, a gorgeous Welsh girl who I'd met on holiday, to ask if she would be my plus-one. My invite sagged under the weight of names I dropped: Jennifer Saunders, Dawn French, Lenny Henry, Adrian Edmondson, Rik Mayall – the cream of the alternative comedy circuit when comedy was emerging as the new rock n' roll. How could she say no? She agreed to travel to London and join us there for the trip down south.

The drive from London would take about two or three hours and I thought this was well within the capacity of my trusty Vauxhall Chevette, so I gamely offered to pilot one of the convoys making the journey.

We started out early under the cloudless sky of a perfect summer's day, with Cormac, Grimmo and John-Boy squeezed into the back, and Jayne in the passenger seat. A dog-eared map, spread out on the bonnet of the car, was consulted before we embarked. Grimmo took the opportunity to roll several joints for the trip on top of the squiggly lines marking roads in the south-west peninsula. Not to be outdone, John-Boy produced a tartan holdall, packed with lager and cider cans. And off we went.

Feeling that my own sobriety was in everyone's best interests, I declined the offers of libation being proffered from the back seat, but I woefully miscalculated my patience and generosity of spirit.

By the time we joined the M3 at Winchester, I resented the hell out of all my fellow travellers. The hijinks continued apace in the back, the volume and affability increasing with the intake of fluids and hash. Charm offensives were targeted at the fair Jayne, who not really knowing anyone, was at a loss as to how to react. The longer the trip went on, the more I convinced myself that these ingrates were deliberately baiting me. But the real cause of my resentment probably had more to do with the onerous driving duties that prevented me from getting wasted with the rest of them.

Soon we were navigating the narrow back roads and lanes of the West Country. The old car struggled up steep hills under the weight of a full load, which added to my consternation. Local cars seemed to swing round blind bends at an alarming speed and on my side of the road, causing me to hug the already encroaching stone walls (parked vehicles were notable for the absence of wing mirrors, attesting to the lack of leeway). All the while, the lads howled for the music to be turned up on the radio. I ground my teeth a little harder.

When we reached our bed and breakfast, I threw off the seat belt, leapt from the car and hurled the car keys at Cormac, the soberest of the trio: 'I'm off duty. Lock up!' Grabbing our room keys, a joint, a can (and Jayne), I headed off to find the church.

The Richardson family home was nearby, and the brightly striped marquee where the reception was to be held was easily spotted from a distance, so we made a beeline for it. I hadn't eaten all day but had enough sense to anticipate the impact of a day's serious drinking. Food was definitely required.

In the marquee they were still setting up for the reception later. In one corner, behind the caterers, was a mountain of freshly prepared strawberry punnets. Beside them, stacked from the grass to the high canvas dome, were wooden crates stamped 'Moet'.

I sheepishly advanced. 'We're with the wedding party. Do you think I could get something to eat?'

'All we have here is champagne and strawberries. Take as much as you want!'

When I woke up much, much later, I was back in my car.

My mouth was caked with scum and my jacket coated in my own dried sick. My head ached abominably. I used the steering wheel to pull myself upright. The car was still parked outside the bed and breakfast but outside it was totally dark. A Bic lighter lying on the seat helped me to read the clock on the dashboard: 4.23 a.m.

What the fuck had happened? Where had the day gone? Where were the others? Where was Jayne?

I cupped my hands around my eyes as I strained to look beyond my own reflection in the side window. Pain shot through my neck and shoulders from sleeping in an outlandish position. How long had I been here?

Images began to drift back to me and the more I remembered, the worse I felt. There I was, cheesy grin, clutching a bottle of Jack Daniels, emboldened by gallons of champagne and a glut of strawberries, walking unsteadily down the aisle to greet the happy couple. With mounting horror, I recalled the looks of disbelief on the faces of the congregation.

Then at the marquee afterwards I vaguely remembered John-Boy and Grimmo scaling the central pole and being coerced down by polite but clearly intimidated members of the bride's family. Cormac's face swam into view, scowling at me from above. 'Never drink angry!' he counselled too late, then washed his words down with a deep swig from his own bottle of Moet.

Oh my god, I thought, and rubbed urgently at my eyes.

A whiff of sick wafted up from my clothes ... or was it the car's upholstery? My gut tightened, and I urgently clawed for the handle to open a window. I retched violently but nothing came.

'Christ!' I blurted out aloud. I'd abandoned Jayne. She knew no one here. Had she made it back okay?

I lurched from the car and as quietly as I could, made my way to our room. Mercifully, she was there, tucked up in bed, her blonde hair framing her perfect face, her breath gently rising and falling.

Well, I thought, my libido reviving somewhat, there's still Jayne. But as I moved quietly toward the bathroom to clean myself up, my stomach flipped again. That smell ... *that vomit smell.* I turned on the light and instantly realised that I must have visited this bathroom already at some point in the evening.

And what a state I'd left it in. Projectile spewing had evidently been in full force. Broad brush strokes of bright red sick adorned the mirror, the sink, the bath, the floor. It looked like the shower scene from *Psycho*.

'Red! RED? Christ, BLOOD! I'm dying!'

I caught my reflection in the mirror. What a mess! My eyes were slits. Beads of sweat were running down my face and my heart was knocking hard in my chest. I moved closer and tentatively prodded a red lump of sick with a finger. Strawberries!

Bile rose from gut to gullet in one easy surge and champagne acid exploded from my mouth and my nose. Mercifully, Jayne slept on, oblivious and indifferent.

I lurched from the room, desperately craving the night air. Try as I might to stay in the room and join Jayne in bed, I could not. The sights, but mostly the smells, drove me straight back out and kept me there until I woke, cramped and cold next morning, lying on the back seat of the car.

I've only recently reconciled with strawberries. And as for champagne ... never again!

On Sunday morning, our English hosts behaved impeccably toward us. No one so much as mentioned the embarrassing excesses of the previous day to me. *Everyone* was nursing some kind of a punitive hangover.

Slightly fortified by a light breakfast of tea, dry toast, honey and walnuts, I joined the others for a prearranged get together at the Richardsons' home.

Green and pleasant land

It was a spectacularly beautiful morning. I found it hard to imagine a bluer sky or greener grass. The marquee had already been disassembled and the lush green meadow seemed to stretch for miles. Delightful children of family and guests were bedecked in white linen outfits, the little girls adorable in lace-trimmed frocks and sun hats, the boys in white trousers and pin-striped waistcoats.

With abandon, they ran around an area close to the rear of the house, where wood-and-rope swings and a roundabout had been erected. The sound of their laughter drifted in the rising heat of that June mid-morning. You couldn't imagine a more archetypal portrait of England's green and pleasant land.

A sizeable pond, traversed by a modest bridge, stood a little way off, and it was there that I went to lick my wounds and leisurely watch the world go by.

An irate Jennifer Saunders, face like thunder and perhaps somewhat the worse for wear herself, tugged two young children, screaming, across the bridge, admonishing them that they had had quite enough ice cream.

Gradually, others from the Irish contingent drifted over to join me. We moved off a little distance from the main house and made ourselves comfortable on the ground, our backs against a large oak tree. Our one-time road manager and fellow guest had driven his vintage Saab down a dirt track near to where we were sitting and opened all the doors wide. From there he played *Sketches of Spain* by Miles Davis and this became the soundtrack to our glorious Devonshire Sunday.

As we lazed around in the rising heat, I watched a figure dressed in white peel away from the group of guests by the house and make its way toward us. It was Adrian Edmondson, dressed in cricket whites and pads. Genially, he wanted to know if any of us would like to join them for a game.

We looked at each other a little uneasily, not wanting to offend but aware of our ignorance regarding the thwack of leather on willow. As I searched for plausible reasons to graciously refuse, Miles's sublime horn refrain was interrupted by the sound of radio stations being tuned in and out. Looking up, I saw Grimmo's rear end jutting out from the driver's side. Eventually, he found what he was looking for – live coverage of the UEFA European Championship game between the Republic of Ireland and England from the Neckarstadion in Stuttgart. It was Ireland's debut at a major international tournament.

He moved to the boot of the car and, opening it, produced a football. 'We were just about to ask you guys if you'd like to join us for a kick around,' he said.

Ade politely declined and returned to the crease.

And so with the match commentary wildly acclaiming Ray Houghton's goal, Jack Charlton's tactics and Ireland's unexpected victory, we passed the afternoon kicking the ball around that immaculately cut meadow, ecstatic that Ireland had got one over on the 'auld enemy', but crestfallen that our hosts and fellow English guests seemed not to care one jot.

31

The return of the native

On returning to Battersea first thing Monday morning, I booked my passage home on the Liverpool ferry. It partly felt like an unconditional surrender, a half-hearted acceptance of defeat. I didn't have the stomach for another painful resurrection of the band, nor was I inclined to continue to serve as a lightning rod for everything my fellow band members despised about London, the music industry ... and me. Once I made the decision, there were no second thoughts. But there certainly was trepidation.

Thatcher's government had just announced that the Harland and Wolff shipyard was to be privatised, and the IRA had just planted a booby-trap bomb on a school bus in an attempt to kill the driver, a member of the Ulster Defence Regiment (UDR). The driver and some school children – one of them Arlene Foster who would go on to lead the Democratic Unionist Party and become First Minister in later years – were injured in the explosion.

Despite all this, I still wanted to go home. I had come to the conclusion that I could not make a living in the music industry. I had none of the safety nets afforded by affluent patrons or parents, so I was going home to join the ranks of supply teachers in Belfast's inner-city schools to get by.

Wild colonial boys

The little yellow hatchback was once more dragooned into service. It always surprised me how I could get my entire material world into the confines of its modest interior. Records and cassettes were boxed up, and clothes pressed into holdalls and a ropey suitcase belonging to my parents. I even managed to squeeze my drums, stands and cymbals in there.

Now that I had made my mind up, I was eager to get going. A 5 a.m. start would get me to Liverpool in about four hours, giving me most of the day to look around the city and still be in good time for the 6 p.m. sailing. A pre-dawn departure from London would also ensure no goodbyes from my flatmates, and that was just fine by me. I wouldn't have been able to pick Alison out in a line up, so few were the times we'd actually spoken. Barry McIlheney knew of my intentions and wished me well in advance. But I would be leaving as I arrived – alone.

Barry also was well placed to provide a particular service at my request. I didn't move in the right circles, nor did I usually have a preference for that most popular of recreational narcotics – cocaine, but as this would be my last opportunity to flirt with the decadence of the bright lights and the big city, I reckoned what the hell.

And so with the prospect of an early drive and a long road ahead, I foolishly twisted Barry's arm for a couple of lines of the old Bolivian marching powder, just to speed me on my way, so to speak. A wrap was left for me on the sideboard with a note wishing me bon voyage. I had also secured a sizeable lump of hashish, which I secreted among my belongings in the boot of the car for personal use on my return home.

Despite my superficial indifference regarding my return from exile, I attached a good deal of emotional significance to my journey home. For such an epic expedition, I felt

The return of the native

I needed the appropriate soundtrack to accompany me, and as I could only listen to cassette tapes in my car via my Sony Walkman, considerable thought went into creating the right compilation mix tape.

Van Morrison had long been derided by punk rockers. Synonymous as he was with our hometown, as teenagers we had roundly dismissed him as a hippy and a dinosaur. It was John-Boy who years later encouraged me to 'listen to those horn arrangements. Listen to those strings! The man's a fuckin' genius!'

And he was right, of course. Mick Glossop, too, who had worked extensively with 'The Man', was similarly moved to sing his praises. As a result, I had spent months cramming on Van's back catalogue and now had all the evangelical zeal of the convert. So Van, along with a selection of punk classics, featured heavily as my musical accompaniment back to the old homeland.

Battersea was virtually deserted at 4.30 a.m. I had loaded the car the night before and was ready for the off. Passing through the empty streets of the capital felt dreamlike. Sitting at the junction of a normally manic thoroughfare – now empty – waiting for the traffic lights to change from red to green was surreal.

And the drugs *did* work! With a manic grin plastered all over my face and Van's 'Full Force Gale' belting out on the headphones, I was away. As the sun rose over the miles of tarmac, likely laid down by a thousand Irish exiles before me, I felt nothing but good about going home. Waving and smiling inanely at the drivers of HGVs and supermarket delivery trucks, I convinced myself that 'the healing had begun'.

Chemically elated but not entirely intoxicated, I still knew the importance of watching the clock and reading the motorway signs. A ship was in the harbour, preparing for the voyage and it wouldn't wait for me.

Some miles along, I considered pulling into one of the many service areas for something to eat and a piss break. But I knew I hadn't built in much wriggle room, so I kept on, struggling to change tapes with one hand. By 9.20 a.m., a little knot of doubt had worked its way into my gut. Shouldn't I have seen a signpost for Liverpool by now? To make matters worse, I noticed that a gauge on the dashboard showed that the temperature of the car's engine was rising. An hour later there was no doubt – the needle was now firmly lodged in the red. I knew that I had no time to pull into a garage to check the water level or let the car cool down.

The coke that was still in my system had morphed from 'feel-good' to 'hyper-anxiety'. Where the fuck was the sign for LIVERPOOL!?

By 11.30 a.m., I was cruising at 70mph and still no sign for fucking Liverpool. The needle, lodged hard right in the red, hadn't lied. Smoke began to seep out from under the bonnet, white at first, then grey, then turning darker and thicker. Boiling water mixed with oil sprayed the windscreen. I put the wipers on full blast, but that only smeared the glass and made it impossible to see the road ahead. There was nothing else for it but to pull over onto the hard shoulder.

I was fighting to stay calm, to push down the adrenaline, the chemically induced dopamine, the stimulant. As I sat on the hard shoulder, smoke belching from under the bonnet, endless traffic hissing by me, I tried to consider my next move. Then, in my rear-view mirror, I saw a large 4x4, with its yellow and blue chequered pattern and POLICE insignia, pull in behind me.

My heart soared. They had come to rescue me, get me to a garage. Maybe I'd make the sailing that evening after all.

The return of the native

'And what about the lump of hash in your trunk?' whispered a little voice in my head.

The burly policeman took his time emerging from the vehicle. Then he pulled on his hi-vis jacket, adjusted his peaked cap and made his way slowly to my side window, motioning for me to roll it down.

My story came tumbling out as I wrestled my driving licence from my wallet. 'I've travelled up from London to catch the Liverpool ferry for Belfast.' I could see him look me up and down and peer exaggeratedly into the back of the car. I almost blurted out, 'I'm not a terrorist, you know!'

Grinning, he put a hand on the roof of the car and leaned in. 'Liverpool? You're in West bloody Riding lad!'

Another look at the livery on his vehicle confirmed it. High on Van and Barry's parting gift, I had somehow sailed past the turn-off for the M56. I now found myself on the wrong side of the Pennines in a broken-down car, under the influence and in possession. How easily my universe had completely flipped.

'We'll need to get you off the motorway and to a garage,' he said and went back to his vehicle to radio for a tow truck.

'Thank you. I'm really sorry to be a trouble. Thank you!' I was talking to his back now and gushing with relief.

I don't remember the name of the Yorkshire village they brought me to but it was small, with an antiques shop, a pub, a post office and, crucially, a garage. The mechanic instantly diagnosed the trouble as a blown head gasket, which he could fix – but, unsurprisingly, he would have to send for the part and it would cost.

Having missed my sailing and with my mind speeding manically as I trod repeatedly up and down, up and down, the one street of this tiny Yorkshire hamlet, I would likely have paid him anything to be on my way.

Presently, once the car was fixed, a strange calm descended as I set off once again for Liverpool. With a kind of Zen-like grace I accepted that the universe had put me in my place. Proper order. I deserved it!

Locating the first hotel with a secure carpark, I checked in. I would make the next evening's sailing for sure. But as the night wore on, I became hyperconscious that all my worldly belongings were in the car parked at the back of the hotel; Liverpool, rightly or wrongly, has a bit of a reputation for spontaneous redistribution of wealth. There was no sleep to be had that night.

Or the next, for the ferry was an overnight sailing and I hadn't booked a cabin.

No amount of squirming and repositioning on the hard, functional seats gave me a comfortable position for slumber.

Feeling chastened and cosmically schooled, I fell in and out of a doze. Half images of London and my escapades there formed, then disappeared. It was as if they had already become distant memories.

Next morning, the rain-soaked deck of the ship proved an inhospitable host. The leaden sky and unremitting wind and rain ensured that I didn't remain out there for very long. Instead I sat by the fogged-up Perspex window, legs drawn into my chest, searching beyond my own distorted reflection for land. For home.

Then I detected a subtle change in the engine noise and vibration. As we turned into the channel that led to Belfast Lough, the ship seemed to shudder, as if cross-currents threatened a deviation from her path. My pulse raced a little for it signified the home stretch.

I remembered then this journey in reverse, when we had crossed from Belfast to Liverpool for the Sense of Ireland gig that now seemed like an eternity ago.

The return of the native

The rain had stopped, and the clouds broke in one or two places. Early morning shafts of sunlight struggled through. A few of my fellow passengers bravely ventured out on deck and I watched them pointing off into the distance. Gulls were in evidence as well. A daily routine for them, of course, banking and wheeling overhead, their loud screeching signifying 'land ahoy'.

I reached for my Walkman. The batteries were low but surely it would hold long enough to play me home. Clamping the headphones on and pushing against the heavy door with my shoulder, I emerged on deck to be buffeted by the strong winds that swept the channel. Immediately I could see green fields and hills. Groomsport on one side, perhaps Whitehead on the other, then Cavehill, so redolent with history. Napoleon's Nose unmistakable.

It was time. I had known all along what my musical accompaniment would be for this particular moment. I pressed play.

> When that foghorn blows
> You know I will be coming home
> Yeah when that foghorn whistle blows
> I gotta hear it
> I don't have to fear it.[1]

The wind was making my eyes tear up. And so was Van.

All my emotions regarding my homeplace came welling up now. This lovely, deadly, contradictory, enigma of a land and its people. This ancient crucible of love and hate, flawless wisdom and empty rhetoric, unthinkable cruelty and boundless compassion.

The sun kissed the crags of Cavehill, and in that moment I was awash again with self-doubt. That no-nonsense, Ulster perspective was demanding to be heard. Had I lost my way and lost the run of myself? Had I become both manipulator and manipulated? Had I sought to rejuvenate a mortally wounded creature to breathe life into something that was never destined to live that long?

Yes, Ruefrex had reared up for a short while in anger and defiance, but we had been slowly bleeding out from the wound left by TC's exit. The band was composed of four immutable constituent parts. How could I ever have come to believe otherwise?

Clarkey, that chaos of contradictions, that exasperating bundle of blind fury and energy, tempered only by a voice that ran the gamut from declamation to sorrowful loss.

Forgie, who poured his self-doubt and crippling angst through the overdrive and reverb of his power chords, and who would only find peace in the conservative conventions he so bitterly derided.

And TC, my first best friend and mentor, who had had the vision and arrogance to believe it could be done but, in the end, not the conviction to do it himself.

Others had come and gone but only us four could truly be said to embody the blueprint, the crusade, *the band*.

The green hills gave way to the gantries and warehouses of Queen's Island, to the shipyards of Harland and Wolff and to Short Brothers where I'd served an apprenticeship of sorts. I thought again about how I might make a living back here. I thought about my friends and family, how I'd turned my back on them to follow my heart's desire. Would I be shunned as a dreamer, an also-ran, or welcomed as a prodigal?

What I couldn't know then was that in less than a year I would be tilting at new windmills, driving my doughty old Chevette, packed to the hilt once again with all my worldly goods, this time from Stranraer down through the north of England to Oxfordshire.

The return of the native

And as I stopped on that early midsummer morning to watch the sun slowly rise on the cattle standing up to their udders in the low Cotswolds mist, I again had my headphones clamped to my ears and the perfect soundtrack prepared.

The theme from the TV show *Brideshead Revisited* seemed an entirely apt accompaniment for my most unlikely elevation as a student to the dreaming spires of Oxford University.

Exhausted from the journey and held in a sublime instant of pastoral splendour, I was fleetingly lost in a trance.

But the reverie ended abruptly as, with a hiss and a crackle, the original recordings I'd made on that cassette broke through the lush orchestration taped over them. It was Dave Vanian of The Damned with *'New Rose'*. And as if offering a cue to where and when it had all begun, he once again asked 'Is she really going out with him?'

And the music played on.

NOTE

1 From 'Into the Mystic' by Van Morrison, from the album *Moondance* (1970).

Coda: Legacy issues and the perils of misremembering

It's no fun being the ghost at the feast, to let light in upon magic, to call out the nakedness of emperors, or comment on the presence of Dumbo or Nellie in the room. People generally don't like it when you do.

Northern Ireland, of course, faces particular problems with all of this. The whole 'legacy' debate on how we deal with the past continues to torment, pulling in one direction the urge to (perhaps) forgive but not forget the awful inhumanity of our recent history, hauling in the other, the generational and pragmatic tug to simply move on. Powerful actors in this drama find uncomfortable narratives, retroactive and limiting.

Just ask the countless victims' families and victims' groups who fight to ensure that the memories of their loved ones are not sanitised from the historical account decreed by Tory legislators, or rewritten by those revisionist ex-terrorists – many now politicians – who seek to justify the merciless horrors they inflicted upon innocents, or, indeed, those commercial interests who simply want to 'draw a line under the past and move on' for the good of tourism and commerce.

Coda

It is not surprising then that when the arts throw up a sanitised or simplistic representation of our past (for example, Kenneth Branagh's Oscar-winning movie *Belfast*), there is a considerable clamour to affirm that narrative.

Another misrepresentation of recent history, polished and repackaged for more palatable consumption locally, nationally and internationally, is the dubious beatification of Terri Hooley and the Good Vibrations label.[1]

In 2019, Belfast academic, novelist and screenwriter Glenn Patterson penned an article for the *Irish Times* celebrating the proud dissenter tradition, which has existed in Belfast most notably from the late eighteenth century.[2] To do this, he evoked some worthy luminaries (to which he might usefully have added Van Morrison and Alex Higgins). Included, however, were Mary Anne McCracken and the United Irishmen, George Best and ... the Belfast punk rock phenomena. In referencing the latter, he acknowledged that the punk rock movement in the city – blue memorial plaque and all – is now forever inextricably linked with the Good Vibrations record shop, its label and their owner, Terri Hooley.

In most respects, it came as no surprise to see Hooley, the 'Godfather of Belfast Punk', elevated to the pantheon of my hometown's greatest (much in the manner that Tony Wilson is synonymous with the Manchester music scene).

A concerted effort by a coterie of Belfast's broadcasting establishment – and music and film movers and shakers – has ensured that he shares a pedestal with those other luminaries of that era – John Peel, Malcolm McLaren, Bernie Rhodes, Geoff Travis, Alan McGee and so on. This saw its culmination in the production of a well-received if somewhat fanciful movie about his life and times, *Good*

Vibrations. (It was also no surprise that Patterson, one of the screenwriters for *Good Vibrations*, should glorify Hooley in this manner.)

The movie bears only a passing resemblance to the Belfast punk scene (and to the man himself) that *I* remember. The 'real' Terri was not a particularly talented, egalitarian, philanthropic, politicised or entertaining individual, as he is portrayed in the myth-making movie. He did not shambolically stumble from one financial crisis to the next, all the while driven only by his overriding love for music and 'the scene'. It is more accurate to say he was an opportunist who saw his chance and took it. Subsequent financial setbacks owed more to hubris and mismanagement than any 'punk' rejection of the music business ethos.

Sub-cultures like the Belfast punk scene of the 70s develop as often as not through deliberate shaping by 'scene makers', those key players who just happen to be in the right place at the right time and can fashion things in their own image. What made the Belfast punk scene of that period different from others, however, was that the macro-narrative in which it took place was a much larger and disputed one. Therefore, in a society as contested as Northern Ireland, we would do well to ask ourselves, 'why is the Good Vibrations' account of the Troubles era the only one that everyone seems to agree on?' Surely that raises some cause for suspicion?

We would do well to be sceptical. For the orthodox narratives surrounding Belfast punk are entirely problematic. Hierarchies were created and privileges jealously guarded to this very day. The cultural politics of Belfast are rarely given over to scrutiny. Many of those who came of age during that time went on to hold prominent positions within the local and national cultural elite. And these

Coda

'myth-makers' are heavily invested in the non-sectarian, affirming narrative of Belfast punk that now uncritically passes as gospel.

Many who cast themselves as self-styled 'outcasts' and 'rebels' were intent from the beginning on becoming the new cultural establishment. And in this they have largely succeeded, principally by reducing the larger and more complex story of Northern Irish punk to vacuous generalities and sloganeering, and an infantile determination to wish social and political problems out of existence.

While bands like The Outcasts, Rudi, and yes, even Stiff Little Fingers, may have postured as something radical, they were in fact very liberal indeed. The Outcasts sang songs that were unashamedly misogynistic, while Rudi's lyrics rarely rose above the inane. Stiff Little Fingers addressed their reality a little more directly, if rather one dimensionally. (I have dealt with this elsewhere in the book.)

But to fit the prevailing narrative, cultural gatekeepers continue to act as apologists for both The Outcasts and Rudi, citing the former as 'comic-book' punk (whose less than acceptable representation of women is not to be taken seriously), and the latter as somehow sublime punk pop in the style of The Undertones or Buzzcocks. (It is not.)

Conversely, if, like Ruefrex, your songs named names or took sides (or even more provocatively, insisted there should be *other* sides to take) then the establishment tended to overlook you. Thus Ruefrex were consigned to the margins of the Good Vibrations story and Belfast punk history in general, and these prejudices endure to the present day.

Given the band's second-time-around success, it is likely that Ruefrex – via Stiff, MCA and RCA Victor – have easily outsold both The Outcasts and Rudi internationally. Yet

Wild colonial boys

Good Vibrations and the standard bearers of Belfast punk rarely cite the band in any official or historical context. (The sales of the *One by One* EP on Good Vibrations have never been shared with me; in any case obtaining a credible tally from Hooley would prove futile.)

Occasionally, the self-appointed keepers of the Belfast punk flame are compelled to give Ruefrex their due. But even then, it is done begrudgingly and in a manner (inexplicably, even now) designed to give offence.

The Ruefrex song 'The Perfect Crime' features a prolonged overdriven guitar introduction, loaning itself to use as film incidental music. It had been employed in John T. Davis's *Shell Shock Rock* in this way to great effect. When I was approached by the producers of the *Good Vibrations* movie to request its use again, I agreed in the hope that perhaps at last, Ruefrex would be granted their place in the celluloid story of the punk scene in Belfast.

So I was both disappointed and angered when, without my permission, the song was not employed in its original recorded format as agreed but re-recorded by someone called Jason Faulkner and (re)produced by David Holmes.

While the song was employed in the film at its climax, this skulduggery ensured that the movie remained a Ruefrex-free zone, with no mention of the band throughout or even on the soundtrack credits. Such wilful disrespect is hard to fathom.

It is my belief that this level of congratulatory self-regard and nostalgic misremembering has consequences, not just for historians, sociologists and musicologists (of whom there are legion researching this period), but for the ordinary men and women, participants on the scene at that time, who deserve better.

Coda

NOTES

1. See also Chapter 5, Bad Vibrations.
2. Glenn Patterson, 'Two fingers from Belfast: A centuries-old culture of dissent. From Mary Ann McCracken to George Best, dissent runs in the city's blood', *Irish Times*, 12 January 2019. www.irishtimes.com/culture/books/two-fingers-from-belfast-a-centuries-old-culture-of-dissent-1.3738399.

Appendix 1
Song lyrics referenced in text

All lyrics copyright Thomas Paul Burgess

Poppies

Gather round and watch them plant their crosses,
And remember them – the men who forced the forces.
Did they have to fight? Did they have to die?
Your work well done ... they didn't even ask to know why.

You've paid your cash, to prove that you've remembered,
Bits of red paper, to prove you're not self-centred.
Well, my lapel is bare and I don't care,
About the future plight of arms and the modern warfare.

Poppies! Remember what you're tryin' to prove,
Paper Poppies! Monarchists would no doubt approve.
Happy! Now you've done your little bit?
Feel free, to pin on your little bit of shit!

Six feet under, don't smell no flowers,
Now it's back to the club for brandy, cigars.
Would you rather be red? Would you rather be dead?
Or would you sleep much better if the people weren't so easily led.

Leave it well alone, let the gullible rest in peace,
What's it worth to stop the Cossack hoards of the East?

Appendix 1

Well, twenty years on, will your poppy be gone?
Or stained with the blood of another generation's young?

Poppies! What about the German dead?
Paper Poppies! Will they stop the flying lead?
Easy, to forget it for another year.
Admit it, your money don't make you sincere.

Communism

Why change your name if your views stay the same?
I bet you'd throw it all away for riches and fame.
How much you'd sacrifice is a political game,
It's just the New Testament, by any other name.

Ideals and raw deals can't keep you alive
Yes, money can be funny, never mind the nine to five.
Politics hurls stones and sticks, while think tanks just contrive,
To blind us all with morals. Human folly knows no sides.

Karl! Karl! You must have meant well.
But you were naive, weren't aware of the smell.
That stinking, selfish stench that gives us all away.
Your equality is heaven but it's hell down here today.

No Mother Russia, you don't fool me at all.
No peasant farmer heard the Communist call.
No frightened land needs your enlightenments maul.
If everyone is happy then there's no need for a wall.

Don't Panic (in a Siberian climate, cuz the pendulum swings both ways)

Butter,
What a novelty.
TC turn it on to fuzz,
Cuz I must be going mad.
Dad just phoned the audio.
Oh, I get but I don't want.
Wanton boys must flies accept,

Septic throats and sticky buns,
I must be going mad.
What's so wrong with that?
I hoped you'd understand.
All around,
I'll round it all.
All I want is all you'll get.
Getting pretty in your pantry,
Panting at your window pane.
Pain I love,
But painful silence?
Silent science says it all.
I must be going mad.
Yeah, I must be going mad.
What's so wrong with that?
I hoped you'd understand.

One by One

'Shall we sit down together for a while, here on the hillside? Where we can look down on the city in the sunset, so old, so sick with memories. Old woman, some they say are damned, but you I know will walk the streets of paradise. The old woman said no.'
From the forward to *Strumpet City* (James Plunkett)

One by one,
See the mighty all have fallen. The townspeople hide and cry.
Bodies laid under tarpaulin, there were many more to die.
Seeking refuge in the basement, helping no-one 'cept yourself
Orphaned children seek replacement, cyanide escape upon the shelf.

Panic, panic, respected citizens are on the run.
Panic, panic, all the kings and queens are dying one by one.

One by one,
Metropolises painted still. Standards slump where chaos reigns.
Seeking Hamlyn's sacred hill, frozen snakes in traffic lanes.

Appendix 1

Believers climb the only towers. Bibles clutched in bloody hands.
Authorities clear the grounds of flowers, to bury friends of Uncle Sam.

Panic, panic, masses try to find a chosen one.
Panic, panic, false prophets profit always one by one.

Capital Letters

'Take a letter, Comrade Kulov, mark it "White House, USA",
now attach it to this warhead,
that's the price they'll have to pay.'

'Take a letter, Miss Morretta, and dispatch it right away.
Please inform supreme headquarters,
that tomorrow is the day.'

Make your peace with God, forgive your debtors,
Cuz they're keeping the airwaves open, for Capital Letters.

Take a letter, wrote the Lord Mayor, on his desk of
varnished teak, and inform the county council,
that the townhall's closed next week.

'Take a letter,' moaned Herr Schmidt, as he read zinc fell again,
'that I've cancelled all appointments,
cuz the whole world's gone insane.'

'I've read the letters,' cried the newsman,
to the hushed and captive crowd,
'and they tell of word from Moscow to expect a mushroom cloud.'

'We've read the letters,' wailed the children,
in their final throes of pain,
'and so we've paid our postage duties. Christ's been crucified again.'

Wild colonial boys

April Fool

Today, it's never been greyer before.
Delay, in bus queues and chilled to the core.
I know those eyes, they're watching me still.
I can't help but feel that they're stalking their kill ... I'm not
  alone.

Tonight, car noise spoils the calm of my room.
In fright, lone dogs close their ranks and resume,
To howl and let me know I'm not alone.
Alright, so who's on the end of the phone ... I'm not alone.

Despair, it's twelve o'clock, was that the door?
I'll swear, a footfall was heard on the floor.
Okay, whoever is down there come out.
If that's you, then you better stop messing about ... cut it out.

Oh no, I don't think that's funny at all.
Oh oh, there's a man with a mask in the hall,
Keep calm, remember to maintain your cool,
What's that? What do you mean April Fool ... April Fool!

Is it a trick or treat?

Paid in Kind

MacLaverty lies drunk, in doorway fifty-one,
his state conceals the mission, his coat conceals the gun.
To kill the last man on the foot patrol, is what the orders say,
and soon,
'No sweat about it, we'll have ya down on Galway Bay.'
The street lamps wash blue silhouettes,
dogs bark and howl somewhere,
for effect MacLaverty warbles 'The Londonderry Air'.
Strangled notes that slur together,
forgotten words are forced to rhyme,
shop front windows, 'Cut Price Discount',
the only witness to the crime.

Appendix 1

On down the road, in single file,
hugging shadows, feeling lost,
more statistics, more reminders,
of a weary, pointless cost.
Now MacLaverty shakes with readiness,
his hand is on cold steel,
for the animal that he's become has forgotten how to feel.
'Are ye alright mister?' comes from nowhere,
'Are ye hurt or anything?'
MacLaverty's finger on the trigger,
voice forgotten how to sing.
From the depths of a too large parka,
all curious and brassy bold,
comes the voice of Eamon Duffy, eyes of blue and ten years old.
Now the men are near upon him,
English oaths and English talk,
but little Eamon Duffy declines to take a walk.
Instead he sits right down beside him,
'Hey mister, what's your name?'
And all MacLaverty's thinking is, 'I'm not the one to blame.'
Two young boys died for nothing, in that mindless senseless act.
Another in the riots of the twisted, tangled facts.

And MacLaverty just ran, and never looked behind,
to finish three months later in Armagh and paid in kind

The Perfect Crime

The wait was long,
I took my time,
as stealth befits the perfect crime.
My mind made up,
the seed they'd sown,
and all that time I'd never known,
my wife, my joy, I'd loved so much,
lay naked to my best friend's touch,

Wild colonial boys

for I was taken unawares,
as early home I climbed the stairs.
I heard their breath, their talk of love,
I heard it clearly come from above.
I'll play for time,
yes I will wait,
and then decide their perfect fate.
I'll lure them to this empty street,
while promising old friends we'll meet,
and as my blade
shines and sings,
I'll pass them on to better things.
For it is written, it is said,
adulterers are better dead,
because the bible tells me so,
God's will be done,
for God will know.
And if in chains ye shall bind me,
the Holy Ghost will set me free.
A great reward in heaven I'll gain,
though men will point, accuse insane.
Oh, I'll be gentle as a feather,
and after all they'll be together.
Ah, here they come now,
right on time,
and so to work,
the perfect crime.

The Wild Colonial Boy

Well I'm the Emerald Isle's own son,
I was born on stateside, Wisconsin.
And your troubles sound like Hollywood,
they sound real good to me.

The rush to be Irish now is on,
the queue is standing ten miles long,
and would be green men stand in line,
to swap their stories tall.

Appendix 1

Well I have traced my past right back,
I've even checked and double checked,
and I'm as sure as ever now that I'm a leprechaun.

And I know that if I get my chance,
that I can jig, and reel, and dance,
cuz in between the killing that's what all us Irish do.

and now a word from our sponsor:
'Eat up all our TV dinner,
open up your wallet wide,
and let your green be seen.'

A people cannot live that way,
or so the songs and leaflets say,
and all this time we're trying hard,
to keep the black man down.

What with collection time and all,
with charities, functions and balls,
it really gives me such a thrill,
to kill from far away.'

The Ruah

(*Journeys through the Pentecostal Prayer Halls of West Belfast, in search of the Lost Tribe of Israel.*)

A whisper on the breeze, has stirred the loose tent flap.
There's nothing there at all.
The overhanging trees, on the window lightly tap.
There's no one there at all.

And so the Ruah comes,
With no sound nor shape nor form.
As a silent messenger,
Brings the calm before the storm.

And the sand will turn to glass, and the day will turn to night,
But there's nothing there at all.

Wild colonial boys

And the dumb shall speak in tongues, and the blind regain
   their sight,
No there's no one there at all.

And so the Ruah comes,
In a way that no one thought.
Casting pearls before the swine,
Giving gifts that can't be bought.

When the wind becomes a hurricane that rages to the sky.
There's nothing there at all.
And blows away the falsehoods of a life that lives a lie.
There's no one there at all.

And so the Ruah comes,
When our efforts have been spent.
Pay homage to the spirit,
The temple veil is rent.

In the Traps

Starting prices favour failure,
gates are open, heads are down.
No tails wag with paper seizure,
a silent pause, a cheated frown.

Off and running, jumping questions,
stroking comma's flustered brow.
Wished I'd taken running lessons,
barked up wrong trees, too late now.

What's the odds they're going to give?
Certificates are now held high.
Some must die so you can live,
your leash, the hallowed old school tie.

Competitors gain thoroughbred,
your kennel owners only mumble,
pointed ears still hear what's said,
'You warped, unwanted, wasting mongrel.'

Appendix 1

Mister Renfield Reflects (with apologies to William Blake and Bram Stoker)

Oh little fly, thy summer's play, my thoughtless hand has brushed away.
And if a spider had spied thee, what better end from him than me.
Open flower, thy bouquet sweet, induces bees to come and eat,
And if I've spoiled their glutton feast, have I then given where life has ceased?

'Hosts of angels look away from my face, the misery I bring,
Kindred spirts come to stay, captured, cut and dried, now there's a thing.'

Speckled thrush, thy song so clear, doth never change from year to year.
And if you die and I survive, then what price death if I'm to thrive?
Human race the love thy bear, cause dormant feelings now to stir.
Despite my needs I know the crime, to steal away your numbered time.

'Sleepless days and nights in jackets, straight and stiff and white I spend.
While plotting my behaviour, they can't know that he and I still plot their end'.

Little fly they summer's play, my thoughtless hand has brushed away.
And if it's souls that I hold true ... then am I not a fly like you?

Flowers for All Occasions

The tests had come back positive, it rained all that April day,
They could stay and face the banns or they could leave and run away.

Wild colonial boys

Now her mother's found the letters, there was nothing more to say.
In a gown one size too big, she swore her youth and life away.
There were flowers for all occasions,
As the bridesmaids gathered around,
Confetti, petals, broken dreams lay scattered on the ground.

Midnight snacks became a nuisance, morning sickness came and went,
She worked hard to fix the spare room, he worked hard to pay the rent.
While she laboured in the ward, he kept his panic stricken seat,
Sweater pulled on inside out, odd shoes on different feet.
There were flowers for all occasions,
And cigars and smiles and sighs.
He's got his daddy's temper, he's got his mammy's eyes.

The child was not to know his father, who would die one winter's day,
In a dark and stinking alleyway, always the innocent who pay.
And the clergy sang it out, their damnation and their prayers,
And police and politicians blame sectarian affairs.

There were flowers for all occasions,
As they shouldered heavy grief,
Sickly sweetness filled our senses, they had kept the service brief.
There were flowers for all occasions,
Floral tributes to the dead.
Orange lilies, shamrock green,
Bloody scarlet poppy red.

By the Shadowline (Patrolling the Peace)

'Hold hard and fast,' the captain said,
'give us this day our daily bread.'

Appendix 1

'If the tide turns now we'll all be dead.'
By the shadowline.

All down below deck hummed a sad refrain,
Of love and death and life and pain.
When you reach rock bottom you come up again.
By the shadowline.

Some will be lost, some will be found,
Some will be spared and some will be drowned,
But the cabin boy laughed and the mate just frowned.
By the shadowline.

Loose your innocence as the wall clocks chime,
Loose your sweet young life when it's in its prime,
And never forget the march of time.
By the shadowline.

So set the sails with no course in mind,
Leave the hopes and the dreams and the doubts behind,
And return at last to your very own kind.
By the shadowline.

Shane MacGowan's Smile

A bottle of rum and a bottle of port,
At nine in the morning, a breakfast of sorts,
So now I'm believing in all the reports,
Of Shane MacGowan's smile.

He comes at me slowly, with one in each hand,
Says he likes Belfast, my songs and my band,
And offers a pull with a cheery command,
of Shane MacGowan's smile.

I don't wish to be haughty, seem stuck up or proud,
But his teeth and his slobbers have rendered me cowed,
And a group of well-wishers have now formed a crowd,
Round Shane MacGowan's smile.

Wild colonial boys

So I take a deep slug, first of one, then the other,
He slaps my back hard and he calls me his brother.
And I see right away, what no one can smother,
That's Shane MacGowan's smile.

Playing Cards with Dead Men

To keep us down in days gone by
you played the Orange card,
and European fields of war, like sheep,
we'd rush to guard.
Six county men have looked to you
in past and present strife,
six county men again have found
you're betting with their life.

'And you're playing cards with deadmen
but you're losing every hand,
you cheat my people past and present,
have lived and died upon this land.'

You've used our home, a testing ground
for ballot box and gun,
you've raised our wages, bought our souls,
we're learning one by one.
You've dealt us all the Easter card
now come and count the cost,
you've gambled with democracy,
you've gambled and you've lost.

'And you're playing cards with deadmen
but you're losing every hand,
you cheat my people past and present,
We'll live and die upon this land.'

Political Wings (Clipped 1969-????)

Were all disillusioned with the way that we live,
Your policies to me seem all receive, no give.

Appendix 1

Why don't you pick your fights with the social elite,
Cos the people that your struggle's for can't even walk the streets.
Both our sides have a common link,
We could save the situation if you'd just stop and think.
Ideology and martyrdom are meaningless bluff,
When the people that you're fighting for have died for you enough.

'You, you're not killing on my behalf!
What are you, street people or military staff?
It's all been done before, in your favourite folk lore, in bygone days of yore.'

Unite the people through the ballot box,
Give them all peace and not tenement blocks.
Sectarian crime's not my socialism,
Do the people that you're fighting for want *you* to liberate them?
The bombs that you plant every once in a while,
Blind the Irish eyes that find it hard to smile.
You leave behind a trail of frightened, crying mothers,
And the children that you're fighting for are fighting one another.

'You, you see it all so clear cut,
Press release: "It's so regrettable, but ..."
Don't you go by any laws, look for a round of applause?
But then it's all for the cause'.

Playing Adult Games

All the rest voted yes, so I thought that I'd better agree.
With the lad from the Kesh and the man at the back we made three.
I wanted to ask them why they wouldn't do ...
The things that they wanted me to go through.
                    And they said ...

Wild colonial boys

'Oh, you're playing grown-up cops and robbers now.
Oh, you pay your dues, your oath, your pledge, your vow.
Oh, never worry, cuz worry never helps,
Just playing adult games, collecting cowboy scalps.'

It was square and small and squat and brown-paper clad,
And I thought of the things that I'd done and the times that
   I'd had.
I've visions of mayhem as I closed the pub door,
Still cannot believe this would even a score.
                            And they said ...

'Oh, we've told you son, you're not to think that way.'
And don't forget about the trigger-switch delay.
Oh, you faceless men, you'll answer for this yet.
Just playing adult games, deserving what you get.

On the line at the top, it said 'Prime and retire right away'.
And they knew that I knew, so you can bet that I didn't delay.
The room it revolved with the sound of a bang,
My fate was resolved, my hospital ward sang ...

                       And they sang ...
'Oh, you've played their game, you must have been insane.
Oh, just inhale, forget about the pain.
Oh, you've got more, than you've bargained for,
Just playing adult games and no one's keeping score.'

Moving counters, throwing dice, playing adult games.
Moving counters, throwing dice, playing adult games.
Naive children pay the price, fulfilling someone's aims.
Moving counters, throwing dice, playing adult games.

Days of Heaven (Rites of Passage, Shankill Road, 1969)

A burned out pub, a playground for the bored,
A Cyclops skylight offers sanctuary.
A boy peeps through the corrugated iron,
From the safety of his world within a world.

Appendix 1

Far away from sirens in his shell,
Days of heaven, nights of hell.
Little fortresses of common love,
Footballs burst on glass-topped backyard walls.
'Johnny 7','Hunts' and 'Hide 'n Go.'
'Best prices paid for copper and for lead.'

But with darkness the stones and rubble fell,
Days of heaven, nights of hell.

A generation built from red-bricked streets
All proud, and hard, and honourable men.
One same purpose, that of right and wrong,
Family and jobs their main concern.

Another side the newsmen seldom tell,
Days of heaven, nights of hell.

The Ballad of Kingsmill Road

Ten Protestant civilians were killed by the Republican Action Force (RAF), believed to be a cover name for some members of the Provisional Irish Republican Army (PIRA), in an attack on their minibus at Kingsmill, near Bessbrook, County Armagh. The men were returning from work when their minibus was stopped at a bogus security checkpoint.

The factory whistle screams an end to toil,
the work day done.
Their minibus, it idles done the lane,
to home they run.
Oh, what's for dinner, what's for tea,
there's football on TV.
On Kingsmill Road, no prayer for the dying.

Some frightened men are standing in a line,
but none know why.
Eleven workers pray to god above
but ten still die.

Wild colonial boys

While carnage fills a country lane,
their families wait in vain.
On Kingsmill Road, no prayer for the dying.

That massacre is frozen in his mind,
a stark nightmare.
The birds, the trees, the scattered memories,
still lying there.
So must Christ hang his head in shame,
they murder in his name.
On Kingsmill Road, no prayer for the dying.

Appendix 2
Ruefrex discography

Albums

Flowers for All Occasions (9 versions). Kasper Records / David Pentland (design and art).

Capital Letters: The Best of Ruefrex. Cherry Red Records / Jim Phelan (design and art).

Wild colonial boys

Singles and EPs

One by One EP (5 versions). Good Vibrations Records / Alan McQuade (design and art).

Capital Letters (7-inch). Kabuki Records / T. P. Burgess (design and art).

Paid in Kind (2 versions). One by One Records / David Pentland (design and art).

Appendix 2

The Wild Colonial Boy. Kasper Records / David Pentland (design and art).

The Wild Colonial Boy (4 versions). Kasper Records / Simon Ryan (design and art).

In the Traps (2 versions). Kasper Records / Simon Ryan (design and art).

Wild colonial boys

Political Wings (12-inch). Flicknife Records / David Pentland (design and art).

List of illustrations

Side 1

1. Ad for debut gig at the Trident in Bangor, 14 December 1977 — 49
2. Recording the *One by One* EP in 1979 — 64
3. 'ArtRat' — 69
4. With the late John Peel at *that* Good Vibrations gig — 87
5. Still from the BBC documentary *Cross the Line*, 1980 — 97
6. 'Gang of Four' — 112
7. Angry Clarkey — 113
8. 'Enter The Dean' – the peroxide days — 117

Side 2

1. 'The Wild Colonial Boy' cover — 124
2. UK Chart — 139
3. Portrait for *Melody Maker* World Cup feature — 171
4. Dingwalls gig, 1985 — 187
5. Ruefrex crest for 'In the Traps' (Kasper Records) — 219
6. *Playing Cards with Dead Men/Political Wings* EP (Flicknife Records) — 229
7. The final line up, Primrose Hill — 230

Dedications, acknowledgements and thanks

This book is dedicated to TC, Clarkey, Gordy, The Dean, Forgie and all the other comrades who fought together in the punk rock wars. Respect to Colin Coulter, Barry McIlheney, Mick Glossop, Alastair and Angus Graham, Grimmo, Henry Cluney, Davy Simms, Bernard Griffin, Larry and Richard Cudden, Mo Lawrence, Davy McLarnon, Tony McGartland, Alex Ogg, Ken McCue, Jim McGarry, Joe Zero, John Watt, Stuart Bailie, Colin and the Faloon family, Elaine & Fergy, Richard L Jordan and Gareth Mulvenna. Special thanks to Averill Buchanan. And to Matthew Smith at Exprimez. I am grateful for the input of Kim Walker, Alun Richards and all at MUP. And to Laura Macy and Dawn Preston at Newgen. A moment of meditation on the memories of Henry McDonald, Gavin Martin and Cathal Coughlan, who played a part in this story and passed away, too soon, during the telling of it.

Index

Advert, Gaye 85–6
Adverts, The 85
  Queen's University (Belfast),
    gig at 86
Agency, The 185, 186
All Children Together (ACT)
  76, 77n2
Anderson, Kenny 26
  Ruefrex, and role in 29, 50
Androids, The 65, 87
  Dandelion Market (Dublin),
    gig at 87–9
Anglo-Irish Agreement 134
Apex Jazz Band 27
Archie Adam's grocery store 58
Ardoyne neighbourhood 13, 35
  Alliance Avenue 35
  Pride of Ardoyne Flute Band
    33–4, 35, 37
Ask Mother 87, 88
Atlantic Bar (Brixton) 200–2

'Ballard of Kingsmill
  Road' 228
  lyrics 269–70
Ballysillan 10, 13
  Playing Fields 36–7
Barry, Peter 220
Bates, Simon 139

Battle of the Bands (Ulster Hall)
  86, 87, 91n3
BBC Radio 1 139–40
  Roundtable 156–8
Belfast
  Belfast Boys Model School 4, 9
  Belfast Primary Schools' Choir
    and Orchestra 27–9
  punk scene in 43–4, 47, 250–1
  Queen's University, The
    Adverts gig at 86
  return to 239–46
Black Catholics 104
  Mansion House (Dublin) gig,
    and presence at 106
Blackstock, Billy 93–4
Blackwell, Chris 191
Blair, Gordy 42, 155–6
  Ruefrex, and role in 180, 185,
    218, 223, 228
Bono 90
Burchill, Julie 86
Burgess family
  David (brother), 5
  Ruby (mother), 5–6, 31
  Tommy (father), 5–6
Burns, Caroline 20
Burns, Jackie (Jake) 20–1, 25,
  82–3, 103–4

Butcher, Bleddyn 174–5
'By the Shadowline' 196–7
   lyrics 264–5

Cable News Network (CNN)
   interview 178
Campbell, Sandra
   'Whatname' 20
'Capital Letters'/'April Fool' 111,
   272, 274
   lyrics 257–8
Carnmoney Hills 7
Catlin, Andy 148
Chambers, George 27
Chevron, Phil 205–6, 213
Chocolate Factory Studios
   (London) 226
Clarke, Allan 57n4, *64*,
   113, 117
   background of 54–5
   Bowie, David, and persona
      of 52–3
   character and personality 55–6
   Ruefrex, and role in 53, 56–7,
      99, 113, 147, 154, 186–9,
      223, 228
   stage presence and
      performance 53, 154
Clayton, Adam 90
Clerk, Carol 169
Cliftonville Road 13
Cluney, Henry 29
Cogan, Višnja 90
'Communism' 255
Complete Control (fanzine) 26
Cook, Paul 220
Cooper, Alice 196
Cork City Hall gig 108–9
'Correct Your Fireside
   Manner' 196
Costello, Elvis 208, 213–14
Coughlan, Cathal 152
Coulter, Colin xiii

Coulter, Tom 3–4, 10, 15, 21, 25,
   56, *64*, 79, *117*
   background and family of 4–5
   Debonairs, leader of 4
   London appearances 154–5
   Ruefrex, formation of and role
      in 25–7, 29, 49, 100–1,
      115–18, 141–2, 147,
      155, 180–4
   work and career of 114
Creaney, Norman 67
'Cross the Line' 68
Cross the Line (documentary)
   52–3, 76, 96, 97n3, 97
'Croucher' (aka 'Steamer') 80–1
   Debonairs, membership of 16
   Ruefrex roadie 80
Cudden, Larry 130
Cult, The 221–2
Cure, The 170
Cuthbertson, Neil 135,
   138–9, 156–7
   wedding of 231–8

Damned, The 25
Dandelion Market (Dublin) 88–9
   Androids, The, gig at 87–9
'Days of Heaven' 5, 227–8, 229
   lyrics 268–9
Debonairs 4, 14–16, 25, 79
   'Croucher' (aka 'Steamer'),
      member of 16
   Highfield Bootboys, conflict
      with 17, 19, 22
   Mawhinney, Jim 'Musky,'
      member of 15, 18–19
   McIlvenney, Norman 'Heckle,'
      member of 14
   McKeown, 'Stinkleroot,'
      member of 15
   Mills, Stephen, member of 15
   territory wars and teenage
      gang warfare 16–17

Index

Dickens, Rob 159–60
Dingwalls (Camden Town) 159, 185
  gig at 184–5, *187*
Doherty, Billy 45
'Don't Panic' 67
  lyrics 255–6

early years 5
  Rathern housing estate, move to 6–7
  sectarian violence, and experiences of 8–9
  Sunningdale housing estate (Ballysillan), move to 10
Eden Way 117
Edmondson, Adrian 237–8
education
  All Children Together (ACT) 74, 77n2
  anti-sectarian approaches to 74–5
  Belfast Boys Model School 4, 9
  secondary school xvi–xvii
  teacher training and teaching jobs 133–4
  university xiv, 95–9, 114
'Even in the Dark Hours' 196

Faloon, Brian 29–30, 104
Fanning, Dave 115
Faulkner, Brian 7
Ferris, Gary ('The Dean') *117*, 123, 154, 178
  Ruefrex, and role in 116, 218, 223, 228
Firm, The 192
Fisher, Billy 38–40
Flickknife Records 225–6
Flowers for All Occasions 176, 180, *271*
  Music Works Studio, tracks recorded for 195–7

'Flowers for All Occasions' (single) 196
  lyrics 263–4
Forgie, John Hepburn 64, 69, *117*
  background and character of 58–60
  marriage and children 154
  nicknames of 59
  political views 181
  Ruefrex, and role in 59, 68, 100–1, 116, 177–8, 180–4, 223, 228
Foster, Willie 117
  Ruefrex, and role in 101

Galvin, Martin J. 123–4
Giffin, Howard 19–20, 21
Glenbryn neighbourhood 13, 35–7
  Alliance Avenue 35
  Glenbryn Park, and move to 35
  Jolly Roger community centre 36, 39–40
  paramilitary activity 35–6
Gloder, Frenchy 226
Glossop, Mick 183, 192, 217, 241
  Music Works Studio, recording at 193–5
Good Vibrations (film) 47, 250
  'Perfect Crime, The,' and use of in 252
Good Vibrations (record shop and label) 45–8, 65, 249–50
  Battle of the Bands (Ulster Hall) gig 86, *87*
  GOT-8 66–70
  Ruefrex, and relationship with 45–6
Goodman, Martin xiv, xviii

279

GOT-8
  recording of 66–70
  release of 71
Graham, Bill 175–6, 179n6
Gray, Gregory 126–7,
  128–9, 129n2
Greene, Barry 26–7
  Ruefrex, and role in 50
Grimmo 198–9, 238
  Karen, and flat share
    with 198–9

Haçienda (Manchester) 159, 166
  gig at 181–3
Harp Bar (Belfast) 61–2
  Ruefrex, gigs at 62–5
  sectarian violence at 63–5
Hawkwind 226
  Space Ritual 36
Heaney, Seamus 172–3
Heaven 17 209
Heinz, Lyn 20
Higgins, Lily 6
Highfield Bootboys 17
  Debonairs, conflict with
    17, 19, 22
  'Sledger,' leader of 17
Highway Star 20, 25
Holmes, Robin 88
Hooley, Terri 45–6, 65, 249–50
  Good Vibrations (film)
    47, 250
  Good Vibrations (record shop
    and label), role in 46–8
  relations with 70–1
Hot Press 175–6

'In the Traps' 196, 217–18,
  219, *273*
  lyrics 262
Ireland, Sammy 31
Irish Northern Aid Committee
  (NORAID) 124, 129n1

Irwin, Colin 106, 169, 186, 215
Island Records 162, 166n1
  Sarm East and Sarm West
    studios 191
  Stiff Records, link to 162–3

Johnston, Norman ('Jonty') 139
  Kissed Air, role in 130
  Olive Road, Cricklewood,
    resident at 144–6
  personal life 159, 212
  Ruefrex, and role in
    156, 158–60
Jones, Allan 169

Kabuki Records 111
Kasper Records 136, 142
  'In the Traps,' production and
    distribution of 217–18, *219*
  'Wild Colonial Boy,'
    production and
    distribution of 136
Kelly, Danny 174–5, 179n3
Kelly, Ivan 50, 59
  Ruefrex, and role in 25–7, 50
Kissed Air 111, 114, 130, 134–6,
  143, 156
  'Out of Night'/'Change of
    Attention' 135
  Video Palace (London),
    employment at 135–6

Lagan Integrated College 74
Lennox, Ronnie 92–3
Lerwill, Paul 126
Ligoniel Road 13, 80
London residency 142–4
  Battersea, and move to 224–5,
    231, 239
  Brixton 198–200
  gigs in 185
  new musical ventures
    in 153–4

Index

Olive Road, Cricklewood 143–7, 154, 218–21
Long, Janice 206–7
'Lucky' (Gordon, Aloysius) 202–3, 204n1–n2
Lynch, Martin 75–6
Lynch, Seamus 75–6

MacGowan, Shane 205, 211–12
MacKean, Muir 168
Mansion House (Dublin) 104
  Black Catholics, presence at 106
  Ruefrex, gig at 104–8
  Stiff Little Fingers, gig at 105–7
Martin, Gavin 96, 174
Mawhinney, Jim 'Musky' 20
  death and funeral of 79–81
  Debonairs, membership of 15, 18–19
McClelland, Colin 42
McGartland, Tony (Ernie Badness) 70
McGlinchey, Dominic ('Mad Dog') 145
McGlinchey, Mary 145
McIlheney, Barry 148, 169, 222–3
McIlvenney, Norman 'Heckle' 14–15
McKenna, Joanne 74
McKeown, 'Stinkleroot' 15, 21
McMordie, Ali 42
Melody Maker 148, 169–70
  interview with 214–16
  Ruefrex review 170, *171*, 186
  'Wild Colonial Boy, The' article, and impact of 148–50
Miami Showband attack 13
Microdisney 152
Milligan, Roy 'Spike' 35–6
Mills, Stephen ('Lambsy') 15, 19–20

Morley, Paul 101–2
Morrison, Van 241
'Mr Renfield Reflects' 196
  lyrics 263
Murray, Frank 205, 216
Music Works Studio 192–3
  recording at 193–5, 203–4
  tracks recorded at 195–7
musical influences 9–10, 17–18, 42–3

New Consensus 75, 78n3, 211
New Socialist, 179n7
  article and review 176–7
Nilsen, Dennis 153
NME
  article and photo shoot 174–5
  review in 168
North Circular Road 13
Northern Ireland Housing Executive 6

Ogilvie, Gordon 42
O'Hagan, Sean 144, 152
Omagh gig 70
'One by One' 96, 195, *271*
  lyrics 256–7
  recording of *64*, 65, 68
One by One Records 116
Orange marching bands 33–4
  membership of 33–4
  Pride of Ardoyne Flute Band 33–4, 35
  rivalry between 37–8
  Shankill Flute Band 37
Orange Order 34
Oxford
  Christchurch College (Oxford University) xiv–xv, xviii–xx
  St. Cross College (Oxford University) xiv
  university career 247

Wild colonial boys

'Paid in Kind' 116, 196, *272*
  lyrics 258–9
Patterson, Glenn 249–50
Peckham, George 135, 137n5
Peel, John 86, 87, 96
Pentland, Davy 125–6, 228
'Perfect Crime, The' 110, 116,
  126–7, 252
  Good Vibrations (film), and
    use of in 252
  lyrics 259–60
  Shell Shock Rock (film), and
    use of in 252
'Playing Adult Games' 227
  lyrics 267–8
'Playing Cards with Dead
  Men' v, 226–9
  'Ballard of Kingsmill Road'
    228, 269–70
  'Days of Heaven' 227–8, 268–9
    lyrics 265–6
  'Playing Adult Games'
    227, 267–8
  sleeve design 227–9, *229*
  'Your Political Wings
    (Clipped 1969-????)'
    227, 266–7
Pogues, The 205–6
  Ruefrex, support act for
    206, 212
'Poppies' 31
  lyrics 254–5
Pound, The (Belfast) 61
Pride of Ardoyne Flute Band
  33–4, 35, 37
  members of 37
  Ulster Volunteer Force,
    association with 37
Prince Far-I and the Arabs 99
Provisional IRA 13–14
  actions of 13–14, 137n2
  Newry RUC base,
    attack on 134

punk rock
  Belfast scene 43–4, 47
  emergence of xvii–xviii, 24

Queen 203

Rathern housing estate 6–7
Red Wedge 177, 179n9, 207, 209
Reilly, Jim 104
Richardson, Sophie 231
Riviera, Jake 162
Robinson, Dave 160–1, 162, 192,
  205, 206
  Stiff Records, foundation of
    and role in 162
Robinson, Tom 209
Rock Garden (Covent Garden)
  gig 183
RTÉ radio session 115
'Ruah, The' 195, 208
  lyrics 261–2
Rudi and The Outcasts 44–5,
  70, 251
  Queen's University (Belfast)
    gig at, 80
Ruefrex ix–x, *112*, *117*
  Agency, The, contract
    with 186
  band members 26–7, 50,
    64, *230*
  Battle of the Bands (Ulster
    Hall) gig 86, 87, 91n3
  Cork City Hall, gig at 108–9
  Cross the Line (documentary),
    52–3, 68, 76, 96, 97n3, 97
  cultural legacy of xi–xii
  Dingwalls (Camden Town), gig
    at 184–5
  early practices and
    performances 29–31
  Flickknife Records,
    discussions and recording
    with 225–6

Index

formation of 25–7
Good Vibrations (record shop and label), and relationship with 45–6
Harp Bar (Belfast), gigs at 62–5
legacy of 251–2
London relocation, and new approaches to 154–5
management of 156, 212–13
Mansion House (Dublin), gig at 104–8
media reviews and interviews 138, 168–9, 170, 174–7, 178
Melody Maker review 170, *171*
naming of 31, 50–1
negative stereotyping of xi
New Socialist article 176–7
NME review 168, 174–5
Omagh, gig at 70
part-time status of 114–15
Pogues, The, support act of 206, 212
principles of and influences on 42–3
punk scene, and view of 44–5
record labels, pitching to and showcase gigs for 158–60
recording records 66–70
RTÉ, radio session at 115
Sounds of Ireland (Sense of Ireland) gig 98–100
stage presence and performance 53–4
Stiff Little Fingers, support act for 48, *49*, 102, 103–10
Stiff Records, discussions and recording with 163–6, 183–4, 217
Tube, The, appearance on 207–9
Turf Lodge (West Belfast), gig at 76–7

Venue Club (London), gig at 101–2
Ryan, Gareth 111, 130, 135
Ryan, Simon 217, 218

Sarm East and Sarm West studios 191
Saunders, Jennifer 237
sectarian conflict 76
  Black Catholics 104, 106
  childhood experiences, and view of 8–9, 148–9, 150
  Glenbryn neighbourhood, and paramilitary activity 35–6
  'killing fields' of North Belfast 12–13
  paramilitary organisations, and membership of 14
  Provisional IRA, and attacks by 134
  romantic relationships, and religious divisions 72–3
Securicor 131–3
  Cash in Transit, and employment with 131–2
Self-Conscious Over You (film) 91n3
Sense of Ireland (festival) 98
Sounds of Ireland 98–100
Sham 69 63
'Shane MacGowan's Smile' 265–6
Shankill Butchers 76
Shankill Flute Band 37
Shankill Road 6
Sharpe, Ruby 5–6, 31
Sharpe family 5
Sheehan, Tommy 169
Shell Shock Rock (film) 252
Short Brothers & Harland xvii, 30, 92–4
Simms, Davy 111
Sinn Féin 75, 148, 149, 177, 229

'Sledger' (Highfield Bootboys) 17
Smith, Davy 66
Smith, Mark E. 222
Smith, Robert 170–2
Smith, T.V. 86
Smithfield Bus Station 8–9
Social Democratic and Labour Party 7–8
Spence, Bobby 37
Spence, Gerry 37
Spence, Gusty 37
Stewart, Nick 163–4
Stiff Little Fingers 25, 29, 42, 45, 82, 251
  band members 42
  'Johnny Was' 82
  live performances arranged by 185–6
  Mansion House (Dublin), gig at 105–7
  Reilly, Jim, role in 104
  Ruefrex, support act for 48, 49, 102, 103–10
  'Suspect Device' 83
  Ulster Hall, gig at 103
  'Wasted Life' 82–3
Stiff Records 160
  demise of 217–18
  Island Records, link to 162–3
  Riviera, Jake, foundation of and role in 162
  Robinson, Dave, foundation of and role in 162
  Ruefrex, discussions and recording with 163–6, 183–4, 217
Stormont
  Direct Rule, reinstatement of 13–14
  power-sharing administration, and collapse of 7–8, 13–14

Stranglers, The 43
Strummer, Joe 43
Sunningdale housing estate (Ballysillan) 10
Sunningdale Disco 17, 20–1, 22
Sutherland, Steve 169

That Petrol Emotion 177
Thorn, Tracey 172
Tohill, Cormac, 130, 145
Tolhurst, Lol, 172
Toner, Frank, 144
Troubles, The xi, 6, 75, 78n4 *see also* sectarian conflict
  funding of 123–4
Tube, The 207–9, 210n1
Turf Lodge (West Belfast) 75–6
  Ruefrex, gig at 76–7

U2 90–1
Ulster Defence Association
  meetings of 7
  Shankill Flute Band, association with 37
  Sunningdale Disco, run by 17
  Ulster Workers' Council strike, role in 7
Ulster Hall
  Battle of the Bands gig 86, 87, 91n3
  Ruefrex, gig at 110
  Stiff Little Fingers gig 103
Ulster Volunteer Force
  Miami Showband, attack on 13
  Pride of Ardoyne Flute Band, association with 37
Ulster Workers' Council
  strike 7–8
  Ulster Defence Association, role in 7

Index

Undertones, The 45, 54, 177
Ure, Midge 157–8

Venue Club (London) gig 101–2
Verlaine, Tom 183
Video Palace (London) 135–6

Watt, Ben 172
Watt, John 130, 137n1, 144
WEA Records 159–60
'Weeble' 15
'Wild Colonial Boy' 102, 124–6, *124*, 195, *272–3*
   BBC Radio 1 *Roundtable* review 156–8
   chart position 138, *138*

Kasper Records, production and distribution of 136
   lyrics 260–1
   media reviews, and reaction to 138–41
   recording of 126–9
Wizard Studios (Donegall Street, Belfast) 65, 66
   drum kit at 66–7
   recording at 66–7

'Your Political Wings (Clipped 1969-????)' 227, *273*
   lyrics 266–7

Zero, Joe 65

EU authorised representative for GPSR:
Easy Access System Europe, Mustamäe tee 50,
10621 Tallinn, Estonia
gpsr.requests@easproject.com